The
Oil Card

Global Economic Warfare
in the 21st Century

James R. Norman

THE OIL CARD: GLOBAL ECONOMIC WARFARE IN THE 21ST CENTURY
COPYRIGHT © 2008 JAMES R. NORMAN ALL RIGHTS RESERVED.
PRESENTATION COPYRIGHT © 2008 TRINE DAY, LLC

Published by:
Trine Day LLC
 PO Box 577
Walterville, OR 97489
1-800-556-2012
www.TrineDay.com
publisher@TrineDay.net

Library of Congress Control Number: 2008906667

Norman, James R.
The Oil Card—1st ed.
 p. cm. (acid-free paper)
Includes references and index.
(ISBN-13) 978-0-9777953-9-0 (ISBN-10) 0-9777953-9-X
1. Petroleum industry and trade—Political Aspects—History—21st
century. 2 Petroleum industry and trade—Military Aspects—History—21st century. 3. World politics—21th century. 1. Title

FIRST EDITION
10 9 8 7 6 5 4 3 2 1

Printed in the USA
Distribution to the Trade by:
Independent Publishers Group (IPG)
814 North Franklin Street
Chicago, Illinois 60610
312.337.0747
www.ipgbook.com

Publisher's Foreword

The Eternal Fire of Baba Gurgur, outside the northern Iraqi city of Kirkuk has been burning for all of recorded history. Said by some to have been the "burning fiery furnace" into which Babylonian King Nebuchadnezzar cast Shadrach, Meshach and Abednego, these flaming natural gas fields became the home of Iraq's first oil well. Even before that occurred in 1927, geopolitics and the arcane agreements between interested nations, warring sheikdoms and oil companies had provided the framework of Iraqi history: a tale of controlling who has access to that oil and whether it just stays in the ground or ...

James Norman aptly brings this story into the 21st Century with a seasoned understanding of the national, international and market forces at play. Norman's long experience reporting on the oil industry has given him insights beyond the screeching rants of crisis-mongers, the hackneyed soliloquies of investment advisors and punditry of talking heads.

Time is moving fast, things change, people shift jobs and prices go up and down, but as has been noted, "The only reason for time is so that everything doesn't happen at once." And things are *happening*. The real query that Norman brings to us, is just *how* are they happening?

Is there a covert economic war being waged? On whose behalf? Does the required secrecy turn our free markets, our democratic republic and our free press into hidden handmaidens of international cartels? Or are the cards being played for sincere long-term geopolitical goals? Do those ends justify the means? These are questions this book brings to mind. And mindful most of us will be — every time we fill up our gas tanks.

Deeper than our wallets and the astounding transfer of wealth, more fundamental, more elemental questions arise, for when secrecy rules, lies are king. Whom can we trust? With our press — whose freedoms are enshrined in our Constitution — part of the obfuscation, how long will the flames of liberty and freedom flicker in our noble experiment with a government of, by and for the People?

Read on, MacDuff.

Kris Millegan
July 4, 2008

This book is written in memory of my father, Ronald G. Norman. It is dedicated to my mother, Winifred, and to my patient wife, Laurel. My thanks go out to all the many industry and other sources over the years who have given me these insights into how the world works. In particular, thanks go to "the shoeshine boy" in Houston.

— James R. Norman

Table of Contents

Welcome to the front lines of economic warfare.

Impossible!

As outrageous as it may seem, the price of even a global commodity like crude oil can be managed – dramatically up or down – in defiance of free-market principles. And it can be used as a weapon of economic warfare. We have been witnessing just that since the late 1990s as oil prices have climbed 12-fold in under 10 years.

Whatever the geopolitical goals, this wholesale enrichment of the oil "haves" and impoverishment of the "have-nots" amounts to larceny on an unimaginably grand scale. If oil at $100 a barrel is overvalued by, say, half, or $50 a barrel, this now equates to a global wealth transfer annually of about $1.5 trillion. At $150 a barrel, that's about $3 trillion a year of money diverted. Even if, one way or another, the United States is buying much of that oil from itself, or its friends, the redistribution of income is immense, imperfect, and destined to have long-lasting effects.

Such upward price management, stretching over a decade or more, would require not only acquiescence but also neck-deep participation of governments. In particular, the US at the highest levels of its national security apparatus would have to be an active organizer and lead player. So would the Saudis, the Brits and the Russians. At the least, the CEOs or other top officials at the handful or so of world-scale integrated oil majors would have to be willing accomplices, wittingly or unwittingly restricting capital spending and holding down oil production. It would have to involve concerted monkeying with commodity prices on the New York Mercantile Exchange (NYMEX) and other futures and option bourses, requiring some level of awareness by key players at the nation's biggest brokers and banks, as well as by regulators.

Impossible! No one could organize such a conspiracy, let alone sustain it and hide it for a decade or more, you would argue: "The gummint ain't that smart!" But as you will see, the US accomplished all of that and more in the 1980s. Then it was done in reverse: driving down oil prices by half or more for more than a decade, as part of a broad effort to cripple the Soviet Union, depriving it of hard currency from its main export commodity. In the end, the old Soviet system simply ran out of money and went out of business. It was a nearly bloodless triumph for the US and its Western allies.

Now the US is faced off against its other longtime Communist rival, and the only nation posing any serious challenge to America's superpower status in the foreseeable future: the People's Republic of China (PRC). The tables now are turned. China has gone from being a modest oil exporter in the early 1990s to being a voracious consumer of crude. Its aging domestic oil fields and bureaucratic petroleum industry have been unable to keep up with soaring demand for fuel to stoke the double-digit economic growth China needs to employ its huge and uneasy population.

Desperate for energy, the PRC has quickly become the second largest world importer of oil, and forecasts indicate it will buy abroad some 70% of nearly 10 million barrels a day needed by 2010. It is all but impossible to grow a modern industrial economy like that of China without ample supplies of affordable energy, particularly petroleum for motor fuels. Oil pricing and availability are thus key pressure points for China, leading it on a relentless foraging expedition among the world's more marginal, pariah states. China has courted Sudan, Yemen, Iran, Syria, Venezuela, and most notably Iraq during the last years of the Saddam Hussein regime. And wherever China has gone looking for oil, trouble has followed.

Is the "Oil Card" now being played in reverse fashion against the Chinese? I think the evidence is compelling: Yes.

Among other key assertions of this book: the US and allied invasion and occupation of Iraq in early 2003 was likely a direct response to the threat of the People's Liberation Army, in the guise of oilfield technicians, preparing to take over and garrison two of the largest undeveloped Iraq oil fields upon the approaching end, later that year, of United Nations sanctions. Unwilling to tolerate such an encroachment by China into Middle East oil reserves in violation of the 1980 US "Carter Doctrine," and unable to sustain UN sanctions by diplomatic means, President George W. Bush reluctantly opted for what was sure to be a messy, costly but dramatically effective invasion and occupation of Iraq, which persists more than five years later, with no end in sight.

In addition to blocking China from establishing a client-state relationship with Iraq, which would have been far more threatening than what China achieved in Sudan, the Bush Administration's takeover of Iraq has also prevented about 3 million barrels a day of crude oil from going to market. That amounts to about 4% of potential world output, tightening an otherwise sloppy world oil supply/demand balance and allowing dramatic price escalation.

While most view the US foray into Iraq as an unmitigated economic, military and human disaster, it may in reality be the exact opposite. The preemptive occupation of Iraq to block the Chinese has deferred and maybe avoided altogether a near-term direct military confrontation between the US and China.

Yes, Virginia, the Iraq war was about oil. But not in the way most people assume. Rather than aiming to enrich oil industry friends of the Bush family, the purpose of the war and occupation has been to keep Iraqi crude in the ground and away from the Chinese. It is the "Great Game" of keep-away. And if it has averted direct US-China military confrontation, the Iraq occupation has most certainly been a bargain in money and lives, no matter what its huge expense proves ultimately to be.

Given the extremely high geopolitical stakes, it should not be surprising that none of the key players in this game are willing to talk about it. Indeed, the public has been fed all manner of blather and lies about why oil prices are so high, about why the US invaded Iraq, and about the supposedly cordial state of US-China relations. The Chinese leadership, quite aware of what is being done to them, is also loath to complain too loudly for fear of rousing their historically volatile populace to demand a greater response. It is hard to overestimate the sheer volume of deception and perception mismanagement the world has been subjected to while these giants circle each other. Though it may be for what is claimed to be the highest possible reasons of state, to avert global thermonuclear war, we are nevertheless being played for patsies. Again.

The cherished "free market" assumptions with which we have been inculcated for decades are, in reality, probably all wrong. Markets *can* be managed, if not outright manipulated, by a relatively small number of high-level collaborators armed with sufficient funding, information and geopolitical clout. Even deep global markets in highly fungible commodities like oil can be driven up or down and sustained above or below normal clearing prices for protracted periods.

Oil, metals, foodstuffs and other raw materials now have their prices set by nameless, faceless financial "speculators" rather than producers and consumers. Pricing in these commodities has been largely de-coupled from actual physical supply and demand fundamentals, becoming a plaything for whoever has deep enough pockets, an ability to dictate world events, and the will to take big risks. Thus, the price of oil is now less dependent on the actual supply and demand for "wet" barrels than on the huge sums of money pouring into NYMEX futures from pension and other investment funds, tacitly enabled and encouraged by US regulators. Daily oil volumes on the NYMEX now dwarf global physical oil consumption.

Anybody who is anybody in the oil industry, government or the analytical community will no doubt officially deny and scoff at my thesis. But then, this is to be expected. Yes, I've gotten confirmation from some "spook" sources I believe to be in the know about what's going on. But none of them dare be quoted, and might not be believed if they were. In the end, perhaps the strongest evidence in this case may be the deafening silence, inaction and seeming helplessness of the US government in the face of runaway oil prices. That is, as Sherlock Holmes would note, "The dog that didn't bark."

We are thoroughly immersed in a new kind of Cold War. In place of armies and navies lined up on opposing borders and the pervasive threat of sudden ICBM attack, we have an economic struggle waged with money and markets while the combatants offer smiley-faced pleasantries for the news media. Don't believe them. This is mortal combat, as the former Soviets will attest.

James R. Norman
July 4, 2008

Glossary

ADR................... American Depositary Receipt. The US-traded equivalent of a foreign company's common stock.

ASEAN.............. Association of Southeast Asian Nations.

b/d...................... barrels per day.

Backwardated... A phenomenon in commodity futures markets in which near-month prices exceed quotes for contracts farther out on the forward curve. The condition is usually rare and would be expected to revert to a more normal "contango" market, in which future prices reflect near-month quotes plus a cost of storage.

bbl...................... barrel, or "blue barrel" as set by Standard Oil, of 42 gallons.

Bcf...................... billion cubic feet.

boe...................... barrels of oil equivalent. Generally, 6 Mcf of natural gas have the same energy content on a Btu basis as one 42-gallon barrel of crude oil.

CalPERS........... The California Public Employee Retirement System.

CBM.................. Coalbed methane. Natural gas produced from coal seams.

CFMA................ The Commodity Futures Modernization Act of 2000.

CFTC................. Commodity Futures Trading Commission.

CNOOC........... China National Offshore Oil Corporation. It is the smallest of China's three upstream majors. State-owned parent CNOOC owns 70.6% of publicly traded CNOOC Limited, which is listed in New York under symbol CEO and had an equity value of $68 billion in early 2008.

CNPC................ China National Petroleum Corporation. China's largest integrated oil major. It is wholly-owned by the People's Republic of China (PRC) and owns 88.21% of PetroChina Company Ltd. its main domestic operating arm. PetroChina has been publicly traded since 2000 and is listed in New York under the symbol PTR with an equity value in mid-2008 of $235 billion.

CUCBM............China United Coalbed Methane Co. Ltd., state-controlled Chinese onshore coalbed gas producer.

DJ-AIGCI.........The Dow Jones-AIG Commodity Index.

Downstream.....Oil and gas activities associated with refining and marketing.

E&P...................Exploration and production. The "upstream" side of oil and gas.

EIA.....................US Energy Information Administration. Part of the Department of Energy.

ESF.....................Exchange Stabilization Fund. Money set aside since 1934 by the US Treasury and managed by the Federal Reserve Bank of New York to damp volatility in the currency market.

ESPO..................Russia's East Siberia-Pacific Ocean pipeline system.

ETF.....................Exchange Traded Fund.

GDP...................Gross Domestic Product. The basic measure of a nation's economic activity level.

GSCI..................The Goldman Sachs Commodity Index, now managed by Standard & Poor's.

GW.....................gigawatt. 1,000 megawatts or 1 million kilowatts.

GWOT..............Global War on Terrorism

ICE.....................IntercontinentalExchange.

IEA.....................International Energy Agency.

IFRS..................International Financial Reporting Standards.

LME...................London Metals Exchange.

Mcf.....................thousand cubic feet.

Mcfe...................energy equivalent of 1,000 cubic feet of natural gas. Generally, one barrel of crude oil has the Btu equivalent of 6 Mcf of methane.

MMcf.................million cubic feet.

MoU...................Memorandum of Understanding.

mt.......................Metric tonne. 1,000 kilograms or about 2,205 pounds. One short ton is 2,000 lbs and a long ton is 2,240 lbs. Roughly 7.3 barrels of relatively light crude oil weighs one metric tonne. One mt of ethanol equates to 7.94 barrels or 333 gal.

NDRC................China's National Development and Reform Commission, which has broad planning control over the Chinese economy.

NSC....................US National Security Council, an arm of the White House.

NSDD .... National Security Decision Directive. Nomenclature during the Reagan Administration for major policy positions, usually classified as secret. Terminology changed with later administrations and now seldom used.

NYMEX .... New York Mercantile Exchange.

OECD .... Organisation for Economic Co-operation and Development. The Paris-based group of 30 free-market democracies which constitute the bulk of the developed world's economy.

ONGC .... India's state-owned Oil and Natural Gas Corp., the country's largest producer and parent of wholly owned international upstream affiliate ONGC Videsh Ltd. (OVL).

OPEC .... Organization of Petroleum Exporting Countries.

OTC .... Over-the-counter. Off-exchange deals to handle customized energy and other futures and derivative transactions.

PKZ .... PetroKazakhstan, acquired by CNPC in 2005.

PLAN .... People's Liberation Army Navy. China's seagoing military service.

ppm .... parts per million.

PPP .... Purchasing Power Parity. A system that measures a country's GDP in terms of the value of goods and services produced as if they were sold in the US and priced in dollars. Chinese PPP was thus pegged at more than $10 trillion vs the US' $13 trillion in 2006, although at China's official exchange rate its GDP was only $2.5 trillion that year.

PSA .... Production Sharing Agreement.

ROACE .... Return on average capital employed. A conservative financial measure of corporate performance favored by ExxonMobil and other integrated oil majors. Calculated as net income plus interest expense as a percent of a company's total debt and equity.

SEC .... Securities and Exchange Commission.

Sinopec .... China Petrochemical Corporation, known as Sinopec Group, is China's second-largest integrated oil major and largest refiner and petrochemicals company. It is wholly owned by the PRC. Sinopec Group owns 75.84% of China Petroleum and Chemical Corporation, also known as Sinopec, which has been listed in New York since 2000 under the symbol SNP and in early 2008 had equity value of $74 billion.

Tcf..................... Trillion cubic feet.

Upstream........... Oil and gas activities associated with finding, developing and producing hydrocarbons at the wellhead.

VLCC................. Very Large Crude Carrier, able to carry 200,000 to 320,000 dwt of oil (1.5 to 2.3 million bbl).

WGFM .... Working Group on Financial Markets, or the President's Working Group on Financial Markets. Also dubbed the "Plunge Protection Team."

WMD................. Weapon of mass destruction.

WTI................... West Texas Intermediate, the benchmark US light, sweet crude on which NYMEX futures are based.

WTO.................. World Trade Organization.

XOM .... Trading Symbol for ExxonMobil

yuan .... The base unit of the Chinese currency, their "dollar."

元 .... Symbol for the Chinese currency. Called the renminbi ("people's currency") or yuan, its exchange rate to the US dollar at mid-year 2008 was around 6.92:1.

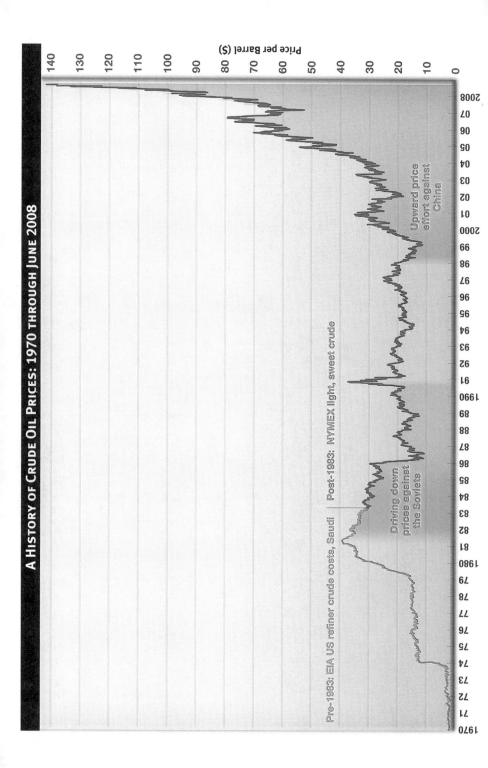

A History of Crude Oil Prices: 1970 through June 2008

Pre-1983: EIA US refiner crude costs, Saudi | Post-1983: NYMEX light, sweet crude

Driving down prices against the Soviets

Upward price effort against China

Price per Barrel ($)

Introduction

Since the end of 1998, the price of light, sweet crude petroleum had staged an amazing rise of more than 12-fold from barely $10/barrel to near $140 in mid-2008. This, for a commodity locked in a trading range around $20 per barrel for the prior 15 years. What changed and what drove this huge increase?

We are told by a growing throng of doom-and-gloomers that the world is quickly running out of oil, and threatened with global conflict over the looming scarcity of this essential resource. This "Peak Oil" mantra has become embedded in public perceptions, and it is now seemingly accepted without question as conventional wisdom. This in turn is said to be the basis for a torrent of speculative buying in crude oil futures on the New York Mercantile Exchange, where the global benchmark price for oil now is effectively set. Without any undue outside influence, we are assured by economic commentators, the invisible hand of Adam Smith has been relentlessly driving up the cost of oil in an entirely rational free-market pricing process.

But it was not that long ago when the world oil industry was languishing in what seemed to be a perpetual glut of the black stuff. In the 1980s, after a brief price spike in the late 1970s that peaked in 1982, world oil demand was in a state of stagnation and even decline, led by oil's biggest consumer: the United States. Long after the 1970s OPEC-driven price and supply scares had abated, US car and truck fuel economy rules took effect in the 1980s, curbing gasoline consumption. High oil prices in the 1970s and new US air pollution rules helped rub out the burning of fuel oil to make electricity, replaced by nuclear, coal and natural gas-fired power generation. Overall North American crude oil demand eased steadily from more than 20 million barrels per day in 1978 to barely 16 million barrels a day (b/d) in 1983, and did not regain its 1978 level until 1998, 20 years later.[1] That was despite steady growth in US cars on the road and miles driven.

Oil supply also surged in the 1980s, despite what were then soaring costs to find new oil, falling oil prices and minimal industry profits. In sharp contrast to current capital-stingy corporate strategies, Western integrated majors like Exxon, Mobil, Royal Dutch Shell and British Petroleum were spending heavily to bring on new production in the '80s. They were able to maintain volume growth at a roughly 5% annual clip, even though profit margins and earnings were slim. Red ink and write-offs were rife throughout the decade, and the 1980s saw a wave of oil industry bankruptcies, mergers, takeovers and financial distress. Still, there was a mad and successful scramble to boost oil production.

The cost of finding and developing the production of each new barrel of crude oil in the early and mid 1980s soared to a range of $15 to $18, running higher than market prices at times. Nevertheless, the US and international majors were plowing back profits into the ground at a breakneck pace to grow their output. Debt levels rose as companies reinvested more than the cash being generated by their upstream oil and gas operations. Oil share prices languished, and General Electric displaced Exxon as the most valuable US public company. Wall Street came to despise oil companies as lumbering behemoths seemingly bent on destroying shareholder wealth by over-investing in an already abundant commodity, merely trying to mindlessly maintain output volume growth. Raiders like T. Boone Pickens Jr. and Carl Icahn had a field day, hounding Gulf Oil into the arms of Chevron and forcing Phillips Petroleum to buy back stock and recapitalize. Getty Oil was bought by Texaco, steel giant USX bought Marathon Oil, Occidental Petroleum bought Cities Service. Mobil bought upstream independent Superior Oil.

Adding to the surfeit of crude in those years, Saudi Arabia turned on the spigots in 1985. As linchpin of the Organization of Petroleum Exporting Countries, the Saudis claimed to be more worried about maintaining market share and in discouraging development of competing fuels than about falling oil prices. Abandoning its role as OPEC's "swing" producer, and refusing to absorb all the produc-

1. US Energy Information Administration, International Petroleum Monthly, April 2008, Table 4.6.

2

tion cuts needed to prop up the market price, Saudi Arabia boosted its output from under 4 million b/d to around 9 million b/d by the early 1990s. Meanwhile, both Iran and Iraq were pumping oil like mad in the 1980s to fund their bloody eight-year war. Epitomized by the sight of flaming tankers in the Persian Gulf leaking their oily cargos on the nightly news, it seemed the world was literally awash in cheap crude with oil to burn.

A new factor also came into play in 1983 that had the effect of throwing "paper" barrels on an already weak market to further drive down prices: the launch of the New York Mercantile Exchange futures contract for light, sweet crude. With uncanny timing there quickly emerged a wave of speculative "short" sellers in NYMEX crude futures. That further undercut the price of physical crude or "wet" barrels, which traditionally had been pegged by the US refining majors, the biggest natural users of crude oil. With the NYMEX futures, the "tail" of paper oil trading began to wag the "dog" of physical crude pricing.

Where all that futures selling came from in the early 1980s was never clear, since the ultimate buyers and sellers of NYMEX contracts were known only to the brokers handling their trades. Even then, the identity of futures buyers could be disclosed as no more than a nominee in the Cayman Islands. With only a 5% margin requirement, or performance bond, per 1,000-barrel futures contract, even relatively small amounts of cash persistently deployed on the NYMEX by the "shorts" had a snowballing effect. NYMEX futures prices fell and dragged down with them the price of real barrels. Oil prices became de-coupled from immediate physical supply-and-demand fundamentals. Ever since, they have been more a function of fickle, highly-levered financial speculation: a deep-pockets money game controlled by interests perhaps far removed from the oil business itself. The shorts made out like bandits in the 1980s, as if they knew the price of oil was heading downward.

Driven by those four factors — weak demand, aggressive output growth by the majors, the ramp-up in Saudi production and selling pressure in the futures market — oil prices staged a stunning collapse in the 1980s. In nominal (then-current) dollars, the spot price of benchmark light, sweet US West Texas Intermediate (WTI) crude fell from an average $37.96 per barrel in 1980 to under $11 in July 1986. It then hovered around $20 a barrel for the next decade, then dipped even further to average $14.39 a barrel in 1998. [2] The NYMEX near-term futures hit a record low of $10.72/barrel on December 10, 1998.[3] In inflation-adjusted terms, the collapse was more than twice as dramatic. Stated in 2004 dollars, that average WTI price cratered from the equivalent of about $82 per barrel in 1980 to about $15 in 1998, losing more than four-fifths of its value.

Whether or not the world was heading toward an eventual cliff by exhausting the earth's petroleum reserves, it seemed an old economic rule was relentlessly asserting itself: that commodities tend toward glut. Somehow, the scare-driven scarcity that had pushed up oil prices to their 1980 peak had spawned a global surplus of the stuff, pulling prices down to rock bottom.

But then that was not all that surprising in the 1980s, which were imbued with the "supply side" conviction that free markets, low taxes and minimal regulation would naturally lead to an abundance of goods, and low inflation. Barring collusion or regulation to restrict output and prop up prices, most commodities do gravitate toward their marginal cost of production. That is, in a really free and competitive marketplace, suppliers will keep increasing output until prices fall to the cost of delivering that last incremental unit of volume.

In fact, in capital-intensive industries like oil, with significant sunk costs already invested in finding the reserves and building production facilities, cash-strained or debt-heavy players can be tempted to keep on boosting output even at an all-in loss if it generates positive, immediate cash flow. By ignoring non-cash costs like depreciation and amortization of past investments, producers can be prone to boost output until prices fall to marginal cash-only operating costs, even if that means reporting an overall bottom-line loss. That's why commodity industries, unless propped up by protective laws, tariffs or collusion, tend to consolidate around very large players able to use economies of scale to gain the lowest cost structures, sustain bouts of destructive price collapse – and then damp excessive production.

---

2. BP Amoco Statistical Review of World Energy, June 2000, p.14, and EIA Web site, Petroleum Navigator.

3. EIA, Petroleum Navigator

This tendency toward commodity gluts has been the bane of economics ever since the days of Malthus and Ricardo. Even if gluts eventually correct themselves, extended spates of oversupply and low prices can be devastating to small or weak producers. And there has been persistent concern they could spread to general economic sickness: over-production, waste, loss of buying power, recession or even depression. The view from Houston in the 1980s was certainly just that: impending doom. Not only were oil prices heading into the tank, but interest rates ran up into the high teens in the early 1980s under Federal Reserve Chairman Paul Volcker. The value of the US dollar soared, damaging export industries. The price of gold and other minerals and agricultural commodities also fell. Real estate languished and farmland went begging for buyers. Instead of the inflationary environment of the prior decade, much of the US heartland's commodity-based economy was seeing for the first time since the Great Depression actual price *de*-flation. Or as economists euphemized: dis-inflation.[4]

The oil industry, in particular, has long been vulnerable to this commodity boom-and-bust tendency, even amid chronic worries over the years that the discovered quantities of oil might soon run out. Ever since the first commercial oil well, drilled in Pennsylvania by "Colonel" Edwin L. Drake in 1859, the oil business has been generally characterized by a history of careful production management by government and industry to try and prevent destructive price collapse. If you will, the oil business has long been subject to *de facto* government sanctioned cartel behavior.

This was epitomized for many decades by the Rail Road Commission of Texas, which was given authority to set the allowable rates of oil and natural gas production in that state. That was prompted by the rampant over-production by independents after their discovery of the big East Texas Field in 1930, which drove the price of crude from $1/bbl to $0.13 by 1931, when the governor ordered the Texas National Guard into the field to control the output.[5]

When Texas was eclipsed as the world's chief repository of marginal crude in the 1970s, the production restraint levers were taken over by the Organization of Petroleum Exporting Countries,

4. "American's Deflation Belt," *BusinessWeek*, June 9, 1986.
5. Julia Cauble Smith, "East Texas Oilfield," The Handbook of Texas Online.

dominated by the Saudis. This was not an altogether unwelcome development for the industry, or for the US government. Indeed, had OPEC not emerged on its own, the US would probably have had to invent it. And maybe it did, given the close relationship between the Saudi kingdom and the US national security establishment. The main reason for the formation of OPEC in 1960, led by Saudi Arabia, Iran, Iraq, Kuwait and Venezuela, was to rein in newly emerging independent producing states like Libya, and generally raise the price of crude. So long as the international majors still controlled the downstream end in refining and marketing, and could pass through higher crude prices, they prospered from OPEC cartelism.

The major oil companies themselves also have had a rich history of collusion to prevent desultory price wars ever since their discovery of massive crude reserves in Iran and Iraq in the early 1900s. Classic in that regard is the "Achnacarry Agreement" or "As Is Agreement of 1928." Forged at Scotland's Achnacarry Castle by the heads of Royal Dutch Shell, BP, and the predecessor of ExxonMobil, that pact aimed to avert price competition, restrain capital spending and cement in place the relative market shares of those giants in perpetuity.[6]

Achnacarry was followed up with three supplemental agreements by 1934, and in 1948 was replaced by the Heads of Agreement, when Exxon and Mobil bought a combined 40% of Saudi-based Aramco from Chevron and Texaco. Gulf Oil had its own deal for Kuwaiti oil. Under those pacts and other arrangements, the "Seven Sisters" of international oil were effectively able to control world crude prices for decades. Though such pacts are officially disavowed now by each of those oil majors, guess what? The proportionate shares of world refined product sales by ExxonMobil, Shell and BP have remained virtually unchanged after lo these 80 years. By coincidence, of course.

In 1952 President Harry S. Truman, over the objections of his national security advisors, ordered the Justice Department's antitrust arm to begin a grand jury investigation into monopolistic oil industry activities. But under pressure to keep the oil majors on board with efforts to block Russian inroads in Iran, Truman agreed as he was leaving office to limit the criminal antitrust case to a civil proceeding. After protracted investigation and negotiations during

6. John M. Blair, *The Control of Oil*, Random House, 1977, pp. 54-76.

the Eisenhower Administration, the oil majors agreed to a nominal consent judgment in 1960.[7] They have never since been broadly challenged on anti-trust grounds.

History shows the quintessential problem of the oil business *not* to be how to find and produce enough oil to meet world demand at the lowest necessary price. Rather, the industry's quiet obsession as been how to keep oil in the ground, or at least enough of those marginal barrels so as not to trash the global price structure.[8] The available supply of oil has almost always tended to outrun immediate demand, requiring concerted efforts over the years to restrain production to keep prices above break-even levels for the major producers.

For some reason, it seems the self-stabilizing mechanism for oil prices in the 1980s completely fell apart. All the major players were over-producing and showing no signs of their former or natural restraint. Futures prices were allowed to plunge under pressure from murky short-sellers. And the world's primary consumer of oil, the US, went on a fuel-efficiency binge despite bargain basement prices. Why?

Bringing down the Soviets

The answer is that while the oil industry lumbered under low prices and high costs during the 1980s, no producer fared worse than the creaking Soviet Union. It had grown to count on high prices and large crude exports for the lion's share of its badly needed hard-currency income. Moscow suffered an economic "perfect storm" in the 1980s, as the price of both oil and gold, its other primary hard-currency earner, tumbled.[9] That problem was magnified by the collapse of the US dollar in the mid-1980s, further devaluing Soviet hard-currency earnings from its commodity exports.

As we will see, the collapse of world oil prices in the 1980s was not a coincidence and was not simply the result of a natural market balancing of supply and demand. It was economic warfare. The US national security establishment under Ronald Reagan, with the help of Saudi Arabia, the oil majors and futures trading, set about to sys-

---

7. Burton I. Kaufman, *The Oil Cartel Case*, Greenwood Press, 1978, pp 93-103.
8. "Petrodollars," *Platts Oilgram News*, Vol. 84, No. 1, Jan. 3, 2006, p 4.
9. Gold went from $850/oz in nominal dollars in January 1980 to $300 in late 1982, and hovered in that range for the next 20 years. Since 2005 it had spiked to more than $1,000 in early 2008, with 5-year futures approaching $1,100/oz.

tematically drive down oil prices to hurt the Soviets. The effort was devastatingly successful, as Russian economists now admit.

To be sure, the oil price collapse was part of a multi-pronged assault on the USSR, which included a vastly expensive arms build-up. That included a "Star Wars" effort to militarize space, all but daring the Russians to try and keep pace. By the end of the decade the Russians were bust and the Soviet Union soon crumbled to dust with nary a shot being fired. Supposedly, the CIA had no clue the collapse was coming. Sure.

Now 20 years later the world's crude oil mindset has done a 180-degree turn. We are consumed with fears that we are on the verge of exhausting world oil supplies, even though world reserves remain as robust as they were two decades ago, and the cost of finding more has plunged. We worry that distant terror or political events will choke off oil flows, although most US imports come from neighbors Canada and Mexico. We fret over the slightest reported decline in weekly commercial inventories, even though it may simply indicate the industry is operating ever more efficiently and needs less inventory sitting around.

The big international oil majors like ExxonMobil, BP and Shell now seem chronically unable to get any more oil out of the ground, despite a torrent of profits from record high prices. The Saudis and other OPEC members are showing astounding discipline and unprecedented production restraint now, despite a long history of rampant OPEC quota-cheating. "Peak Oil" propagandists claim Saudi and other world oil reserves are now vastly overstated and quickly running out. US government policy has all but ignored the wasteful fuel use of oversized sport utility vehicles and worsening automotive mileage performance. Even with oil prices at nose-bleed levels, the US keeps buying prodigious amounts of crude to sink back in the ground as "strategic" reserves, refusing to release those vast stores to ease price spikes. At any given time there are at least half a dozen hot spots of war or civil unrest involving key oil export countries, from Iraq and Iran to Nigeria, Sudan and Venezuela, and the US seems to inflame those festering boils rather than salve them. Even tanker rates have soared. Compared to the 1980s, the world's thinking about oil has been completely turned on its head.

Is the world really in dire risk of running out of liquid hydrocarbons in the span of a few years? Unlikely. Except for the US and some other well-worked venues, the earth's crust remains relatively unexplored for oil. Vast areas in Asia, Africa, South America and offshore around the world remain essentially undrilled and unprospected with detailed seismic analysis. Where substantial drilling has already occurred, much of it has been to only shallow depths. And where oil has been found, relatively little of the volumes calculated to reside "in place" have been actually produced or booked as proved reserves. That leaves vast amounts of already technically discovered oil awaiting enhanced recovery methods such as water flooding, injection of CO_2 or polymers, horizontal drilling and even high-pressure air injection to free up remaining oil and sweep the rocks clean.

Moreover, there is much to be said for the theory that petroleum is "a-biotic." That is, that its formation deep underground is not the result of unrenewable decomposing dinosaurs and buried vegetation from eons ago. Geoscientists increasingly are leaning toward the contrary notion that the earth is continually manufacturing hydrocarbons like methane that are then trapped and baked into longer molecules to form oil and gas liquids. This is evidenced by recent large oil finds at depths below 18,000 feet in rocks predating fossil deposits. Given the underground findings of carbon dioxide, helium, hydrogen sulfide and other gases, the internal grinding away of the earth's core must be continually churning out hydrogen and other light elements that find their way to the surface to combine with carbon. Petroleum may be far from the finite resource of the Peak Oil Chicken Littles.

ExxonMobil, arguably the industry leader in technical oil analysis, has consistently challenged the doom-and-gloom crowd regarding oil supply. Even without game-changing technological breakthroughs, it notes there are probably another 2.2 trillion barrels of conventional oil to be found and produced, on top of the trillion barrels of known reserves and the 1 trillion barrels or so already consumed in the past 150 years.[10] And it sees yet more trillions of barrels available down the road from technical improvements and the processing of less desirable heavy oil deposits.

10. ExxonMobil, 2006 Financial & Operating Review, p 8.

In fact, the cost of finding and bringing into production a barrel of crude oil has been on a downtrend for the past 25 years, thanks to steadily improving technologies and the economies of scale in large offshore oil developments. From costs ranging into the high teens in then-current dollars per barrel in the early 1980s, the industry average finding and development, or F&D, cost fell fairly steadily to around $10 a barrel in the late 1990s, despite inflation that roughly halved the currency's value. ExxonMobil, for instance, has said its cost of replacing each barrel of proved reserves it produced in 2006 was just $7. And that included all the expensive steel and hardware needed to bring those replacement barrels on line. The cost of just finding or acquiring rights to new oil has been under $0.50/bbl in recent years, down from almost $4/bbl in the 1980s.

Helping to hold down oil industry operating costs until recently was a lingering surplus of thousands of over-built drilling rigs and oilfield service hardware left over from the early-'80s boom. Eventually rust, service-industry consolidation and the torches of scrap metal dealers gradually worked off the hardware overhang or took it off the market. Prominent in that consolidation effort as a dealmaker and advisor was Houston investment bank Simmons & Co., led by Peak Oil chief advocate Matt Simmons. [11] Ironically, Simmons in the 1980s was preaching an opposite doom-and-gloom view of perpetual oil patch depression, due to abundant oil and chronically low prices as far as the eye could see. "The grim reality is, there will be no recovery" in oil prices, Simmons told *BusinessWeek* in 1985. Now his best-seller *Twilight in the Desert* warns of a coming cataclysmic oil shortage, claiming Saudi Arabia's reserves are vastly overstated and running out fast.[12] Simmons' brother Laurence is a principal in buyout firm SKF Partners, which now stands to make a killing from selling its accumulation of oilfield service firms acquired in the doldrums of the market.

Along with ample and cheap hardware, the oil industry has benefited from much better seismic data, vastly greater computing power and improved geophysical analysis. These have allowed ex-

---

11. "Matt Simmons: Doctor to the oil fields' walking wounded," *BusinessWeek*, Nov. 4, 1985, p. 82.
12. Matthew R. Simmons, *Twilight in the Desert: The Coming Saudi oil shock and the world economy*, John Wiley & Sons, 2005.

plorers to "see" many more likely oil and gas deposits underground, at deeper levels and even under salt formations that used to block seismic response. Satellite and aerial remote sensing have also improved, opening up new oil provinces and lessening the odds of a dry hole. Drilling systems and techniques have gained sophistication, allowing much deeper wells, in deeper waters, directionally steered to precisely hit even small oil accumulations. Doom-and-gloomers bewail the declining volumes of hydrocarbons found per well. But another way of looking at the data is that lower costs and better technology have made it economical for prospectors to go after much smaller pools of oil. That means a geometric increase in potential targets versus shooting for "elephant" sized fields. And those giants are still being found, from what could be a multi-hundred-billion barrel find at Kashagan in the Kazakh Caspian Sea[13] to huge new claimed discoveries in China's Bohai Bay, offshore Brazil and in the deepwater Gulf of Mexico.

Despite these upbeat supply considerations, oil prices abruptly ended their nearly two decades of slumber in late 1998. Like the bend in a hockey stick, prices began a rapid and determined escalation. After bottoming at under $12 a barrel in December of that year, the price of NYMEX light, sweet crude futures marched up dramatically. Within six months they were trading at nearly triple that price, above $30 a barrel, for no readily apparent reason. There was no impending supply disruption. Inventories were in line with historical trends. Costs for finding, developing and producing oil remained low and under control.

As late as September 2004, with spot-market US light, sweet crude trading at $50/bbl, Bear Stearns analyst Frederick Leuffer was still saying oil should be in the $20s/bbl based on supply and demand fundamentals. The sudden price premium of more than $20, he concluded, was due merely to "speculation."[14]

Along comes China

Now, for some reason, oil prices have risen 12-fold over the past nine years to nearly $150/bbl, with almost none of what could

13. "Petrodollars," *Platts Oilgram News*, Vol. 79, No. 48, p. 3, Mar. 12, 2001.
14. Frederick P. Leuffer, "The Oil Bubble," Bear Stearns integrated oil equity research, Sept. 30, 2004.

be expected to be a normal supply response to put more oil on the market. What has changed? Geopolitics.

The alignment of world economic and military power by 1998 had taken on a dramatically different orientation from the 1980s. The US had emerged as the seemingly unchallenged global superpower. Russia was in eclipse, foundering in confusion and corruption, and reeling from continuing bouts of credit and currency collapse. But the slumbering People's Republic of China was rapidly emerging from centuries of war-torn chaos, totalitarian rule and economic hibernation. Though still tightly controlled politically by a one-party Communist elite, it had de-collectivized farming, and since 1978 had been adopting the market incentives of capitalism in a massive effort to jump-start economic growth and employ its huge and restless population. By wooing foreign industrial investment with tax breaks and cheap labor, and undervaluing its currency to encourage exports, it was rapidly transforming itself into a modern industrial giant, and it is now the world's leading maker of steel, cement, aluminum, glass and a raft of other goods.

China was making itself into a serious strategic rival for neighbor Russia, the US and its Western allies. But in doing so, the long-self-contained and self-sufficient Chinese economy was becoming vulnerable to external supply constraints. It is seriously short of key raw materials like iron ore and bauxite. By 1993 China had gone from being a small exporter of crude oil to a net importer. Its intake of foreign crude in 1998 was still a modest 800,000 b/d, about 1% of world supply, for 20% of its needs. But that demand was projected to soar with the eventual proliferation of cars and trucks as incomes rose. Moreover, China's industrial and power sectors were notoriously inefficient, still burning costly fuel oil in many cases to make electricity, and consuming much more oil per unit of GDP than the US or other developed nations.

By 2006, China was importing more than 3.4 million b/d of crude, or almost half its 7.3 million b/d of oil needs. The US Energy Information Administration predicts 2008 Chinese petroleum use to average more than 8.1 million b/d, with 52% having to be imported.[15] The growth of Chinese oil demand is fast outrunning forecasts by the International Energy Agency (IEA), which in 2003

---

15. EIA, Short-Term Energy Outlook, Dec. 11, 2007, table 3a.

had been expecting China to reach the 7 million b/d demand mark only after 2010, and then need only 40% of that as imports. Even so, the IEA's conservative forecast projected Chinese oil demand to top 12 million b/d by 2030, and require 80% of that to be imported. Sooner or later, oil would become a critical pressure point for China if crude prices were to rise.

And rise they have.

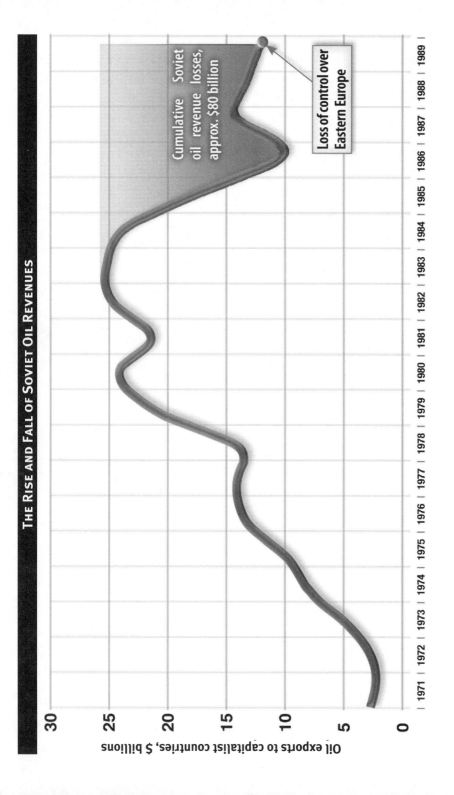

The Rise and Fall of Soviet Oil Revenues

Cumulative Soviet oil revenue losses, approx. $80 billion

Loss of control over Eastern Europe

Oil exports to capitalist countries, $ billions

30
25
20
15
10
5
0

| 1971 | 1972 | 1973 | 1974 | 1975 | 1976 | 1977 | 1978 | 1979 | 1980 | 1981 | 1982 | 1983 | 1984 | 1985 | 1986 | 1987 | 1988 | 1989 |

—1—

Breaking the Soviet Union with Oil Prices

Warfare in the future is going to be fought mainly through economic means.
— Jian Luming, National Defense University (China), 2001[1]

Supreme excellence consists in breaking the enemy's resistance without fighting.
— Sun Tsu, The Art of War, 6th Century BC

In the age of nuclear-armed super-powers, war ain't like it used to be. Direct military confrontation by two countries has always been the least attractive and last resort of wise and prudent leaders. But with the risks now of rapid escalation to global thermonuclear missile exchanges, a tacit understanding seems to have emerged among nuclear-armed powers that head-to-head conflicts which could lead to overt shooting engagements are to be avoided at all costs. They are a no-win proposition.

That does not mean the Big Guys do not have serious differences, gripes and conflicting national interests. It just means that sanity requires these conflicts to be pursued by means other than direct military action between nuclear-armed states. Even if direct military conflict cannot be averted, its outcome is usually sealed years in advance in the relative economic strength and strategic political positioning of the belligerents.

Now, with the stakes so high in any great-power military conflict, much more emphasis is placed on non-military forms of coercion, dominance and conquest. This can include ideological or psychological warfare, covert operations, efforts to compromise or undermine an opponent regime, or the use of third-party or surro-

1. Jiang Luming, "Certain Issues on China Countering Future Economic Sanctions," The (Chinese) National Defense University, Military Economics Study, Nov. 2001.

gate military or paramilitary groups aimed at creating havoc without overtly revealing the real adversary. Such may be the origins of "Al Qaeda" and any of the dozens of supposedly indigenous rebel and guerrilla organizations active to varying degrees around the world. What are the odds any such movement could long survive, let alone pull off elaborate terror events, without some form of state sponsorship?

But those kinds of peripheral, nuisance activities may have little real impact on a major nation state with internal controls and a strong military. What is instead gaining increasing attention in statecraft is the non-military equivalent of conventional attrition combat: large-scale economic warfare. In its overt form, this can include embargoes or blockades of strategic goods and commodities, tariffs, trade sanctions and legal battles under trade rules. But more corrosive over time could be the long-term effects of more subtle manipulation of currencies, interest rates, commodity prices and other markets, aimed at limiting an opponent country's economic growth and fomenting social unrest.

Like a skillful torture which leaves no visible bruise marks, clever application of such principles could make it appear that Adam Smith's free-market "invisible hand" was responsible for delivering the blows. Successfully waged by a strong opponent, long-term economic warfare could thwart an opponent's ability to amass the wealth and power needed to sustain direct military confrontation. It might even achieve relatively bloodless regime change in a weak rival state unable to keep its populace fed and employed.

That was the fate of the Union of Soviet Socialist Republics.

Popular perception, mostly promoted by American commentators, is that the USSR disappeared in 1991 due to the inherent weakness, contradictions and corruption of its totalitarian, collectivist and centrally-planned economic system. Some analysts credit the costly US Strategic Defense Initiative embarked on by conservative Republican President Ronald Reagan in the 1980s for outflanking and out-spending the Soviets to the point of bankruptcy and surrender. Others credit US diplomacy and arms agreements. Others laud US support for the Taliban in waging a costly, painful and humiliating guerrilla war against Soviet forces in Afghanistan.

No doubt all those factors had some role. But the most persuasive explanation of the mortal blow delivered to the USSR is revealed in a book written in 1994 by Hoover Institution fellow Peter Schweizer: *Victory: The Reagan Administration's Secret Strategy that Hastened the Collapse of the Soviet Union.*

The death of the USSR at the end of 1991 was not an accident, nor was it foreordained. It was the outcome of a long and hard-fought economic struggle. Citing three key national security directives signed by Reagan in 1982 and 1983, plus interviews with Reagan's top national security insiders, Schweizer detailed a concerted US and allied effort to pressure and ultimately collapse the Soviet Union by starving it for money and technology. The

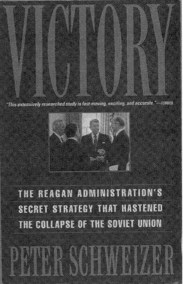

directives amount to a manifesto of economic war. The most important element of the strategy involved what Schweizer found to be "*a campaign to reduce dramatically Soviet hard currency earnings by driving down the price of oil with Saudi cooperation and limiting natural gas exports to the West.*"

Using oil as a geopolitical economic weapon is not new. It is well recognized that the single most provocative factor prompting the Japanese attack on Pearl Harbor in 1941, officially bringing the US into World War II, was the *de facto* oil embargo imposed on Japan by the US.[2] After Japan occupied Northern Indochina in 1940, the US had embargoed exports of iron, steel and scrap to Japan. When the Vichy French allowed Japan to also occupy Southern Indochina in 1941, the Roosevelt Administration froze Japanese assets in the US. That became a *de facto* oil embargo after July 25 of that year, because the US, then providing upwards of two-thirds of Japanese oil product imports, balked at issuing export licenses that would let the

2. Akira Iriye, *The Origins of the Second World War in Asia and in the Pacific* (New York: Longman, 1987), pp. 149-150. The passage is noted in a 1997 review by Brad DeLong, professor of economics at the University of California, Berkeley.

blocked funds be used for payment. Japan then shifted from a plan to attack the Russian East to a southward move on oil-rich Indonesia, including hits on the Philippines and Hawaii in December 1941.

Oil was also used as an economic bludgeon in the 1970s by Arab exporting states to punish the US and allies with what became a five-month embargo for their support of Israel in its 1973 war with Egypt and Syria.[3] That ushered in a decade of economic turmoil, inflation, currency gyrations and major global energy policy changes that put pressure on the oil-hungry US, and created a windfall for the crude-exporting Soviets.

Oil and energy would next figure prominently in the Reagan Administration's retaliatory campaign to bust the Soviet "Evil Empire."[4] Of the three major covert policy decrees Reagan signed to launch the anti-Soviet campaign, Schweizer cites National Security Decision Directive-66 as most pivotal in launching the oil price war against Moscow. Its main author, then-National Security Council staffer Roger W. Robinson, described it in *Victory* as "tantamount to a secret declaration of economic war on the Soviet Union."[5] It was signed by Reagan on November 29, 1982.

A six-page version of NSDD-66 was declassified in 1995, a year after *Victory* was published. It discloses that after meetings with then-Secretary of State George Shultz, the US and allies Canada, Germany, France, Italy, Japan and the UK had agreed on a framework of "security-minded principles that will govern East-West economic relations for the remainder of this decade and beyond."[6] It listed four "principal objectives":

- No new contracts to buy Russian natural gas beyond the first strand of a new Siberian pipeline and accelerate development of alternate Western energy supplies (especially Norwegian gas).

3. Daniel Yergin, *The Prize: The Epic Quest for Oil, Money & Power* (New York: Simon & Schuster 1991), pp. 588-612.

4. President Reagan's speech before the National Association of Evangelicals, Orlando, Florida, Mar. 8, 1983.

5. Peter Schweizer, *Victory: The Reagan Administration's Secret Strategy that Hastened the Collapse of the Soviet Union* (New York: The Atlantic Monthly Press, 1994), p. 126.

6. US National Security Council, National Security Decision Directive-66, Nov. 29, 1982.

- Expand the list of technology and equipment banned for the USSR under COCOM controls, with better enforcement.
- Beyond COCOM, restrict sales of other advanced technology and oil and gas equipment.
- "Substantially" raise interest rates on credit to the USSR, requiring higher down-payments and shorter maturities.

Note that nowhere in the declassified document is there specific mention of driving down oil prices or enlisting the aid of the Saudis. Indeed, an attached "summary of conclusions" reached by the allies specifically notes "it is not their purpose to engage in economic warfare against the Soviet Union" and "trade with the USSR must proceed on the basis of a strict balance of advantages." Knowing the document was likely to soon reach Soviet hands, the official wording may have been intentionally misleading. Robinson's "economic war" declaration is no doubt a better characterization of what NSDD-66 was really all about, with the devil in the details of more secure follow-on documents. Certainly, economic war is what it spawned.

NSDD-66 launched a huge effort, which marshaled the CIA, the Pentagon, Treasury and other government agencies to devise ways to increase economic pressure on the Soviets. It gave rise to a series of studies aimed at identifying and exploiting Soviet economic weakness. Among them, Schweizer found, was a "massive secret study on international oil pricing" concluded by the US Treasury Department in early 1983. Based on an oil price of $34/barrel, the study found the US was paying $183 billion for 5.5 billion barrels a year, of which 1.6 billion barrels were imports. A price drop to $20/barrel, Treasury concluded, would save $71.5 billion a year. It would be like a huge tax cut, benefiting the entire US economy except, of course, the upstream oil industry.[7]

More importantly, *Victory* claims that Treasury calculated the Soviets would be devastated, relying as they did on oil for as much as half their hard-currency earnings. Each $1/bbl change in the oil price meant $500 million to $1 billion a year for the Russians. They would be crippled by a price drop to $20. In addition, the stymieing of construction and expansion of the Soviets' planned new Siberian

7. Schweizer, pp. 140-144.

natural-gas export pipeline to Europe would have a serious effect. By various means, including probably sabotage, US policy managed to delay start-up of that Yamal line's first pipe by two years, depriving the cash-strapped Russians of up to $20 billion of hard-currency revenue. Its second pipe, which would have doubled those revenues, was delayed for more than a decade. Moreover, Washington was able to thwart over-funding of the Yamal line's construction by Western banks. Previously, the Soviets had been able to borrow twice the cost of an initial gas line to Europe, the Orenburg Pipeline, and divert the excess cash to other party uses.[8]

Before NSDD-66, Reagan had signed NSDD-32 in March 1982.[9] Partially declassified in 1996, it included various anti-Soviet goals, eg.: "contain and reverse the expansion of Soviet control," "increase the cost of Soviet support and use of proxy, terrorist and subversive forces," and "neutralize the efforts of the USSR to increase its influence."

The third key anti-Soviet document, signed by Reagan in January 1983, was NSDD-75.[10] Like its predecessor NSDDs, a nine-page version of that document declassified in 1994 makes no specific mention of forcing down oil prices. But authored primarily by former Harvard Russian history professor Richard Pipes, it lays out the most aggressive blueprint to that date for not merely containing, but even rolling back Russian influence. It declared US policy would be to loosen the Soviet hold on Eastern Europe and "promote ... the process of change in the Soviet Union toward a more pluralistic political and economic system in which the power of the privileged ruling elite is gradually reduced."[11]

---

8. Norman A. Bailey, *The Strategic Plan that Won the Cold War: National Security Decision Directive 75*, (McLean, VA: The Potomac Foundation, 1998), p. 17.
9. US NSC, NSDD-32, May 10, 1982.
10. US NSC, NSDD-75, Jan. 17, 1983.
11. Subsequent US administrations have greatly restricted the use of such broad national security policy documents, regularly changed their nomenclature and boosted their classification status to keep a tighter lid on planning. Under George H.W. Bush they were termed National Security Directives. President Clinton called them Presidential Decision Directives and George W. Bush has called them National Security Presidential Directives. So far, according the Federation of American Scientists, nothing similar to NSDD-66 has surfaced in regard to US-China economic warfare goals. But that does not mean such directives might not be in place.

In what seems to be a mandate for at least defensive market intervention in European gas, and world oil, prices against the Russians, NSDD-75 set out to "minimize the potential for Soviet exercise of reverse leverage on Western countries based on trade, energy supply and financial relationships."

Moscow promptly obtained the wording of NSDD-75 and within two months, a few days after Reagan's noted "Evil Empire" speech, began openly railing against such an aggressive US posture. But the meatier details of the new US policy may have been reserved for more secretive supporting documents, including oil price aspects of the economic war. As former Reagan National Security Advisor John Poindexter, perhaps coyly, told *Victory's* Schweizer, "I would be surprised if in NSDD-75, an NSDD after that, or a covert action finding about Saudi Arabia there wasn't something ... to reduce the foreign price of oil because of the effect that it has on the free world economy but also the impact on the Soviet Union."[12]

After NSDD-75, according to *Victory*, at least one more national security decision directive involving economic warfare against the Soviets was drafted and signed by Reagan, in April 1984. There is no record of such an NSDD on that subject at that time, according to an inventory maintained by the Federation of American Scientists. But there was an NSDD-139 signed April 5 of that year relating to contingency planning for a step-up in the Iran-Iraq war. A partially declassified version was released in 1994 with several redacted sections, including blacked-out portions regarding a "plan of action designed to avert an Iraqi collapse." A second Iran-Iraq war NSDD-141, was signed in late May, and remains entirely classified.

Victory says the April 1984 NSDD was drawn up particularly to respond to the threat that oil prices might jump again that year. Assigned once more to draft it was Roger Robinson, along with oil expert William Martin. They were tasked by National Security Advisor Robert McFarlane to "outline an alliance-wide strategy that would send the right signals to the market to prevent a sudden rise" in oil prices.[13] Among its recommendations if prices threatened to run up: a concerted plan for early release of strategic crude stockpiles by key

---

11. Schweizer, p. 218.
13. Ibid., p. 174.

allied countries in order to flood the market. "Speculators were going to be thrashed this time around," Robinson told Schweizer.[14]

Reagan never did have to resort to releasing crude from the US Strategic Petroleum Reserve, which had been set up after the mid-1970s Arab oil embargo and was budgeted to hold 750 million barrels by 1990. Instead, word of the implied threat to do so was spread generously around the oil markets to ward off bullish speculators and encourage the bears. It appears to have been mainly a jawboning effort, *Victory* says, with US officials "dispatched to keep markets calm."

But as early as 1983 the Reagan Administration cut by one-third its crude purchases going into the SPR, to 145,000 b/d. That had the effect of adding more barrels to an already increasingly sloppy crude market, indicating there was a more active and multi-faceted effort afoot beyond mere talk to push down oil prices. We will look further at the uses of strategic reserves in oil price manipulation in a later chapter.

Exactly how the US and its allies succeeded in driving down the price of oil in the 1980s is not explained in Schweizer's book, except to note the Saudi decision in August 1985 to open the floodgates, slash its pricing, and pump more oil into the market. Schweizer credits that crucial Saudi decision to the personal assurances by President Reagan to Saudi King Fahd in early 1985, during a White House visit, that the US would protect Saudi Arabia against any military

---

14. It is interesting to note that Roger W. Robinson Jr., the primary author of NSDD-66 while a member of the Reagan National Security Council, went on to become chairman of the Congressional US-China Economic and Security Review Commission (www.USCC.gov). Formerly the loan portfolio manager for Chase Manhattan Bank in the Soviet Union, Central and Eastern Europe, Robinson was also personal assistant to former Chase Chairman David Rockefeller. Under Reagan he was Senior Director of International Economic Affairs at the NSC from March 1982 to September 1985. Robinson now heads private investment risk analysis firm Conflict Securities Advisory Group, which monitors corporate involvement in rogue states like Iran, Sudan, North Korea and Syria. In presenting the USCC's strongly worded and highly critical 2005 report to Congress, Robinson seemed to echo NSDD-66 by urging the US to "reach out more creatively and involve its allies – such as Japan and the European Union – in addressing mutual trade- and security-related concerns with China." He noted the need for "meaningful upward revaluation of the Chinese currency" and proof China is really a "market status economy." He initially agreed to be interviewed by this writer about NSDD-66 but later declined.

moves by Iran. Straining under the costs of its desultory war with Iraq, Iran had been pressuring the Saudis to prop up OPEC oil pricing and was threatening to expand attacks on Persian Gulf tankers.

Other administration officials, including Defense Secretary Caspar Weinberger, Energy Secretary John Harrington and the CIA's William Casey had been quietly raising the issue of lower prices with the Saudis for many months before that. And there were similar efforts afoot with Kuwait and other US-friendly Persian Gulf states to support a major price drop.

Curiously, not long after the dramatic Saudi price-cut move in 1985 there was a flurry of major oil-find or reserve upgrade announcements in the Middle East that served to further assure the world it was facing no near-term crude shortage. Iraq, Iran, Abu Dhabi, and Venezuela all claimed to have roughly doubled their prior estimates of proved reserves, with the Saudis also taking a big write-up around 1990 to more than 250 billion barrels.[15]

Oil economists have generally attributed the 1985 Saudi price cut and resulting downward global "oil shock" to the kingdom's own economic self-interest rather than to US arm-twisting. True,

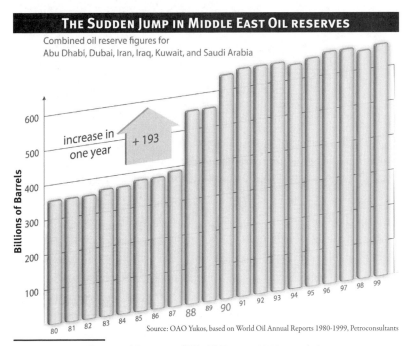

THE SUDDEN JUMP IN MIDDLE EAST OIL RESERVES

Combined oil reserve figures for
Abu Dhabi, Dubai, Iran, Iraq, Kuwait, and Saudi Arabia

increase in one year + 193

Billions of Barrels

600
500
400
300
200
100

80 81 82 83 84 85 86 87 88 89 90 91 92 93 94 95 96 97 98 99

Source: OAO Yukos, based on World Oil Annual Reports 1980-1999, Petroconsultants

15. BP Amoco Statistical Review of World Energy 1999, pp. 4-5.

the Saudi regime was suffering under low export volumes as it struggled to maintain world oil prices. But it seems implausible the Saudis would suddenly undertake such a radical change in their role as OPEC's linchpin "swing producer" without serious prodding and encouragement from Washington.

As the biggest producer and main source of spare capacity in OPEC, the Saudis have been the biggest beneficiary of OPEC price maintenance efforts. But they pay for that by being the first to absorb production cuts if needed to balance supply when demand falls, and to add barrels if demand rises.

OPEC had boosted the price of oil in 1973 from $2.90 a barrel to $11.50 in just a few months, around the time of the Yom Kippur war. In 1978-79, spurred by Iran's Islamic Revolution, the start of the Iran-Iraq war and later the Soviet invasion of Afghanistan, OPEC had pushed up the price of international crude almost threefold, from under $13 a barrel to more than $34 in just two years.

But world demand was starting to drop sharply at those prices, and by mid-1982 OPEC's 31 million b/d of output of the late 1970s had shrunk to 17.5 million b/d. Saudi crude exports ebbed from 10 million b/d in 1981, or almost 43% of OPEC production, to barely 2 million b/d (under 21%) in 1985. Price discounting by Saudi rivals in OPEC was rampant, leaving Riyadh to bear the full load of cartel price maintenance.

New output from the UK North Sea had become a particular threat to OPEC, and led the cartel, under Saudi pressure, to reluctantly trim its official price in mid-March of 1983 from $34/barrel to $29. But that was still a windfall for the exporting USSR, and likely more than could be supported by a continuing drop in world demand. OPEC, and especially the Saudis, continued to lose market share.

Even at its official selling price in that year of a rich $32/barrel for its somewhat less attractive crude, the Saudis began running budget deficits in 1982. And they would get worse. From an estimated $160 billion of financial reserves in 1981, the accumulated Saudi investment surplus had shrunk by 1985 to only $50 billion, after excluding some $30 billion of assets held in the form of doubtful loans to third-world countries.[16]

16. Wilfrid L. Kohl (ed.), *After the Oil Price Collapse; OPEC, the United States and the World Oil Market* (Baltimore: The Johns Hopkins University Press, 1991), pp. 37-39.

In June of 1985, Saudi crude sales to the US had essentially ceased, falling to a mere 26,000 b/d from 1.4 million b/d in 1979. The kingdom's overall output of 2.2 million b/d was half its OPEC quota level, and at times even less that UK North Sea production.

It was amid those grim statistics, and soon after Reagan's meeting with King Fahd, that in the summer of 1985 Saudi oil minister "Sheikh"[17] Ahmed Zaki Yamani began approaching Western oil majors with an offer to boost sales volume of crude using "netback" pricing. Under that scheme, the Saudis agreed to sell crude to major refining customers and bill them later, at whatever price was required to give the refiner an agreed-on profit on finished product, say around $2/bbl.

It was a temporary end to the Saudi swing-producer role, and a move away from price support to market share maintenance. "We want to regain our market power," Yamani commented. Later asked about resuming the Saudi swing-producer role, Yamani quipped, "We all swing together or not at all."[18]

The launch of netback pricing by the Saudis in September of 1985 quickly lifted the kingdom's oil exports back to their OPEC quota level of 4 million b/d, and it triggered an all-out price war, as OPEC price cheaters scrambled to maintain their discounts. By early 1986, US refinery crude acquisition costs had tumbled to near $10/barrel, and some Persian Gulf shiploads were going for as little as $6/bbl there. That was even though the actual volumes of OPEC crude added to the market rose only about 9% and overall free-world crude supply rose only about 3%.[19]

Thrown into panic and disarray, OPEC convened in early 1986. In December of that year it had settled on a new quota scheme with a price target of around $18/barrel. Worried non-OPEC producing countries like Mexico, Egypt and Oman attended as observers. Mexico agreed to cut 10% of production or 150,000 b/d. Norway cut.

---

17. In Yamani's case, an honorific title. That is from p. 639 of *The Prize: The Epic Quest for Oil, Money & Power*, by veteran oil and energy consultant Daniel Yergin. A tome of Biblical stature among oilmen, it won a Pulitzer Prize in 1992. I picked up my more than 900-page hardbound copy at an East Village, New York, second-hand bookstore called The Strand for two-thirds off the cover price. Opening it I was amused to see who had been its prior owner. The signed greeting by Dan Yergin was "To Henry Paulson – Best wishes in the quest for the prize."
18. Yergin, p. 760.
19. Ibid., p. 750.

Even the stunned Soviets made a token contribution to the market stabilization effort by offering to cut 100,000 b/d of exports, though it would prove hard to measure. Netback pricing ended and the oil market settled at around $15 to $18/barrel, having wiped out all the impact of the oil shock of the late 1970s, and in line with the levels targeted by the Reagan Administration.[20]

Over-quota production continued within OPEC, however, and the Saudis had to again cut output as the swing producer. The Saudi restraint, and the dispatch of US warships to protect Kuwaiti tankers from increasing Iranian attacks in the Persian Gulf, helped firm oil prices to above $17 in 1987. But as the price rose, so did the quota-cheating among OPEC members. Iran, Kuwait, Venezuela and Indonesia were well over their allotted volumes and prices ended the year around $14/barrel.

Prices rose slightly in early 1988 to about $18 on signs OPEC would reduce the cheating. But weak world demand and rising non-OPEC output meant OPEC production was still too high. Prices again fell to about $14 in early 1988, and later that year dipped below $10 for Dubai grades amid another wave of OPEC overproduction, this time by the Saudis, Kuwait and Abu Dhabi. Just why the Saudis and Kuwaitis would pour on more barrels at that time was never clear. Some thought they were trying to discipline the Abu Dhabis, or pre-empt cheating by Iran and Iraq. Others suspected the Saudis just needed the cash.[21]

Or might it have been due to yet more encouragement from the US national security team to drive a stake through the heart of a stumbling USSR?

Death blow to the Soviet empire

Whatever the causes and motivations of the 1980s oil price collapse, the damaging impact on the Soviets is difficult to overstate. Russian academic Yegor Gaidar, acting prime minister of Russia from 1991 to 1994 and a former minister of economy, has described it as clearly the mortal blow that wrecked the teetering Soviet Union.[22]

---

20. Ibid., pp. 758-764.
21. Kohl, p. 59.
22. Yegor Gaidar, *The Soviet Collapse: Grain and Oil*, American Enterprise Institute for Public Policy Research, April 2007.

Gaidar notes the struggling Soviet economy had been bailed out by oil in the 1970s. Unable to export manufactured goods due to their poor quality, the Soviets had to rely mainly on raw commodity exports for the hard currency needed to buy foreign wheat, mostly from the US. Luckily, a series of rich oil finds in the Tyumen region of Western Siberia in the 1970s, coupled with a fortuitous quadrupling of world oil prices, provided a windfall of oil export revenues. That allowed Moscow to fund its growing need for imported grain, stemming from the ongoing failure of an agricultural system still reeling from Stalin-era collectivization.

From only about $3 billion a year in oil export revenues in 1972, Soviet hard-currency oil sales to the capitalist world soared to around $25 billion in 1980 and peaked in 1983 at around $26 billion. With Soviet oil production rising to almost 12 million b/d at its peak in 1988 (10 million b/d of that in Russia itself), it was the world's largest producer, and second only to Saudi Arabia as an oil exporter at 4.1 million b/d.[23] As the Reagan oil-price war gained momentum, aided by the Saudi decision to boost output in 1985, Russian oil revenues plunged. Gaidar calculates Soviet oil export income had fallen to $10 billion in 1986, remaining below $15 billion through 1989, despite a mostly futile attempt to ramp-up production and export volumes. All told, the cumulative loss in Soviet hard-currency earnings due to the oil price drop from 1983 to 1989 added up to about $80 billion.

A further effect of the 1985 oil price downdraft was a big drop in Soviet foreign arms sales, another key hard-currency earner, as its biggest customers in the Middle East faced budget strains. To make matters even worse for Moscow, and OPEC, the Reaganites had engineered a steep decline in the value of the US dollar after 1985. So whatever hard currency income they were getting for their crude was plunging in real value. By mid-1986 it took five times as much Russian oil sales volume to afford a given piece of West German machinery than it did a year before. Soviet plans to remake their economy with Western capital goods soon fell apart, and a raft of large industrial projects were derailed.[24]

23. Center for Energy Economics, University of Texas at Austin, "Soviet Legacy on Russian Petroleum Industry."
24. Schweizer, p. 263.

To compensate for the revenue loss a desperate Mikhail Gorbachev began seeking bank loans from the West. As Gaidar observed, "Instead of implementing actual reforms, the Soviet Union started to borrow money from abroad while its international credit rating was still strong. It borrowed heavily from 1985 to 1988, but in 1989 the Soviet economy stalled completely." It then tried to assemble a consortium of 300 banks to fund a $100 billion loan in 1989, but won commitments from only five. The bankers told Gorbachev he would have to negotiate directly with Western governments for what Gaidar terms "politically motivated credits."

To get that funding, Gorbachev had to stand back and allow freedom movements to wrest control of Lithuania, and then the rest of Eastern Europe. Despite weeks of rioting in East Germany, the Soviets held back from sending in troops to crush that unrest, and finally in November of that year the East German government allowed free passage to West Berlin. The wall was soon dismantled, a symbolic end of the Soviet era. The Soviets had been forced to let go of Eastern Europe in return for loans roughly equal to the revenues lost from falling oil prices and delay of the Yamal gas pipeline.

Even with the Western loans, by late1991 the Soviet Union was out of money. "A state that does not control its borders or military and has no revenue simply cannot exist," Gaidar writes, noting the Soviet Union came to an effective end in November 1991 when Vneshekonombank informed Soviet leaders there were no more funds on hand. The USSR simply went bust. Gorbachev resigned on Christmas Day.

Just as happened to 16th Century Spain, with its windfall gold and silver from the New World, the Soviets went from phenomenal sudden oil wealth to losing an entire empire without ever being decisively defeated on the battlefield. Indeed, Gaidar blames Moscow's oil-funded conquest of Afghanistan in 1979, and especially the 1985 escalation of fighting against the Taliban, for solidifying US-Saudi relations. That lead directly, he claims, to the kingdom's oil price-reduction and production-hike that ruined the Soviet financial structure. Certainly, Reagan's team played heavily on fears of Russian plans to eventually dominate the Middle East in enlisting Saudi support for breaking the USSR.

Uncle Sam as oil market manipulator

Whether the 1980s oil price drop was mainly a function of normal market adjustments or was politically driven by US national security efforts can perhaps be debated. The triumphal breast-beating by Reagan NSC types in *Victory* might have been just so much after-the-fact glory gathering for events that just happened to occur on their watch. But it is undeniable that oil prices fell and fell hard in the 1980s, beginning almost as soon as Ronald Reagan's election as President.

Long before its main price shock in 1985, Saudi Arabia had begun an initial price retrenchment soon after Reagan was first elected in November 1980, and even before he was inaugurated. Facing buyer resistance from its traditional US refining customers, the Saudis cut their official selling price of Saudi Light crude from $34 to $32/barrel, and increased production. By year-end 1981 the rest of OPEC had been forced to follow the Saudi lead and trim prices as well. US refiner crude acquisition costs, which had approached $40/barrel in late 1980, began to ease, and by the end of 1982 were under $30/barrel, according to the EIA.

OPEC market-watchers were openly suspicious that the Reagan Administration was actively at work to undermine world crude prices, either through the actions of over-producing Western oil companies or manipulation of the newly-opened New York Mercantile Exchange's crude futures. One secret briefing memo for Secretary of State George Shultz in early 1985, before a meeting with King Fahd, urged Shultz to deal with "allegations the US is manipulating oil markets," according to *Victory*. "OPEC ministers including Yamani have accused the US of engineering a plot to drive down oil prices to some pre-conceived level," the memo said. To which Schweizer's NSC sources replied, "Yamani was only half wrong. The US had no preconceived price."[25]

Given the extraordinary efforts expended by the Reagan Administration on other aspects of the economic war with the Soviets, it is hard to imagine it would have left oil prices to take their own leisurely pace downward, or have relied solely on eventual Saudi cooperation. William Casey, Reagan's Director of Central Intelligence

---

25. Ibid., p. 218.

and perhaps the single most ardent and powerful player in the anti-Soviet campaign, "was keeping an eye on oil prices almost daily," Schweizer reported.

In addition to his notoriously secretive management of aggressive clandestine operations, Casey brought to his CIA role a background as a Wall Street lawyer, international banker and former head of the Securities and Exchange Commission. He knew money. He knew markets. And he was a master at working covertly through front organizations. *Victory* notes even most senior Reagan national security insiders had little awareness of what all Bill Casey was doing in the darkness of CIA covert "ops" to further the cause of Soviet collapse. Most likely, they didn't *want* to know.

In retrospect it seems implausible Casey would have missed the opportunity to quickly begin ratcheting oil prices downward by selling futures on the NYMEX. In March 1983, soon after the OPEC price cut that year to $29/barrel, the New York Mercantile Exchange launched trading in 1,000-barrel futures contracts for the benchmark US light, sweet crude, or West Texas Intermediate.

Planning for the WTI contract had been in the works for four years, and its introduction followed Reagan's lifting of antiquated US oil pricing and tax rules soon after he took office. For the first time, rights to future oil production could be traded and settled strictly for cash without having to physically take or deliver the crude. No longer would the oil price be set just by a clubby network of physical producers, refiners or "wet" barrel traders. Now anyone with enough nerve and cash to put down the 5% margin, could buy or sell "paper" barrels through the anonymity of brokers.

The supply of paper barrels suddenly mushroomed while paper buyers, at high and falling oil prices, were wary. From the start, activity on the NYMEX was characterized by persistent and determined selling of futures contracts by unknown speculators betting oil prices would fall. "It's those damn shorts on the NYMEX!" was a common complaint of Houston oil traders in the early 1980s, as paper prices dragged down the value of real or wet-barrel trades. Were those "shorts" merely brilliant market analysts? Were they just bold and marvelously lucky? Or did they have inside information on the direction of oil prices? Were they perhaps even fronting for government, and playing with CIA- or Treasury-controlled slush funds?

Among the earliest players in NYMEX crude futures was Dutchman John Deuss, a secretive former Mercedes dealer who rose to prominence as one of the more notable global oil traders in the 1970s. Deuss had been particularly involved in trading Russian oil, was intimately familiar with the Russian oil scene and the players there, and would be a prominent figure in the scramble for Soviet oil assets after the USSR's collapse.

Rumors of Deuss' links to the CIA have persisted since at least the late 1970s, when he brazenly reneged on paying $102 million for a series of Russian oil cargos. After a decade of arbitration and litigation, Deuss reportedly settled the case on favorable terms.[26] In the early 1980s he employed Research Associates International, headed by CIA Vietnam clandestine operations veteran and former Miami station chief Theodore Shackley, to help organize crude shipments from Oman and elsewhere to the embargoed apartheid regime in South Africa.

According to former close acquaintances of Deuss, his Transworld Oil organization was one of the biggest early traders in NYMEX futures, and accounted for as much as 30% of the activity there, or about a million barrels per day, in its first few years. Deuss employed a "very sophisticated trading system" using computerized and econometric modeling, according to an ex-associate. But after about five years, in the late 1980s, the system is said to have been abandoned.[27] By then, Transworld's trading program may have been

---

26. "The rise and fall of oil impresario John Deuss," *Platts Energy Economist*, Issue 303, Jan. 1, 2007, p. 27.

27. Interview of a confidential Deuss associate. Ironically, perhaps, soon after London's International Petroleum Exchange began trading paper futures in North Sea Brent crude in 1987, Deuss tried to corner the market in that key light, sweet benchmark grade. He reportedly spent some $425 million to buy up all but one of the 42 Brent cargos slated for sale in January 1988. But Duess is said to have misread signals of a possible OPEC tightening. Western oil majors, reportedly fearing a probe of their own Brent trading, are said to have added more barrels to the market to damp a brief price-run. Spot-market Brent prices jumped from an average of barely $14/barrel in 1986 to almost $18.50 in 1987 before easing back under $15 in 1988, according to *Platts*. Deuss is reported to have sold half his cargos at a profit but lost about $200 million overall on that play.

surpassed by more powerful platforms being developed inside the major brokerage houses and investment banks.

Whether or not John Deuss was gaming the NYMEX crude contract for Casey's CIA or the US Treasury, he certainly had the background, the capabilities and the chutzpah to play a role in manipulating even the huge global crude oil market in the 1980s. And Deuss should have done well. Given the sharp and fairly steady decline in crude prices in the Reagan 1980s, short-sellers on the NYMEX ought to have made out handsomely. Many billions of dollars would have been reaped by those traders lucky or smart enough to know where that market was heading. The oil-consuming US and developed-world economies also benefited mightily from the price drop.

There was collateral damage for the US, however. The large and thriving independent domestic oil and gas industry of 1980 was decimated. Hundreds of companies failed, were sold, or closed up shop. Idle rigs and other oilfield hardware went begging for buyers. In 1984, largely due to energy loans gone bad, the eighth-largest US bank, Continental Illinois, had to be taken over and recapitalized by the FDIC. Scores of other major banks in Texas and Oklahoma also had to be rescued.

The US oil majors, with deep pockets, downstream profit centers, low debt and bloated cost structures that could be trimmed, fared all right, or at least survived with a few scars. In fact, they emerged all the stronger compared to their weakened independent rivals and smaller integrated companies.

A huge run-up to double digits in US interest rates to squelch oil-driven inflation, under 1979 Federal Reserve appointee Paul Volcker, had pushed up the dollar's relative value to other Western currencies by 50%. That had hurt US industrial and other exporters. Housing, land and office building values sagged, and a surge in mortgage foreclosures added to pressure on the savings and loan industry, which went through a painful and messy process of liquidation and recapitalization of almost 750 S&Ls, estimated to have cost taxpayers nearly $90 billion.[28]

---

28. US General Accounting Office, Financial Audit: Resolution Trust Corporation's 1995 and 1994 Financial Statements, July 1996, p. 9.

Whatever the financial costs to the US, however, compared to armed nuclear conflict, the economic war on Russia would have been a bargain at many times its price. It seemed to show that with patience, deep pockets and strong allies, the US could break an enemy and even make a buck or two in the process. A generation of US policy makers was born, steeped in the skills of financial and commodity market manipulation, and imbued with the idea they could alter physical reality to confound any future foe.

It would not be long until they were proudly at it again. In a 2004 article in the *New York Times Magazine*, writer Ron Suskind quoted an unidentified aid to George W. Bush deriding "what we call the reality-based community": the media, academics and others who "believe that solutions emerge from your judicious study of discernible reality." "That's not the way the world really works anymore," the source continued. "We're an empire now, and when we act, we create our own reality. And while you're studying that reality—judiciously, as you will—we'll act again, creating other new realities, which you can study too, and that's how things will sort out. We're history's actors ... and you, all of you, will be left to just study what we do."[29]

---

29. Ron Suskind, "Faith, Certainty and the Presidency of George W. Bush," *New York Times Magazine*, Oct. 17, 2004.

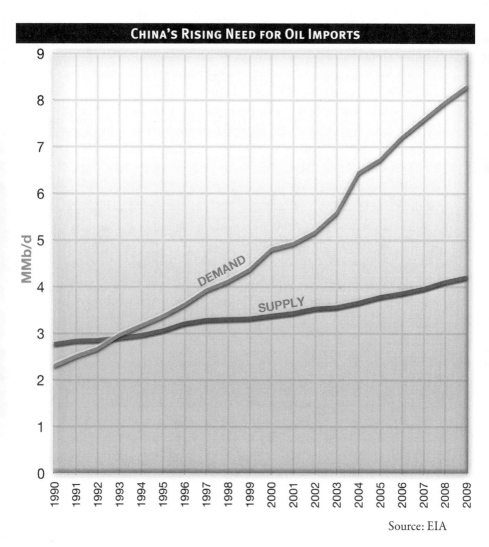

CHINA'S RISING NEED FOR OIL IMPORTS

MMb/d

DEMAND

SUPPLY

Source: EIA

—2—
Next Target: China?

On almost every issue, the Chinese harbor suspicions that the US has malignant plans to restrain the growth of China's power and to take advantage of its vulnerabilities.... In energy security, it is believed that the US deliberately keeps oil prices high and tries to deprive China of cheaper oil from countries like Sudan by demonizing China's policy toward Africa.
— Peking University dean of international studies Wang Jisi, director of international strategic studies institute at the Central Party school.[1]

Given the stunning success of such a bloodless economic war against even the outwardly mighty and nuclear-armed Soviet Union in the 1980s, it is only logical the US might try to play the "Oil Card" again against its other long-standing remaining Big Power rival: the People's Republic of China. Reminiscent of the case with Russia, there is no concrete, documentary or other hard evidence that such an economic war has been launched against the PRC. But there is abundant circumstantial evidence that at least a low-grade version of that conflict is well under way. As with the USSR econo-war, the conflict may again be reflected in the curious behavior of oil and other key commodity prices.

As crude oil futures on the NYMEX hit $100 a barrel in December 2007, a number of respected analysts flatly declared that price to be as much as $50 a barrel too high, based on even the most costly new sources of supply. The culprit: unidentified market "speculators." Particularly outspoken was Fadel Gheit, a managing director and senior oil analyst with Oppenheimer & Co. He told a hearing of the US Senate Committee on Homeland Security and Government Affairs that "current high oil prices are inflated by as much as 100%." Said Gheit, "I don't think industry fundamentals of supply and demand justify the current high prices, which I believe are driven by excessive speculation." As he noted, "most OPEC ministers and the

1. Wang Jisi, "America in Asia: How much does China care?" *Global Asia*, Vol. 2, No. 2, Fall 2007.

heads of major international oil companies" share that view, which has been echoed by even US Energy Secretary Samuel W. Bodman.[2] Bodman would later change his tune, insisting the run-up to an even more astounding price of almost $140 in June 2008 was "strictly supply and demand."[3]

As the price of oil has climbed steadily skyward, OPEC leaders have been adamant they are not to blame. They have repeatedly noted ample supplies of physical crude available globally. They accuse instead nameless, faceless "speculators" for the problem, as well as a chronic tightness in US refinery capacity in recent years, due to lack of reinvestment and new construction here. "In my view, the basic reason for which we have been seeing higher prices since last September is because of speculation," declared OPEC Secretary-General Abdullah al-Badri in a January 2008 interview, typical of the views within OPEC.[4]

As stored tanker-loads of unmarketable Iranian heavy crude were riding at anchor in the Persian Gulf in June 2008, an angry Iranian President Mahmoud Ahmadinejad told an OPEC-related gathering in Isfahan the huge price run-up in world crude prices has been "completely fake and imposed." He blamed "speculation" by "visible and invisible hands" with "political and economic aims."[5]

For several years the Chinese have been railing against unspecified market-manipulation forces driving oil prices upward. In 2005, Xu Ding Ming, director of the energy bureau at China's powerful National Development and Reform Commission, lashed out at the unidentified "international petroleum crocodiles," for jacking up NYMEX WTI futures to what was then $67 a barrel. He accused those unnamed forces of intentionally bidding up crude futures and conspiring to restrict world oil supplies in order to drive up the price.[6]

Who are these unknown "crocodiles"? The general perception is that the managers of private investment pools, "hedge funds," and major investment banks with proprietary commodity trading desks

2. Fadel Gheit, prepared remarks to the US Senate Committee on Homeland Security and Government Affairs, Dec. 11, 2007.

3. Reuters, "US Energy Secretary to attend Saudi oil meeting," June 11, 2008.

4. Michele Kambas, "Speculators drive oil price rise: OPEC sec-gen," Reuters, Jan. 13, 2008.

5. Reuters, "Market full of oil, price trend 'fake': Ahmadinejad," June 17, 2008.

6. "Petrodollars," *Platts Oilgram News*, Vol. 83, No. 156, August 15, 2005, p. 4.

have been bidding up oil futures. But where do they get the confidence and the capital to go so far out on a limb to make such huge bets? To the Chinese and the Iranians there can be only one answer: Somehow the US government is behind it.

Whether or not it is "manipulation," there is ample evidence oil markets are under some form of concerted upward trading pressure. Oil futures over $100 a barrel, against marginal finding and development costs less than half that amount, could be considered *prima facie* evidence of market rigging. The huge volume of futures trading, far beyond the normal needs of industry hedging activity, is another sign. Unfortunately, given the record of admitted US oil price action against the Soviets, the finger naturally points to Washington and New York. As we will see in Chapter 12, the CFTC has clearly aided and abetted the run-up by suspending position limits on commodity index players.

With or without hard evidence, there is a growing conviction among the Chinese masses that oil prices, and probably other raw material and agricultural commodity costs, are being manipulated upward with US encouragement. The goal: to crimp China's emergence as a dominant world economy, or worse. This simmering suspicion was brought out into the open recently by Wang Jisi, director of the international strategic studies institute at the Central Party school and dean of international studies at Peking University. Considered a preeminent Chinese US-watcher, he warned in a lead story for *Global Asia* in late 2007 that the Chinese populace increasingly believes the US is not only propping up oil prices, but also has manufactured the "global warming" scare to force down Chinese carbon emissions. They think the US is trying to force up the value of China's currency, while devaluing its own dollar, to limit Chinese exports.

"On almost every issue, the Chinese harbor suspicions that the US has malignant plans to restrain the growth of China's power and to take advantage of its vulnerabilities," Jisi has said. He himself seems to treat the idea of US oil price manipulation as little more than misguided popular myth, but warns that the perceptions themselves become a force to be reckoned with. Indeed, those notions are not confined to just the uninformed lower rungs of Chinese society, but also permeate to the highest levels of the PRC ruling elite. "Whether or not that's true," former US China ambassador J. Stapleton Roy told me in 2005, "the Chinese leadership believes it."[7]

The Beijing government has made only generalized open complaints about world oil price manipulation in public, and has cautiously avoided trying to pin the blame specifically on the US. It may raise the issue in private with people like Ambassador Roy, but it has made no public formal protest or accusation. Chinese government officials refused to even discuss the issue for this book.

But then, such circumspection is not surprising. Even to suggest they suspect a crime and a likely perpetrator would mean they would have to *do* something about it to maintain Communist Party credibility and control. And if the villain is the world's leading superpower, then best keep silent until you *can* do something about it, or do it on the QT.

The stakes could not be higher. "It would be hard to imagine a more hostile and provocative US policy toward China," noted professors Eugene Gholz and Daryl Press, writing for the Cato Institute in 2007. Stating the Oil Card case in reverse, they wrote, "The only way for the US to stem China's energy consumption would be to significantly slow China's economic growth – a goal that would trigger enormous bilateral tension and, given the importance that the Chinese government attaches to steady economic growth, possibly war."[8] In reality, the strategy may be to force the Chinese to consume yet more energy, and make them pay through the nose for it.

For some forty years under Communism, China's insulated and mostly agrarian economy managed to be self-sufficient in oil and most other commodities. But by 1993, at an oil consumption rate of just over 3 million b/d, a combination of increasing industrialization and flagging output from Chinese fields tipped the PRC from being a slight net exporter of crude to being a slight importer. From there, its imports have risen steadily at a brisk pace. In 2007 they were nearly 3.3 million b/d, or more than the country's total oil use in 1993. Crude imports were up 12.3% for the year and totaled nearly half China's total demand of about 7 million b/d, making China the

---

7. "China may be stalking new upstream prey," *Platts Oilgram News*, Vol. 83, No. 123, June 28, 2005, p. 1.

8. Eugene Gholz and Daryl G. Press, "Energy Alarmism: The Myths that Make Americans Worry About Oil," Cato Institute, Policy Analysis No. 589, Apr. 5, 2007.

world's biggest oil importer behind the US. In just 10 years, China's bill for imported oil has mushroomed from under $3 billion in 1998 to a current rate in mid-2008 of more than $200 billion a year.

Economic war: The Oil Front

If, just *if*, economic war were to break out between the US and China, oil pricing would have to be a primary battle front for the US and its allies. Oil supply, which was a major strength for the Soviets, is a particular weakness for China. It has to import nearly as great a share of its petroleum needs as does the US, but is much less able to afford it. With more than half its forecasted 8.1 million b/d of 2008 oil demand expected to come from abroad, China is already seriously exposed to world oil prices. And that is even before the expected surge in automobile use as more of its population reaches the $5,000 of annual income considered a threshold for increasing car ownership. By 2030 China is expected to require imports of almost 10 million b/d, according to the International Energy Agency, which has been chronically low and after-the-fact in its China oil forecasts.

China's consumption of oil is not very efficient. Much of it goes for what would be low-value uses in the West, such as power generation and industrial heat. China's refineries are generally not configured to run heavy, sour crude, so they must buy more expensive light, sweet grades. And since oil is priced in dollars, China pays a stiff premium when it uses its undervalued currency. High oil prices are a pain in the neck for Americans, but they could strangle the Chinese economy.

Logistically, the bulk of China's 4 million b/d of oil imports comes from the Persian Gulf through the Straits of Malacca. That makes those shipments particularly vulnerable to US interdiction in the event of an oil embargo. Soon after becoming PRC president in 2003, Hu Jintao warned of China's "Malacca dilemma." To circumvent that route would require almost 1,000 nautical miles of added tanker travel. That would add several days and considerable expense per voyage while still facing overwhelming US sea power. That Malacca traffic is also vulnerable to "pirate" attacks, which could be a cover for state-sponsored harassment. In mid-2005 Lloyd's briefly declared the strait a war zone for insurance purposes, sending coverage costs soaring.

Adding to the vulnerability in this reliance on long-distance tanker traffic through insecure sea lanes is the fact that very little of China's crude oil is carried in Chinese ships. More than 90% of China's oil imports come by sea. But in 2004 only about 10% of that moved in Chinese vessels, rising to only 16% by 2006. Meanwhile, the cost of chartering a VLCC from the Arab Gulf eastward had spiked to more than $200,000 a day in late 2007 from about $14,000/d in 2000. They spiked again to more than $150,000/d in May of 2008 and appear headed for a yearly record.[9]

In 2006 China launched a major $10 billion supertanker construc-

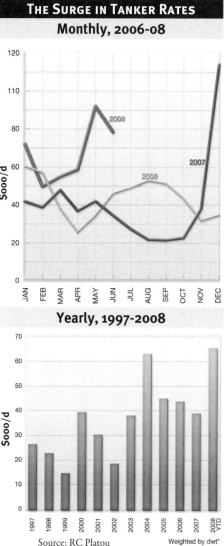

THE SURGE IN TANKER RATES
Monthly, 2006-08

Yearly, 1997-2008

Source: RC Platou   Weighted by dwt*

tion effort aimed at carrying the equivalent of half China's crude imports in Chinese boats. From about 25 VLCCs, China's supertanker count would have to swell to more than 100 such ships by 2015.[10] Even with six yards reported to be fabricating those vessels, and with more shipyards expected to join the effort, rising costs and the logistical problems of such a massive building effort will make it

9. RS Platou Economic Research, Weekly Tanker Rates, June 9, 2008.

10. David Lague, "China begins expanding its supertanker fleet," *International Herald Tribune*, May 16, 2007.

a challenge for China to meet that goal. And it will still be exposed to foreign-owned shipping for half its crude needs.

Except for one costly new and under-utilized crude pipeline from Kazakhstan to remote Western China refineries, China has no overland pipeline access to crude oil. Its deliveries from Russia, running at less than a modest 300,000 b/d in 2007, move almost entirely by slow and costly rail shipments with only about 12,000 b/d allocated by Moscow to China via the Kazakh pipe.[11] Long-pending plans for a major crude pipeline from the Urals region to northeastern China have been plagued by continuing foot-dragging by Russia.

Although China has attempted to create a small strategic petroleum reserve, under prodding from the US and OECD, those new tank farms reportedly held only about 15 to 22 million barrels of crude at year-end 2007.[12] That was less than a week's worth of Chinese oil imports. Only one of four strategic stockpile tank farms along the China coast, at Ningbo, has started to accept oil, according to Chinese news reports. Plans are to eventually store 12 million metric tons, or about 90 million barrels, with additional tank farms at Dalian, Quingdao and Zhoushan. That would be a one-month supply at an import rate of 3 million b/d. But at the 4 million b/d of imports expected in 2008, even a stockpile that size costing $9 billion at $100 a barrel would last only three weeks. That is half the existing days-supply of OECD crude stocks and would be about one-third of the more than 70-day import "cover" in the US Strategic Petroleum Reserve. In addition, much of that tankage is leased to Chinese oil majors, so the oil may function more like commercial inventory than strategic reserves.

In the event of a US-led oil embargo in retaliation for some future invasion of Taiwan or other aggressive act, China would quickly feel the economic pinch of a physical interruption in crude oil deliveries.

But such an embargo would be overt, controversial and could likely be applied by the US for only a limited time. More damaging, over the course of years or decades, could be the effects of very high oil prices. Like a relentless tax, the high cost of foreign oil and other key raw materials would be a steady drain on Chinese wealth

11. EIA, "Country Analysis Briefs: Kazakhstan," February 2008.
12. "China sets up oil reserve center," Xinhua News Agency, Dec 24, 2007.

and capital. In theory, the compounding effect might trim enough of China's GDP growth to stress that brittle political system with unemployment, inflation and social unrest. With no electoral system in place for the release of pent-up pressure, the PRC leadership elite has reason to worry.

Heavily Muslim and resource-rich Xinjiang province in China's far northwestern corner has a history of insurrection. Some published reports say there could be as many as 100 armed separatist or rebel movements of various forms simmering within China. Rapid communications by Internet and cell phone make crowd control a major challenge, and there are periodic press reports of spontaneous uprisings of thousands of industrial workers, or whole rural communities, to vent anger over wages, land seizures, pollution or other affronts of corporations or corrupt government. These hint of a pressure-cooker environment ready to blow. Regime change in China may not be beyond the realm of possibility in the minds of US strategic planners.

China: Vulnerable to economic attack

Chinese military strategists have been preoccupied with the threat of such political and economic warfare, and have warned their country is at a significant disadvantage in a protracted struggle such as the US successfully waged against the Soviets. Giving voice to this concern was a 2001 paper by Chinese military expert Jiang Luming of China's National Defense University, called "Certain Issues on China Countering Future Economic Sanctions." In summary, Jiang wrote, "Warfare in the future is going to be fought mainly through economic means," and he puts "great strategic significance" on "countermeasures against economic sanctions to win the war."

Among the key factors Jiang cited in such a conflict are the overall size of a nation's economy, its available resources and strategic reserves, foreign capital dependency, reliance on foreign trade and the disposition of its international monetary assets. On just about every count he found China vulnerable. "Although China's economy has grown considerably," Jiang concluded, its situation "remains grim in the case of an economic war against a strong power." The unspoken but obvious foe: the US and its allies.

Since Jiang's 2001 assessment of PRC vulnerability to economic warfare, China has certainly strengthened itself. Mainly that has been achieved by unleashing a torrent of low-priced exports on the rest of the world, while continuing to take in a large flow of foreign capital for industrial expansion. That has grown the economy in size and industrial weighting and has provided badly needed jobs. It has also built up a vast war chest of hard-currency holdings, including the reported $1.53 trillion of US-dollar investments at year-end 2007.

In sheer size, at just under $3 trillion a year of GDP at the official exchange rate, China's economy is around third or fourth behind the US, Japan and perhaps Germany. But it is second on a purchasing power parity basis, at more than $7 trillion in 2006, according to the *The World Factbook* of the CIA.[13] Purchasing Power Parity (PPP), though favored by the World Bank, is a suspect and subjective way to gauge economic activity, and in early 2008 the CIA adjusted its estimate for China downward to $7 trillion from $10 trillion. Even so, it is clear that China is gaining rapidly on the $13 trillion-a-year US economy by any measure.[14] Since 1993, China's economy has grown at about three times the pace of US GDP.[15]

China's per-capita income is still only 12% of the US' $43,500, even on a comparable purchasing power basis in 2007.[16] And most of that wealth is concentrated in a few large coastal cities. The wide gulf between rich and poor in China is said to be more akin to that of Latin America than of most OECD countries. About 10% of China's 1.3 billion official population falls below international poverty levels. The US has about a 12% "poverty" ratio, but its population is about one-fifth of China's, its wealth is more evenly distributed, and Americans can go to the polls periodically and "throw the bums out." Or at least feel like they can.

The US also is not beset by a large mass of restive males roaming the country looking for jobs. Some 200 million Chinese rural

13. US Central Intelligence Agency, *The World Factbook*: China, update as of May 1, 2008.
14. CIA, *The World Factbook*: United States, update as of May 1, 2008.
15. C. Fred Bergsten et al., *China: The Balance Sheet*, (New York: the Center for Strategic and International Studies, and the Institute for International Economics, 2006), p. 163.
16. CIA, *The World Factbook*: China.

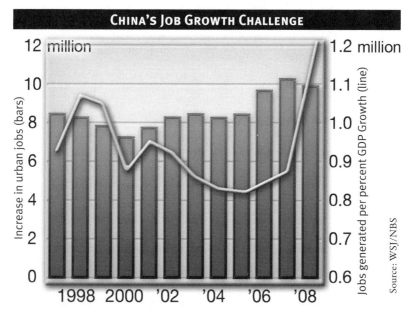

CHINA'S JOB GROWTH CHALLENGE

The PRC has a goal of 10 million new urban jobs in 2008. But at its 2008 target of 8% economic growth that requires a record more than 1.2 million jobs per percentage point of added GDP.

workers have migrated to mainly coastal cities looking for employment, but anywhere from 100 million to 150 million surplus laborers have been "drifting between villages and cities" looking for work, according to a CIA estimate in 2007 (omitted in the CIA's early 2008 China update). That equates to 12% to 20% of China's labor force being grossly under-employed and restive. Unemployment in coastal urban areas is officially only about 4%, but unofficial tallies put it around 13%.[17]

In addition to the problem of assimilating its large surplus of rural workers into urban jobs, China's modernization effort has meant laying off millions of workers from bloated state-owned enterprises to make those businesses at least self-supporting, if not internationally competitive. And though its one-child-per-family policy has turned it into the fastest-aging population on earth, at a growth rate of only 0.6% a year, it will still have a large influx of young working-age people in the next few years. By some estimates, China has to grow its GDP by about 10% a year in the coming decade just to pre-

---

17. "Unemployment in China," *China Labour Bulletin*, update as of Dec. 14, 2007.

vent a worsening of unemployment. For 2008, China has targeted 10 million new urban jobs.[18]

Another Chinese vulnerability, in Jiang's view, is its dependence on imports and exports, almost entirely by sea. Fully 40% of its GDP is generated from exports, and more than 31% is consumed for imports, mainly raw materials to turn into exports. That is by far the highest trade dependency of any major world economy. China's export growth rate continues to sizzle, although it eased in the second half of 2007 to around 22%, down from 29% in the year's first half.[19]

High on Jiang's vulnerability list would be foreign capital dependency. In a mad dash to woo offshore multinational companies in the 1990s, Chinese provincial leaders orchestrated the sale of big equity stakes in many of China's larger private-sector industrial firms. Foreign direct investment in China leaped to 10% or more of GDP. That has now eased with FDI running at about 2% of a much larger Chinese GDP number, but it still rose slightly to $63 billion in 2006 despite some backlash against foreign takeovers. According to a CIA estimate, foreign direct investment in China totaled some $700 billion in 2006. That would mean China, with official GDP at 20% of the US level, would have foreign ownership totaling 40% of that in the US.

Moreover, foreign investment in China has been focused on its most profitable businesses. Ohio State University Professor Oded Shenkar has noted nearly two-thirds of Chinese exports are by companies with some foreign ownership, with that ratio rising to 80% in high value-added categories like information technology.[20] Chinese critics have argued this trend has been turning China into the world's sweat-shop, selling off industries too cheaply and actually undermining local entrepreneurship. In some cases, concerned Chinese officials have now moved to limit US and other foreign investors to only minority ownership positions. In a major 2007 deal, US-based Carlyle Group had to settle for a 45% stake in major Xu-

---

18. "China to create 10 mln jobs in cities, keeping jobless rate at 4.5% in 2008," People's Daily Online, Mar. 5, 2008.
19. "China Ministry Figures Indicate Jan-Apr Exports Up 21.5%," Dow Jones Newswires, May 9, 2008.
20. Simon Elegant, "China's Unwelcome Mat," *Time*, Sept. 18, 2006.

zhou machinery maker Xugong, rather than the 85% it bid $375 million for in 2005.[21]

China and its provinces are still welcoming foreign buyers, and remain hooked on the inflow of offshore capital to expand and upgrade Chinese employment opportunities. But a new Anti-Monopoly Law was to take effect in August 2008. That could subject foreign investments to added review. And under pressure from the US, EU and WTO, China is being prodded to drop the export subsidies which have made foreign investment so attractive there, including large hidden assistance in the form of heavily subsidized energy costs.

Indeed, without subsidies and tax breaks, it is questionable whether even the more profitable Chinese export enterprises actually make money at current raw material cost levels. Some observers calculate that, overall, the Chinese industrial sector has been barely able to break even, and could be racking up significant red ink, if accounted for in a more transparent manner. How much worse could that situation become if commodity prices rise further and are sustained for years and years?

Weijian Shan, a former Wharton School professor and a partner in TPG Newbridge, has argued that since 1999 the total of Chinese debt-to-equity swaps and bank recapitalizations to deal with bad loans has exceeded the sum total of pre-tax profits reported by China's industrial sector. That suggests the only "profit" there has been from lax bank lending.[22] The problem has gotten worse in recent years, as raw material costs have soared while the prices of Chinese exports to the US have fallen. From 2002 to mid 2006, Shan notes, the cost of raw materials rose about 37% while export prices to the US fell 5.2%. "With a deterioration in the terms of trade, profit margins must have severely eroded," he notes, adding, "There is no telling the size of government subsidies included in the final profit number."[23]

China's statistics bureau reported combined net income of industrial companies in China in the first five months of 2008 of 1.09 trillion yuan ($160 billion), up 20.9% from a year earlier. That was half the rate of increase a year earlier, however, and came on a more

21. "Carlyle reduces Xugong bid again," *China Daily*, Mar. 20, 2007.
22. Daniel H. Rosen and Trevor Houser, *China Energy; A guide for the perplexed*, Peterson Institute for International Economics, May 2007, p. 12.
23. Weijian Shan, "The World Bank's China Delusions," *Wall Street Journal*, Sept. 29, 2006, excerpt from *The Far Eastern Economic Review*, Sept. 11, 2006.

than 29% rise in revenues to 18.4 trillion yuan ($2.68 trillion). That gave Chinese industry an apparent overall margin on sales of 6%.[24]

The highly politicized World Bank, for whatever reason, has taken the rosy view that Chinese companies have been highly profitable due to rapidly increasing labor productivity. They have been earning returns on capital in the high teens and building up ample amounts of cash to finance themselves even without easy bank loans or foreign equity investment. But Shan, a veteran in China investment with firsthand awareness of the tenuous profitability of many Chinese ventures, calls this analysis flawed and naïve. "If firms are so profitable," he queries, "where do the billions of dollars of China's reported bad loans come from?"[25] Wall Street economist Stephen Roach of Morgan Stanley sides with Shan, noting "It makes a huge difference if investments are funded internally through surging profits and retained earnings, as the World Bank argues, or if this is a bank-sponsored investment binge."[26]

Perhaps another sign of the poor profitability of Chinese industrial companies is the fact that China's economy is growing at *only* 10% a year or so, despite the stated reinvestment of the country's GDP as running at upwards of 40% and still rising. In addition, there is a big gap in the valuations of Chinese companies trading on the New York Stock Exchange and their inflated stock quotes in Shanghai (where the Dow Jones Shanghai Index has fallen a stunning 50% in the first half of 2008). As Shan notes, "There is no question China's growth continues to be financed by banks. In fact, total investment by industrial firms likely accounts for no more than 20% of the country's annual fixed-asset investment. Bank loans, on the other hand, are greater than China's GDP." Adding off-balance-sheet funding, he calculates Chinese bank credit could be two times the country's GDP.[27]

A horse race to oblivion

In short, it looks as if China is financing a losing poker hand by making lots of bad loans to itself. The US, meanwhile, as propri-

24. Li Yanping, "China's Industrial-Profit Growth Halves on Fuel Costs," Bloomberg.com, June 27, 2008.

25. Ibid.

26. Stephen S. Roach, *The Great Chinese Profits Debate*, Morgan Stanley Global Economic Forum, Oct. 6, 2006.

27. Shan.

etor of the world's reserve currency, can just keep printing money to fund its spendthrift policies, balance-of-payment deficits and costly economic war effort. That sets up a horse race to see who is first to have a "run on the bank." The US appears to be betting China will suffer a financial meltdown and catastrophic banking system collapse before the rest of the world calls a halt to US dollar devaluation by insisting on other reserve currencies.

So far, any covert efforts the US might have had in the works to hold down Chinese economic growth since the late 1990s appear to have been a dismal failure. Chinese GDP has been on a rampage. Since launching its new era of reform in 1978, China has been the world's fastest-growing economy, at an average pace of almost 10%, and is second only to the US on a purchasing-power parity (PPP) basis. Real per capita output in that time has grown nine-fold.[28] In 2007, by Chinese figures, that growth rate reached 11.5%, even after deducting estimated consumer price inflation of 4.5%.[29]

Chinese inflation has been edging up, however. Consumer prices in early 2008 were up 7.1% from a year earlier, for the most rapid rise in 11 years. Producer prices were up more than 6%. Inflation reached 8.7% in February 2008 and has remained above 8% through mid-year. Growth was also slowing to a targeted 8% GDP increase for the year, with steps being taken by the People's Bank of China to tighten credit and rein in aggressive lending by Chinese banks. The more it raises interest rates to curb loan demand, however, the more "hot money" China attracts from abroad, adding to inflationary pressures. This is especially true as the US Federal Reserve has slashed interest rates to stave off recession. Foreign direct investment into China in January 2008 more than doubled from a year earlier to $11.2 billion, after rising 13.6% in 2007 to $75 billion.[30]

The primary way to curb inflation due to the high cost of imported energy and raw materials would be to let the value of the Chinese currency adjust upward to more realistic parity with the dollar. But that could risk choking off the flow of manufactured exports which have been the underpinning of China's growth miracle. Un-

---

28. Bergsten et al., p. 18.
29. International Monetary Fund, *World Economic Outlook*, April 2008, p. 82.
30. Terence Poon, "Inflation Pressures China," *Wall Street Journal Online*, Feb. 19, 2008.

til mid-2005, China kept its currency, the renminbi or yuan, pegged tightly to the dollar, at what was arguably a fraction of its real value. Since then China has allowed a gradual upward move in the yuan of about 15% against the dollar, including a 7% rise in 2007. That currency adjustment, plus regulatory reforms and rising labor costs, is blamed in part for a rash of factory closings in Guangdong. Some 10% of the 60,000 to 70,000 Hong Kong-owned factories in the Pearl River Delta region could close in 2008, according to the Federation of Hong Kong Industries. In 2007 about 10% of footwear makers in that region, which accounts for a third of Chinese shoe exports, closed up shop, relocated inland or moved to other countries.[31]

Even so, the renminbi may still be undervalued against the US dollar by perhaps as much as 100%. That is an extreme view, based on the very rough calculation that its purchasing power parity GDP in 2007 was an estimated $7 trillion or double its nominal GDP of about $3.4 trillion at the exchange rate in early 2008 of $1 to 7.15 yuan. Other commentators put the undervaluation in early 2008 in the range of 15% to 20%, even after the 15% increase since 2005. Some significant undervaluation seems to be confirmed by the rush of foreign investment and speculative inflows of funds into China in apparent anticipation of further upward revaluation of the yuan.

To "sterilize" these huge inflows of dollars to avoid inflation (and to prop up the dollar's value), the People's Bank of China has had to frantically buy up dollars in exchange for yuan. This has built up the massive $1.5 trillion in Chinese dollar reserves, invested mainly in low-yielding US Treasury obligations, ever at risk of devaluation. To boost returns on those funds, China has invested heavily in mortgage-backed "agency bonds," and now holds several hundred billion dollars worth of debt issued by quasi-government lending arms like Fannie Mae and Freddie Mac. But those obligations lack formal US government payment guarantees,[32] and suffered a brief meltdown in value in early 2008 due to the US subprime debt scare.

Chinese policymakers are caught on the horns of a dilemma. Do they let their currency rise to make oil and other raw material imports

31. Mei Fing, Sky Canaves, "Many Factories in China's South Sound Last Whistle," Wall Street Journal Online, Feb. 22, 2008.
32. Max Fraad Wolff, "Sino silence in subprime swamp," Asia Times Online, Dec. 14, 2007.

more affordable? Or do they hold down the currency to encourage exports? Since the main goal is to create and sustain employment, rather than to make a profit, the likely outcome is the PRC will fight tooth and nail to maintain the yuan at a significant undervaluation to the dollar. That will invite concerted US and other western pressure on raw commodity prices in hopes of eventually toppling what could be seen as an economic house of cards built on an antiquated 19th century industrial model.

This means oil prices are likely to remain inflated for a protracted period. If it took a decade to cripple a weak Soviet Union, it might take twice that long for such policies to impact China. But oil many not be the only such commodity pressure point. Just about any basic commodity the PRC must import, from iron ore to soybeans, could be susceptible to similar price manipulation.

By stepping out of the its dark age of Communist isolation, China's leadership elite has stepped onto the same unrelenting treadmill driving most free-world governments: keeping people employed to maintain incomes, order and, above all, political power.

That is where US national security analysts may see oil and other commodity pricing again playing a critical role at the margin. Very high raw material costs could tip China into slow-growth, profit-less "stagflation" that could help breed social and political unrest. By levying what amounts to an oil "tax" on China's economy, the thinking goes, growth rates might be trimmed by one or two percentage points, or more. Compounded over time, along with other negative influences, that modest strain might be just enough to critically stress what Washington perceives to be an oppressive but tenuous political command-and-control structure in the PRC. Without the steam vent of popular elections, the Chinese populace has shown a penchant for taking to the streets *en mass* in what can become violent protests.

By lighting the fire of fast-improving economic expectations under this restrictive Communist socio-political system, the PRC elite are viewed to have created a potentially explosive dynamic risking escalation into widespread civil unrest. Therefore, the PRC leadership's instinctive response to such outbreaks has been repression: quick, massive and brutal. That, in turn, raises the specter of all hell breaking loose at some point if things get out of control. The essence of that view is contained in the title to an important 2007 book by former Clinton-era US Deputy Secretary of State for China affairs, Susan Shirk: *China: Fragile Superpower*.

Shirk concludes it is China's "internal fragility, not its growing strength that presents the greatest danger" to the US. "The weak legitimacy of the Communist Party and its leaders' sense of vulnerability could cause China to behave rashly in a crisis involving Japan or Taiwan," she warns, adding the PRC might be tempted to "wag the dog" in an effort to divert attention from domestic troubles by stirring up military conflict with the US. "China's massive problems, instead of reassuring us," Shirk writes, "should worry us."[33]

But the "State Department" view reflected by Shirk may not be shared by the national security establishment and the CIA. According to one veteran US intelligence operative interviewed for this book, a crackup of political power in the PRC might not be so unwelcome an outcome of economic stress there. Another veteran US national security advisor notes centralized government has been the exception rather than the rule for China over the centuries, and sees an eventual reversion to regional dynasties and "warlordism."

There is already said to be considerable power rivalry between China's central government in Beijing and the regional governments of wealth centers like Shanghai and Guangzhou. Sooner or later, it is felt, the leadership of China will have to be chosen by some kind of popular vote, and perceptions are that China's regional leaders may have more sway with the populace than their Beijing overlords.

As in Russia after the Soviets, life in China after a political meltdown would go on, and could even improve with continued economic and income growth. But government might be less centralized, with elements of democracy. A greater share of business investment could go into consumer goods to improve living standards of the Chinese, rather than to make heavy industrial goods for military hardware and below-market sales abroad. There could be less interest in geopolitical expansion, military spending and force-projection that could confront the US or neighboring countries. Or so goes the thinking in at least some corners of the national security establishment.

---

33. Susan L. Shirk, *China, Fragile Superpower*, (New York: Oxford University Press, 2007), p. 255.

WHEN THE US BUYS OIL...	WHEN CHINA BUYS OIL...
...it mostly comes from friendly neighbors like Canada and Mexico.	...it comes mainly at great distance from the Persian Gulf and from strangers aligned to the West (Saudi Arabia, Kuwait, Oman) or from pariah states (Iran, Yemen, Sudan).
...it can buy the heaviest, sourest grades at steep discounts to light, sweet crude because its refineries are sophisticated and configured with the proper metallurgy.	...it usually has to pay up for sweet crude.
...it arrives mainly by low-cost pipeline.	...it requires long-haul tanker shipments at what have been very high freight rates since 2000.
...there is no Asia premium on tanker rates.	...it pays an extra $2/bbl or so just because its Persian Gulf shipments head East.
...it pays with overvalued dollars, which are still the world's reserve currency.	...it pays with Chinese currency kept 30% to 40% undervalued to the dollar in order to promote Chinese manufactured exports.
...it processes a high percentage of the crude into high-value gasoline, or clean diesel, and leaves mostly just petroleum coke.	...it mostly makes lower-grade diesel fuel with a large cut of low-value heavy boiler fuel which is then mainly burned to make electricity (a poor use of costly liquid fuel vs coal).

3

That was Then.
This is Now.

Genie: I'll grant you any wish, but will give your neighbor twofold.
Farmer: Then pluck out my right eye.

— Old Russian saying[1]

Rising oil prices have hurt China much more than the US, because Chinese energy use is much more inefficient.

— Senior Chinese Official

If a major impetus behind US downward crude price manipulation in the 1980s was to boost the US economy with what amounted to a massive tax cut, while breaking the Soviets, why on earth would the US ever possibly want to push prices *up*? As by far the world's biggest user of crude oil at more than 20 million b/d, or almost a quarter of the entire world's consumption, would not the US be shooting itself in the foot by trying to use a high-oil-price environment to damage some economic foe, such as China?

Intuitively, the US would always try to keep prices low, or at least moderate. But let's consider the problem in more detail, and against certain alternatives in relation to China. What becomes apparent is that high oil prices might give the US a cold, but China could get pneumonia. And the effect on reluctant US allies Saudi Arabia and Russia would be nothing short of wonderful, not to mention the benefit to friends like Canada and Mexico, with whom the US has been eying a possible North American version of the EU.

While US petroleum consumption is high, nearly all of it is for transportation fuels. Generally speaking, that is a high-value use of crude oil. Only a very small 2%, or about 150 million barrels a year,

---

1. As related by Alexander Kalina.

is burned as heating oil, mainly in the Northeast states, with only 7% of the US' 107 million households using oil for heat.[2] A minimal 3.4% of US crude use, in the form of low-value heavy fuel oil left over from refining, is burned to make electricity. Of the gasoline used in the US, only about 35% is work-related. A hefty 25% is considered to be for purely casual or recreational driving.[3]

Granted, the US may be profligate in its use of motor fuels. Driving long distances in gas-guzzling sport utility vehicles for even trivial pursuits may be considered an inalienable right by some Americans. But in economic terms that non-essential driving is a luxury item. It can be curbed with little impact on the country's ability to generate wealth, or GDP. Indeed, US gasoline consumption has seen almost no growth since 2005, at just over 9 million b/d, and was running almost 3% below a year ago in mid-2008.[4] This is despite longer commutes to work, as people move to farther-out suburbs seeking cheaper housing, and generally falling fleet efficiency due to more SUVs. Miles per gallon have also dropped about a quarter of a percentage point due to increased use of less-efficent ethanol, now about 4% of the US gasoline pool.[5]

Even with our outsized consumption of gasoline, at recent prices upwards of $4/gal the share of US GDP allotted to petroleum consumption is very modest. It got down to barely 1% of GDP in the late 1990s. Though it has now risen to around 4%, that is still far less than in 1980 and 1981, when it approached 7% of GDP.[6] Fuel expense as a percentage of the cost of an average new car over its expected life has remained low and falling. So gasoline remains affordable, for most Americans compared to the not-so-distant past.

Fuel costs do hurt airlines and trucking companies. But by and large, these firms have been able to pass those costs through to customers and have thus spread the hurt over the general population.

---

2. EIA, "Residential Heating Oil Prices: What Consumers Should Know."

3. Tancred Lidderdale, "Gasoline Demand Trends; EIA Energy Outlook," Modeling and Data Conference; Mar. 28, 2007.

4. EIA, "This Week in Petroleum: Gasoline."

5. Lidderdale, p. 11.

6. "Oil Price Increases Impact Economy Less Now," Michigan Public Service Commission, Mar. 3, 2000.

China: twice the share of GDP for oil vs. the US

Both the US and China now import roughly the same share of their petroleum needs, at something approaching 60%. At $100/barrel, the US would spend about $400 billion a year to buy foreign crude oil, or about 3% of its GDP. By contrast, imported oil costs are a much bigger deal for China. At $100/barrel, China would have to spend about $150 billion a year on crude imports, or 6% of its GDP at the official exchange rate. At $150/bbl, China's crude import bill swells to above $200 billion, or 8% of GDP. And that is at current Chinese consumption and import rates, which are expected to grow prodigiously as automobile ownership expands.

There are a number of ways in which high crude oil prices are relatively harder on China than on the US. Most notable is the fact crude is priced in dollars. As noted earlier, China's tightly controlled renminbi has been variously estimated to be trading anywhere from 30% to 40% below its fair market value to the dollar. Though China loosened its currency peg to the dollar in 2005, it has allowed the renminbi to adjust only about 15% against the greenback, so as not to crimp its ability to push out exports abroad. So China pays for overvalued oil with painfully but intentionally undervalued currency.

Secondly, China has to pay an inherent cost penalty to buy crude. Most of its imports come from the Persian Gulf region, where the sellers routinely charge an Asia premium of several dollars a barrel on cargos heading east. The oil it buys from Russia comes by high-cost railcar, since Russia, as noted, has continued to drag its feet on building a pipeline.

Third, China is paying for long-haul ocean transportation amid very high tanker rates, which also started to take off about the time crude prices began their upward march in the late 1990s. Freight costs to get Middle East crude to China now add another $3 to $5 per barrel. And most of that oil moves in tankers owned or controlled by Western shipping companies. All of it has to transit key waterways controlled by the US or its allied navies and readily susceptible to blockade or interdiction in the event of an international embargo.

The US, on the other hand, buys most of its crude from neighboring Canada and Mexico, or South America and West Africa.

Much of it arrives by cheap and efficient pipelines or on short-haul tankers through safe waters.

Fourth, Chinese refiners generally have to buy more expensive sweet, or low-sulfur, crude grades, due to the lack of proper metallurgy in most Chinese refineries to handle the corrosion from "sour" high-sulfur crude. That adds considerably to raw material costs compared to the US, where much refining capacity is now geared to process heavy and sour crude, selling at times for $20 a barrel or more below the NYMEX quote for light, sweet WTI.

Fifth, the slate of refined products from most Chinese plants is inherently far less valuable than what is made in the US. China's less-sophisticated refineries mainly are geared to make distillate, or medium-grade fuel oil and diesel to run power generators, trucks and industrial equipment. Until recently, Chinese refiners actually exported unfinished naphtha at a discount rather than upgrade it, due to the dearth of gasoline-powered cars and trucks. Also, a relatively high fraction of each barrel refined in China ends up as low-value heavy fuel oil fit only to fire boilers or to be made into asphalt. US refiners, by contrast, crack most of their "resid" (heavy fuel oil) to gasoline or diesel, ending up with just petroleum coke, almost pure carbon, which can be burned like coal as a boiler fuel or gasified using synfuel processes.

China's declining energy efficiency

The US has been getting dramatically more energy efficient in terms of Btu used per dollar of GDP. Using constant 2000 dollars, the US burned 8.75 Btu per dollar of GDP in 2006, barely half its rate of energy consumption in 1976.[7] And petroleum has dropped over those 30 years from 46% of US energy supply to 40%.[8]

China, on the other hand, has actually been losing energy efficiency. Instead of energy use growing at about half the pace of its GDP over the 25 years after 1978, when it began to seriously expand its economy, Chinese energy demand began to mushroom in 2001. Since then it has been rising at about 150% of its double-digit GDP growth rate, or about 15% a year and twice as fast a most analysts

7. EIA, "Energy INFOcard."
8. EIA, "Annual Energy Review 2006," Table 1.3, Energy Consumption by Primary Energy Source, Selected Years, 1949-2006.

expected. This has mainly been due to China's breakneck push to boost capacity to world-leading status in energy-intensive strategic industries like steel, aluminum, chemicals, cement and glass.

With just 6% of world GDP, China accounts for about 15% of world energy demand. That is not so much from "air conditioners and automobiles," notes Trevor Houser of China Strategic Advisory, but rather from "steel mills, cement kilns and aluminum smelters."[9] In just a decade China has leaped from 12% of global steel production to a market-dominating 35%, and it has gone from being the world's biggest importer to the biggest exporter of steel. Its share of aluminum production has jumped from 8% to 28%. It now accounts for half of global flat glass output. China has been making itself into the world's primary converter of energy into industrial commodities, just as energy and other raw material prices are soaring. Observes Houser: "Much of China's energy demand is used to satisfy consumption outside China's borders, not least in the US."

In 2005, 71% of China's energy demand came from the industrial sector, against just 25% of US energy used in industrial production. Conversely, energy used in transportation was only 10% of China's total 2005 demand, compared to 33% in the US.[10] Oil supplied 21.1% of Chinese energy demand that year, up from less than 17% in 1990.[11] Partly that has been due to the need for costly private oil-fired diesel power generation to make up for spotty availability of cheaper coal-fired utility power. As a result, Chinese oil demand has swelled from a self-supplied 3 million b/d in 1994 to more than 8 million b/d in 2007, of which more than half had to be imported. In short, to mix a couple of metaphors, China has been digging itself into a hole on oil consumption just as prices have gone through the roof.

China's oil demand is already 40% of that in the US. But the real surge in motor fuel demand in China has only begun to be felt. Even though China's passenger car fleet has doubled in the past five years

9. Tevor Houser, testimony before the US-China Economic and Security Review Commission hearings on "China's Energy Consumption and Opportunities for US-China Cooperation to Address the Effects of China Energy Use," June 14, 2007.
10. Rosen and Houser, p. 9.
11. University of Michigan China Data Center, "Total Consumption of Energy and Its Composition."

to 25 million units, it is still only 20% of the US car count. Adding in trucks, its fleet is about 37 million units. But using the same model that has held true for other developing countries as per-capita GDP rises, the Institute for Transportation Studies at the University of Leeds expects China's vehicle population to explode to 10 times that number over the next 25 years, to 370 million units.[12]

To keep its gasoline and diesel within the range of affordability for Chinese consumers, and hold down outrage over inflation, the PRC has employed an awkward system of retail price controls and subsidies to refiners. This has kept the dollar cost of key diesel fuel in China at roughly half the price in the US in recent years. But those subsidies have failed to keep pace with the rising cost of crude oil, and so gasoline prices in China have now climbed to roughly match the US price, at just over $3 a gallon in late 2007. Diesel remains about $0.50/gal cheaper in China than in the US.[13] But China has been plagued with periodic fuel shortages in some regions, causing long lines at filling stations with occasional reports of violence. Refiners have had to be prodded with specific orders from Beijing to step up fuel production or to import finished diesel and gasoline to meet shortage conditions.

In late 2007, for the first time in almost a year and a half, China raised pump prices on gasoline and diesel by 10%, as overall inflation rose to a worrisome 6.5% annual pace in November. Even so, Sinopec, the PRC's largest refiner with about 60% of the country's downstream exposure, had an operating loss of 10.5 billion yuan ($1.5 billion) in its refining operations in 2007 with about 6 billion yuan of that in the last three months of the year. It was expecting about 10 billion yuan ($1.4 billion) in subsidies for all of 2007, up from 5 billion yuan in 2006 and 10 billion yuan in 2005.[14] Instead, in March 2008, Sinopec got only a 4.9 yuan billion subsidy for 2007. It got a 7.4 yuan billion subsidy for first-quarter 2008, but still warned its overall profits for that period would be down 50% from

---

12. Joyce Dargay, Dermot Gately, Martin Sommer; "Vehicle Ownership and Income Growth, Worldwide: 1960-2030," Institute for Transport Studies, University of Leeds, January 2007.

13. Rosen and Houser, p. 22.

14. Aries Poon, "Sinopec to get Chinese government subsidy for 2007 refining loss," Dow Jones MarketWatch, Jan. 4, 2008.

a year earlier.[15] In April, the PRC began making monthly subsidy payments to its refiners with Sinopec getting a hefty 7.1 yuan billion ($1.02 billion). Even so, according to Sinopec Chairman Su Shulin, the government handouts would not "even cover half of the losses" of Sinopec's refining segment.[16]

China is estimated to have paid out about $8 billion in energy subsidies in 2005, with about one-third of that going to oil refiners. That appears to have declined in 2006 and 2007. But at the April 2008 subsidy rate, PRC outlays to refiners alone could be approaching $20 billion a year. In addition, Beijing has had to begin refunding the 17% value-added tax companies pay to import refined products to ease consumer shortages.

Offsetting some of the Chinese government's subsidy costs is a windfall profits tax imposed in early 2006 on upstream oil production above $40/bbl, gradually rising to a 40% levy. Some of those proceeds have been recycled to farmers and transporters hurt by rising diesel and gasoline prices.

Even at $20 billion a year, such subsidies by themselves might not be an undue strain on the PRC treasury. But at oil prices over $150/bbl, China's domestic windfall profits tax falls far short of paying for the downstream subsidies that would be required to hold down retail prices without bankrupting refiners.

China's fuel-subsidy burden has to be viewed in combination with its fast-rising military outlays, and soaring costs for other key raw materials like iron ore, metallurgical coal and bauxite. There is also still a huge overhang of bad debts in Chinese banks and worthless investments held by China's state investment funds, plus what some analysts view as the generally red-ink performance of the nation's overall industrial sector, mentioned in the prior chapter.

Other ways to view the relative cost of crude

According to official statistics, the US last year imported almost 60% of its petroleum demands, or 12 million b/d of crude oil

15. "Petrochina, Sinopec to get state subsidy," *Platts Oilgram News*, Vol. 86, No. 79, Apr. 28, 2008, p. 3.
16. "Sinopec gets $1 billion subsidy for April," *Platts Oilgram News*, Vol. 86, No. 104, May 28, 2008.

and refined product. It was the single largest category of foreign goods purchased and accounted for fully 35% of the US' $744 billion deficit on goods traded internationally in the first eleven months of 2007, up from 32% a year earlier.[17]

But consider where that money really went. Almost half of US foreign crude purchases in 2007 were from good friends: Canada, Mexico and Saudi Arabia. Moreover, much of the equity ownership of the crude bought by the US would have been held by US based companies, or foreign oil majors whose shares are heavily owned by US financial institutions and investors. While it would be difficult or impossible to calculate the real net equivalent ownership share of US petroleum purchases, a plausible case can be made that one way or another the US likely buys the bulk of its oil imports from itself, or from close friends the US would want to support in any case if oil prices were far lower. In fact, in a macro sense, counting US-based equity ownership in global crude production, the US might actually be "long" crude (i.e., a net seller), or close to being so.

China, on the other hand, has very little foreign equity crude ownership through its state oil companies or government investment funds, despite a global spending spree to buy into far-flung ventures from Central Asia and Africa to Ecuador and Venezuela. And China's foreign equity production has had essentially no effect on lowering the overall world crude price level set on the futures exchanges.

One clear beneficiary of very high oil prices has been the new Russia, which has seen its crude and refined product exports rebound to slightly more than 6 million b/d. Its 4.5 million b/d of crude exports equal about 10% of world crude output traded internationally. Russian crude generally sells at a discount due to its gravity, sulfur content and location. But at $100/barrel, Russia would reap a windfall of almost $250 billion a year from foreign oil sales, equal to almost one-third its 2006 GDP using the official ruble exchange rate. On a purchasing power parity basis, those foreign crude sales would still have been some 12% of a $2.1 trillion Russian economy in 2007. At higher prices, well … you get the idea.

---

17. US Census Bureau, Bureau of Economic Analysis, "U.S. International Trade in Goods and Services," March 2008 and December 2007, "Exhibit 17: Imports of Energy-Related Petroleum Products, Including Crude Oil."

Oil exports let Russia boost its hard-currency foreign reserves from $12 billion in 1999 to a massive $315 billion at year-end 2006, by US estimates, and it repaid all remaining Soviet-era foreign debt. By the end of 2007 Russian reserves of foreign exchange and gold had climbed to $470 billion. At year-end 2006 Russian international debt had fallen to 39% of GDP, which grew 6.6% that year as inflation ebbed to less than 10% for the first time in a decade. [18]

If indeed the US were pursuing a high-oil-price strategy against China, one would expect to see exactly that kind of windfall for the Russians. A fundamental axiom of US Cold War policy has been to drive a wedge between Russia and China, to prevent their collaboration against the West, and to ally, when possible, with one against the other. This was clearly spelled out in the Reagan-era NSDDs, which specifically called for close cooperation with China to thwart Soviet expansion.[19] If the US tilt were now against China, it would have to be assumed there would be some equivalent alliance with the Russians that would be paid for in oil profits. This seems to be borne out by the sometimes tense, but generally positive, state of US-Russian relations in recent years.

To the extent the US has been able to "buy" Russian cooperation in China's economic containment with high oil prices, the negative hit to the US balance of payments could be rationalized as a bargain, even at twice the price.

Similarly, a high US balance of payments deficit on crude oil could be viewed as a necessary geopolitical cost for the US to sustain its crucial ally and *de facto* protectorate, the kingdom of Saudi Arabia. The upturn in low oil prices in late 1998, when the economic war with China appears to have begun in earnest, coincided with a looming dire financial situation in Saudi Arabia.

The Saudis had been lumbering under low oil prices, mounting deficits and simmering social unrest for more than a decade since aiding the Reagan Administration in breaking the Soviets. By the late 1990s the Saudis were clamoring for a better price for their main export. From $214 billion in oil revenues in the prior peak year of 1980 (in 2005 dollars), Saudi oil income had plunged to under $37

18. CIA, *The World Factbook*: Russia, May 1, 2008.

19. US NSC, NSDD-32, p. 5.

billion in 1998.[20] Saudi borrowing had climbed to almost 120% of the country's GDP in 1999.[21] One way or another, the US would have had to come to the Saudis' rescue. Rising oil prices provided a miraculous bailout, and Saudi finances are again comfortably in the black on revenues in the range of $200 billion a year.

The bottom line on high oil prices is that they net out to be a troubling but affordable nuisance for the US and a much needed windfall for its key allies Canada, Mexico, Russia and Saudi Arabia. For the PRC ruling elite, high oil prices are a lead weight on a runner struggling to stay ahead of an unrelenting grim reaper, who is forever threatening to overtake them with unemployment, social unrest and regime change.

---

20. EIA, "OPEC Revenues Factsheet," April 2008.
21. Moin A. Siddiqi, *Saudi Arabia: Financial Report*, IC Publications Ltd., 1999.

The Chinese People's Liberation Army Navy's (PLAN) aircraft carrier, the former "Varyag."

The PLAN's new class 094 SSBN

—4—

From Ally
to Adversary

Warfare is now escaping from the boundaries of bloody massacre, and exhibiting a trend toward low casualties or even none at all, and yet high intensity. This is information warfare, financial warfare, trade warfare ...
— Unrestricted Warfare, PLA Cols. Qiao Liang and Wang Xiangsui[1]

After a close but tacit alliance in breaking the Soviets in the 1980s, the US and China have seen a steady rise in tensions and distrust over the past two decades. Without the anti-Soviet glue to cement that partnership-of-necessity, Washington and Beijing have become increasingly at odds. Their dysfunctional relationship is held together mainly by a symbiotic dependence on each other's trade. The US has now aligned itself with a reconstituted Russia to gang up on an uppity PRC. Once again, the economic weapon of choice: oil.

Most of the tension is kept out of sight. But there has been no shortage of overt spats between the US and China in recent years. The brutal slaughter of young pro-democracy protesters at Beijing's Tiananmen Square in June 1989, estimated by some to have numbered between 4,000 and 6,000,[2] provoked world outrage, US condemnation, and a continuing US-EU arms embargo against the PRC. There have been occasional subsequent military dust-ups, from the 1995-96 naval show of force over threats to Taiwan, to the "accidental" 1999 NATO bombing of the Chinese embassy in Bel-

1. Qiao Liang and Wang Xiangsui, *Unrestricted Warfare*, published in 1999 in China by the People's Liberation Army. Excerpted and translated for the US intelligence community and republished in 2002 by Pan American Publishing as *Unrestricted Warfare: China's Master Plan to Destroy America*, p. 162.
2. Edward Timperlake and William C. Triplett II, *Red Dragon Rising: Communist China's military threat to America*, (Washington, DC: Regnery Publishing, 1999), p. 28. The official PRC death toll is 200 to 300.

grade during the Kosovo war, which touched off Beijing rioting that damaged the US embassy and trapped the US ambassador for four days. After a Chinese fighter pilot was killed in a provocative midair collision with a US patrol plane over the South China Sea in 2001, Beijing unsuccessfully demanded a US apology, then shipped the slightly damaged P-3 Orion back to the US in pieces.

An obvious source of US irritation is China's lopsided balance of trade with the US, running at an astounding $260 billion in 2007. What in the 1990s looked like a way to export US inflation and tap China's vast manpower pool for cheap labor has mushroomed into a current-account nightmare that has sped up evisceration of the US industrial base, and seems to make the Treasury Department beholden to Beijing to finance the continuing US budget deficits. China, for its part, is touchy about US meddling in its internal politics by harping on human rights and China's lack of all but token village democracy.[3]

But the real issue is much bigger than money or politics, and all but unmentionable in public discourse. The US national security establishment views China as an inevitable strategic threat, and the PRC is convinced the US is trying to contain its growth in economic and military strength and rightful geopolitical influence. Or worse. Both sides are probably quite right, but can't afford to talk about it openly, or even directly in private. The stakes are extraordinarily high. For the US: continuation of its status as unchallenged world superpower and keeper of the global reserve currency. For China: survival of one-party Communist rule and the small elite behind it.

Outwardly, China has put on the friendly face of an altogether peaceful economic competitor since the 1970s. It officially disavows territorial expansion or external domination and has been concentrating great efforts on a "charm offensive" of "soft power" projection all over Asia and the developing world.[4] But inside the US and Western security establishment, there is an uneasy awareness that China's growth trajectory would put it in eventual position to force and win a showdown over who will dominate Asia and the Pacific. It is viewed as just a matter of time. Chinese leaders have a similar

---

3. James Mann, *The China Fantasy*, (New York: Viking, 2007), pp. 18-20.

4. Joshua Kurlantick, *Charm Offensive: How China's soft power offensive is transforming the world*, (New Haven: Yale University Press, 2007).

view: "War (with the US) is inevitable; we cannot avoid it," according to comments of Gen. Chi Haotian, China's defense minister.[5]

Sooner or later, as China's wealth and military strength grows, it will begin to bump up against US interests and allies in the Far East. The flash point could be Taiwan, a perennial problem, or any of a number of other potential territorial or economic disputes.

While the touchy issue of Taiwan independence seems to have cooled with the recent election victory of the Kuomingtang party there, China has now deployed some 1,000 missiles across the adjoining straits, and has been pursuing a big buildup in amphibious assault ships.[6] In November 2007 there was a tense 28-hour standoff between the USS *Kitty Hawk* carrier battle group and Chinese naval units in the Taiwan Strait, shortly after the PRC had denied the *Kitty Hawk* group a planned Hong Kong port visit.[7]

The acid test could revolve around the summer 2008 Beijing Olympics. Should that extravaganza prove to boost Chinese world stature, the PRC may feel it has a freer hand in forcing the issue of Taiwan separatism and/or pursuing other geopolitical goals.

Taiwan is not China's only friction point with the US and its allies, however. China has simmering boundary disputes in the South China Sea over the Spratly Islands with Vietnam, Taiwan, the Philippines and Malaysia. In the East China Sea it bumps into unresolved boundary issues with Japan. In both cases, it must be emphasized, massive potential oil and gas deposits could be at stake, constituting what one 1968 United Nations survey report dubbed "another Persian Gulf"-worth of energy resources.[8]

In 1974 China attacked and seized the Paracel Islands from Vietnam, then fought a naval battle with the Vietnamese in 1988 at Johnson Reef in the Spratlys, sinking several Vietnamese vessels and killing 70 sailors. Since then, there has been a series of hostile encounters in the region between Chinese, Vietnamese and Filipino forces. Boundary talks coordinated by the Association of Southeast

---

5. Al Santoli, introduction to the US translation of *Unrestricted Warfare* by Liang and Xiangsui, p. x.

6. Charles Smith, "Military Buildup Continues in China," Newsmax.com, Jan. 4, 2008.

7. "Report: Chinese ships confronted Kitty Hawk," Kyodo News Service, Jan 17, 2008.

8. Selig S. Harrison, "Seabed Petroleum in Northeast Asia: Conflict or Cooperation?" Woodrow Wilson International Center for Scholars, 2005, p. 3.

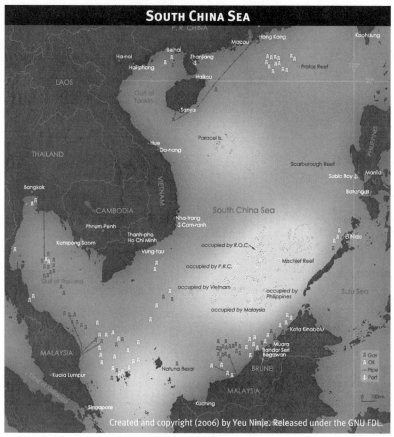

SOUTH CHINA SEA

Created and copyright (2006) by Yeu Ninje. Released under the GNU FDL.

Asian Nations have been inconclusive. But state oil companies from China, Vietnam and the Philippines did band together to split the $15 million cost of a 55,000 square mile seismic survey over the Spratlys in 2005. Chinese firms have said they plan to begin preliminary drilling there in 2008.

A 1993 US Geological Survey estimate put the likely oil potential of the South China Sea at 28 billion barrels, or nearly double China's current proved liquid reserves of 16 billion barrels. More recent Chinese estimates put the potential volume at anywhere from 105 billion to 213 billion barrels of oil.[9] The stakes there are clearly very high.

In the nearby East China Sea, estimated to hold some 100 billion barrels of potential oil reserves and around 200 trillion cubic feet of natural gas in a half-million-square-mile area, China and Japan have been at odds over a nearly 1,000 square mile stretch of ocean

---

9. EIA, "Country Analysis Brief: South China Sea," March 2008.

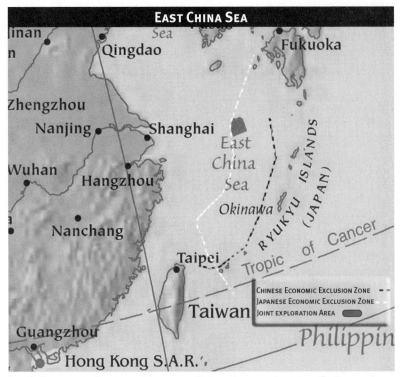

EAST CHINA SEA

Jinan
Qingdao
Sea
Fukuoka

Zhengzhou

Nanjing
Shanghai
East
China
Sea

Wuhan
Hangzhou

Nanchang
Okinawa

RYUKYU ISLANDS (JAPAN)

Taipei
Tropic of Cancer

Taiwan

CHINESE ECONOMIC EXCLUSION ZONE
JAPANESE ECONOMIC EXCLUSION ZONE
JOINT EXPLORATION AREA

Guangzhou
Philippin

Hong Kong S.A.R.

boundary northeast of Taiwan. The disputed Xihu (Chinese) or Okinawa Basin is believed to hold about 20 billion barrels of oil and 17.5 Tcf of gas, and is overlapped by Chinese and Japanese Exclusive Economic Zone claims. Japan administers the Senkaku Islands near Taiwan, but in 2003 China and Taiwan asserted rival claims, followed by a series of protest incidents by Chinese activists.[10] Chinese warships and aircraft have made numerous incursions into Japan's claimed territory.

Chinese majors CNOOC and Sinopec are joint owners in a dozen oil and gas fields on the Chinese side of the basin. But Japan fears that China's new Chunxiao gas development, just three miles from Japan's boundary claim, could drain Japanese reserves. When Japan's Teikoku Oil was awarded an exploration concession there, and sent a seismic vessel to explore Japan's side of the basin in 2005, it was forced to withdraw by Chinese naval units.[11] After years of unsuccessful talks, a summit meeting of Chinese President Hu Jintao

10. Senkaku/Diaoyutai Islands, GlobalSecurity.org.
11. "Japan and China face off over energy," AsiaTimes Online, July 2, 2005, condensed and republished from *Yomiuri Shimbun*.

and Japanese Prime Minister Yasuo Fukuda in May 2008 hinted at a pending deal to allow Japanese participation at Chunxiao. A month later the two countries announced a joint exploration venture over part of the disputed area, but the boundary issue may remain.[12]

China's growing naval power

China has undertaken a major expansion and upgrade of its navy with new ballistic missile submarines, stealthy new nuclear and diesel attack subs, modern frigates and Russian destroyers. Ominously, it recently disclosed plans to deploy three aircraft carrier battle groups over the next 10 years.[13] Construction contracts for two new carriers reportedly were signed in 2006, and one rebuilt Ukrainian carrier could be in service eventually: the former *Varyag* moored at the main PLAN naval base at Dalian. This has touched off talk of a major naval rearmament effort by Japan.

Though too small and of limited capability to project power into the blue-water Pacific, the rebuilt *Varyag* could serve a purpose similar to what had been envisioned by its Soviet designers: to guard ballistic missile submarines in nearby waters.[14] Recent sightings claim the PLAN has two new Type 094 ballistic missile subs, each with 12 missiles of up to three warheads.[15] These would replace China's sole

---

12. James Manicom, "Hu-Fukuda Summit: The East China Sea Dispute," *China Brief*, The Jamestown Foundation, Vol. 8, Issue 12, June 4, 2008.

13. Russell Hsiao, "China navy floats three-carrier plan," Asia Times Online, Jan. 8, 2008.

14. Richard D. Fischer Jr, "China's Carrier of Chance," *China Brief*, The Jamestown Foundation, Vol. 2, Issue 6, Mar. 14, 2002.

The 65,000-ton Kuznetsov-class Varyag was laid down in 1985, but work was abandoned in 1992 when she was 70% complete. It was given to Ukraine. In 1998 the ship was sold for $20 million to Chong Lot Tourist and Amusement Agency of Macau to supposedly be used as a floating casino. Chinese officials at the time denied Chong Lot was acting for the Chinese government. Skeptical Turkish officials held up Bosporus passage for 16 months, and Egypt denied transit through the Suez Canal. When the ship was finally towed around Africa and into China in 2002, it went not to Macau but to Dalian. In 2005 it entered dry-dock at the main PLAN shipyard and was extensively refitted. In the summer of 2007, it was commissioned into the PLAN and renamed for admiral Shi Lang, who conquered Taiwan in 1681.

15. "Type 094 Jin Class Nuclear-Powered Missile Submarine," SinoDefense.com, update May 5, 2008.

remaining SSBN, which was commissioned in 1981 and in recent years has seldom deployed.[16] The other one sank.

Currently, China lacks a credible nuclear deterrent threat toward the US. Its small fleet of land-based, liquid-fuel ICBMs is exposed to a preemptive attack. Some analysts say the US might even have a decisive first-strike ability now to knock out both Russian and Chinese nuclear capabilities.[17] In response to this vulnerability, China has fielded a new solid-fuel, road-mobile DF-31 ICBM, created a plethora of decoy missile sites, and in January 2007 demonstrated its anti-satellite capability by knocking down an aging weather satellite in low earth orbit. In early 2008, the Pentagon's annual assessment of Chinese military capabilities noted the PRC could now have ballistic missiles able to hit US carriers at sea, a major improvement in targeting and tracking capabilities.[18]

Though difficult to quantify, China's military budget has been on a rapid increase. In March 2007, it announced a 17.8% hike for that year to $45 billion. But those figures do not include large outlays for strategic forces, foreign acquisitions, R&D and paramilitary forces. The US Defense Intelligence Agency estimated China's total military spending for 2007 could range from $85 billion to as much as $125 billion.[19] The International Monetary Fund has calculated Chinese defense spending growth from 1996 to 2006 at an inflation-adjusted rate of 11.8%, exceeding China's inflation-adjusted GDP growth in that period of 9.2%. That is still small in relation to US defense spending, but US military planners note this aggressive military buildup belies China's outward posture to the world of being a peaceful partner with its neighbors and having no territorial ambitions.

Pre-empting China's timetable

In the late 1990s, the Chinese believed they had at least a 10- to 20-year window of opportunity to quietly prepare themselves for confrontation with the US. In 1998, according to a prominent Asian

16. Dr. Phillip Saunders, *China's Strategic Force Modernization*, National Defense University, Institute for National Strategic Studies, Jan. 13, 2005, slide 5.
17. Keir A. Lieber and Daryl G. Press, "The Rise of U.S. Nuclear Primacy," *Foreign Affairs*, March/April 2006.
18. Bill Gertz, "Inside the Ring," *Washington Times*, Mar. 7, 2008.
19. US Department of Defense, "Annual Report to Congress, Military Power of the People's Republic of China 2007," p. 25.

diplomatic source close to Chinese thinking at the time, the PRC believed it had a decade or more in which to build itself up economically and militarily to prevail in a toe-to-toe standoff over reunification of Taiwan or some other flashpoint issue. Time was thought to be on China's side. It was getting stronger, and the US was getting weaker.

That thinking appears to have changed dramatically with the US-led 2003 invasion of Iraq, which blocked PRC occupation of two very major oil fields there. That war also prevented development of a likely client-state relationship with the Saddam Hussein regime that would have given China a foothold in the Middle East. As reported then by CNN, the preemptive US assault on Iraq "has convinced the Chinese Communist Party leadership that some form of confrontation with the US could come earlier than expected."[20]

Until late 2002, Beijing thought confrontation with the US could be delayed, and China could focus on economic improvement under Mao successor Deng Xiaoping's "keep-a-low-profile" strategy. "Now, many cadres and think tank members think Beijing should adopt a more pro-active if not aggressive policy to thwart US aggression," CNN quoted a Chinese source in 2003.

Hu Jintao, who succeeded Jiang Zemin as president of the PRC right about the time of the second Iraq war in mid-March 2003, and a year later as chairman of the Central Military Commission, had warned just weeks earlier that China must "make good preparations before the rainstorm." Wen Jiabao, a geologist who became Hu's premier, reportedly told China's cabinet, the State Council, that PRC leaders "must keep a cool head" and "think about dangers in the midst of safety."[21]

Wen's warning came soon after China's belated February 2003 disclosure of a months-earlier outbreak of Severe Acute Respiratory Syndrome or "bird flu." Russian scientists were quick to note the unnatural mix of measles and mumps DNA in the SARS virus, and speculated it might have been man-made. Some China critics raised the specter that the outbreak might have stemmed from a leak in Chinese biowarfare experiments.[22] Chinese Internet posters, howev-

---

20. Willy Wo-Lap Lam, "China readies for future U.S. fight," CNN.Com/World, Mar. 25, 2003.
21. Ibid.
22. Fisher, "SARS Crisis: Don't Rule Out Linkages to China's Biowarfare," *China Brief*, The Jamestown Foundation, Vol. 3, Issue 8, Apr. 22, 2003.

er, were quick to suspect a US bio-weapon attack aimed at damping Chinese opposition to the looming action in Iraq.[23] That sentiment has remained pervasive among the Chinese leadership.

A question of US political will

Beijing has long respected and been wary of US military and technical superiority. But until the Iraq invasion it had viewed the elected US political leadership as lacking the willpower to seriously challenge Chinese ascendancy, particularly since the US' bitter 1960s experience in Vietnam. Moreover, especially during the Clinton Administration, the PRC found venal Washington politicians and thought leaders who could be readily influenced with campaign or other cash. They were subservient to US corporate interests champing at the bit to use China as a low-cost manufacturing base or tap its seemingly vast consumer market. If they could not be cajoled, they could be bought.

Ever since Richard Nixon's détente with Mao Zedong in 1971, forging an alliance against the Soviet Union, the PRC had been getting kid-gloves treatment from Washington. Jimmy Carter established full diplomatic relations in 1978. With Chinese aid instrumental in helping the Taliban drive Soviet troops from Afghanistan, Taiwan independence was downplayed and subsumed in US acceptance of a "One China" foreign policy. This US tilt toward China was most evident in 1989, when George H.W. Bush, after a brief show of anger at the Tiananmen Square killings, went on to approve Most Favored Nation US trade privileges for China, greatly reducing US trade barriers for Chinese goods. Despite its repressive "Communist" regime, Bush formulated a "comprehensive policy of engagement" with the PRC. He also worked to reinstate billions of dollars in suspended China loans from Japan and the World Bank after Tiananmen Square, at a time of severe fragility to China's economic system.[24] "If ever there was a time when the US held considerable economic leverage over China, this was it," observes China scholar James Mann, former Beijing bureau chief for the *Los Angeles Times*.

Bush's successor Bill Clinton, who was lobbied hard by US multinational corporations, pushed for and twice won extension of

23. Lisa Chiu, "Outbreak of rumors has China reeling: Conspiracy theories explaining SARS at epidemic level," *San Francisco Chronicle*, May 7, 2003, p. A-14.
24. Mann, pp. 77-80.

China's Most Favored Nation status. He extolled the prevailing US sentiment that commerce and economic progress were sure to bring along democracy there in tow.

But Clinton later dropped his initial requirement that China show tangible progress in human rights, when it became apparent none was forthcoming. He also allowed a surge of high-tech and potential military exports to the PRC, while taking in large and illegal campaign funding from a raft of dubious Chinese front men. At the end of his troubled administration, after surviving impeachment, Clinton campaigned hard for and won US approval for Chinese entry into the World Trade Organization, formalized in 2001.

Clinton claimed WTO entry would help regularize or prevent rapacious Chinese trade practices, open up China to more US exports, and curb its propensity to militarize. As Clinton declared in a 1999 speech: "Clearly, if it chooses to do so, China could [pour] much more of its wealth into military might and into traditional great power geopolitics. Of course this would rob it of much of its future prosperity, and it is far from inevitable that China will choose this path. Therefore I would argue that we should not make it more likely that China will choose this path by acting as if that decision has already been made."[25]

In reality, the annual US trade deficit with China swelled from about $15 billion when Clinton entered office to about $70 billion when he left in 2000. It was running at a gargantuan $260 billion a year in 2007.[26] China's beggar-thy-neighbor trade practices have persisted, and it has embarked on a steep increase in military spending to boot.

What China could not buy in the way of much-needed technical goods during and after the Clinton years, it has tried to pilfer. Its onslaught of military and industrial espionage has been aimed particularly at computer, missile, submarine, satellite and communications technology. US Immigration and Customs Enforcement has rated Chinese espionage as the leading threat to US technology leadership. Since 2000 Customs has launched more than 400 investigations into illicit export of US hardware and know-how to China.[27] Among the more alarming cases made public was a major security

---

25. "Transcript: Clinton outlines China policy," CNN.com, Apr. 7, 1999.
26. Mann, pp. 80-84.
27. DoD, "Military Power of the People's Republic of China 2007," p. 29.

breech at US nuclear weapon labs discovered in 1995, leading to the indictment of Los Alamos scientist Wen Ho Lee in 1999 on charges of spying for the PRC. The charges were later dropped, but Lee pled guilty in 2006 to a lesser count of mishandling restricted data.

More recently the Department of Homeland Security has reported a surge in cyber attacks on US computer systems, apparently originating from China and aimed at intelligence gathering on sensitive defense-related technologies.[28] "You can kind of connect the dots," Gen. Kevin Chilton, head of US cyberspace defense, told reporters in March 2008. China has denied such charges and chides the US to shed its "Cold War mentality."[29]

Larry Wortzel, chairman of the congressional US-China Economic and Security Review Commission and a former military counterintelligence officer, told a closed-door Congressional hearing in July 2007 that US counterespionage teams are "overwhelmed" with trying to counter Chinese information warfare.[30]

In mid-February 2008 the Department of Justice unveiled separate indictments in two high-profile Chinese espionage cases, involving theft of Space Shuttle technology from Boeing Co. and data on Taiwan arms sales from the Defense Department. DoJ official Kenneth Wainstein, in announcing the charges, called China "particularly adept, and particularly determined and methodical in their espionage efforts."[31]

A history of Chinese influence-buying

Adding to US national security unease over the not-so-successful "nice guy" approach to China during the Clinton Administration was a parade of campaign finance and influence-buying scandals involving Chinese fronts during his presidency. Among the ethnic Chinese names to surface in that regard: Maria Hsia, Ted Sioeng, Yah Lin "Charlie" Trie, the Lippo Group's Riady family, Gene and

28. Sioban Gorman, "Bush Looks to Beef Up Protection Against Cyberattacks," *Wall Street Journal*, Jan. 28, 2008, p. A8.

29. Yochi J. Dreazen, "Pentagon Links China to Hacking," *Wall Street Journal*, Mar. 11, 2008.

30. Bill Gertz, "Beijing espionage poses 'No. 1' threat," *Washington Times*, Jan. 30, 2008.

31. AP, "Arrests Made in Chinese Spying Case," *New York Times,* Feb. 11, 2008.

Nora Lum[32] and others. Some 22 people were eventually convicted of various crimes related to funneling Chinese or Asian money into US political races in the 1990s.

Notable in that list of Chinese money conduits was John Huang, a former Lippo Bank vice chairman and major Democratic Party fund-raiser who was given a sensitive post in the Commerce Department and top-level security clearances under Clinton Commerce Secretary Ron Brown. Congressional investigators found it "vexing" that Huang got his clearance with little vetting, that he got 37 classified CIA briefings, saw some 500 secret intelligence reports with no "need to know," and had at least 67 White House visits. Those included at least one long Oval Office meeting with President Clinton. In Huang's brief and undistinguished 18-month stint at Commerce, his supervisors limited his work to what amounted to an "inconsequential" administrative job, and he was supposedly "walled off" from China matters. Huang nevertheless met various Chinese diplomats. His top-secret clearance was continued for a year after he left to join the Democratic National Committee as a fund-raiser. Huang's boss, Charles Meissner, died in the April 1996 plane crash that killed Ron Brown.[33]

In 1996 the Clinton Administration had moved export licensing control over satellite technology from the State Department to Commerce, just at the time US defense tech majors Loral Space & Communications and Hughes were tipping off China about why one of its rockets exploded while launching a US-built satellite that year. Three classified US studies eventually found US security was harmed by the sharing of technology that would improve the accuracy and reliability of Chinese ballistic missiles. In 1999 Congress shifted satellite export control back to State. Clinton, who counted Loral CEO Bernard Schwartz as a close friend as well as major campaign donor, had signed waivers in 1998 that undermined security

---

32. "Failed Dynamic Energy Still a Focus of US Congressional Fund-raising Probe," *Platts Oilgram News*, Vol. 76, No. 83, May 1, 1998, p. 1

33. US Senate Committee on Homeland Security & Governmental Affairs, "The China Connection: Summary of Committee's Findings Relating to the Effort of the People's Republic of China to Influence U.S. Policies and Elections," part of the "1997 Special Investigation in Connection with 1996 Federal Election Campaigns." See "John Huang at Commerce," p. 12.

efforts by allowing licenses for the technology in question.[34] Loral denied any improper influence from Schwartz' political giving, paid a $14 million fine in 2002, and skirted indictment. Clinton Attorney General Janet Reno declined to appoint a special prosecutor to investigate the Schwartz-Clinton connection.

There is ample reason to suspect the real impetus behind Clinton's impeachment in late 1998, and near removal from office, was concern within the national security establishment about possible compromise of US interests and US-China policy drift, rather than any Arkansas real estate deal or sexual dalliance in the Oval Office. "One issue stands head and shoulders above the rest in terms of the damage his actions did to the nation he was sworn to protect," declared former federal prosecutor, ex-CIA employee and ex-US Congressman Bob Barr, who was among the first in Congress to call for Clinton's impeachment. "That issue is national security, and it remains the foremost reason Bill Clinton should have been impeached and removed."[35]

In the end, however, "Chinagate," "Fostergate,"[36] "Whitewater" and a myriad of other Clinton scandals touching on national security issues were ignored in the public impeachment proceedings.

34. Shirley A. Kan, "China: Possible Missile Technology Transfers from US Satellite Export Policy – Actions and Chronology," Congressional Research Service, Library of Congress, Sept. 5, 2001.

35. Bob Barr, *The Meaning of Is: The Squandered Impeachment and Wasted Legacy of William Jefferson Clinton*, Stroud & Hall, 2004, p. 11.

36. My own reporting at *Forbes*, later published in 1995 in an alternative magazine called *Media Bypass*, confirmed White House Deputy Counsel Vincent W. Foster had been under counterintelligence surveillance at the time he supposedly committed suicide in 1993. Among the suspected (but unproven) buyers of high-level code, encryption and other secrets via Foster's Swiss bank account and Israeli banks: China.

Forbes declined to publish the "Fostergate" story because, I was told by the late Jim Michaels, then editor of *Forbes*, "We can't say this about Systematics." That was a bank data processing and software firm based in Little Rock, Arkansas, which various sources confirmed had been a primary vehicle or front company used by the National Security Agency in the 1980s and early 1990s to market and implant bugged software in the world's major money-center banks and clearing houses as part of the Reagan/Bush "follow the money" effort to break the Soviets. In 1990 private Systematics was bought by Little Rock phone company Alltel, which sold it in 2003 to Fidelity National Financial. Alltel was sold in 2007 to Texas Pacific Group and Goldman Sachs. (footnote continued next page)

His trial in the Senate in February 1999 focused instead on narrow questions of Clinton's truthfulness under oath on sexual matters. For those, he was let off the hook.

Sea-change in the US approach to China

By the end of Clinton's second term, it had become clear the Beijing government was embarked on a much more aggressive agenda. It would be using its new trade powers and undervalued currency to pursue a classic mercantilist export strategy to build wealth and, with it, military power. Well before Clinton left office, and with or without his involvement, the US security establishment appears to have been moving toward a "Plan B" to deal head-on with the China threat. Except for smiley-faced surface-level diplomacy, it would be "no more Mr. Nice Guy."

Rather than accommodate the Chinese timetable for preparing for a US confrontation, Pentagon planners may have decided to take control of that clock themselves, slowing or preempting China's buildup by raising the cost of economic growth and applying stress to what they view as China's rigid social and political system. This sea-change in US-China relations may have been at work in the "accidental" bombing of the PRC's Belgrade embassy in 1998, during the Kosovo conflict, by

Foster's Rose Law Firm protégé Hillary Rodham Clinton and colleague Webster Hubbell were attorneys of record for Systematics in a 1978 federal civil case in which owners of Washington, D.C., bank holding company Financial General Bankshares sued Systematics and its then-owner, Little Rock investment bank Stephens & Co. The Arkansas bond brokerage house had put together a plan to take over FGB on behalf of a group of Middle Eastern investors later identified as front men for the scandal-wracked intelligence and money-laundering operation called Bank of Credit & Commerce International. Among them was Kemal Adham, former head of Saudi intelligence. Stephens' plan was to have Systematics handle all of FGB's data processing, but the merger was blocked by the Securities and Exchange Commission. Eventually BCCI secretly acquired FGB and changed its name to First American, installing former US defense secretary Clark Clifford as chairman. A 1992 Senate report on the BCCI scandal noted the CIA continued to use BCCI and First American to handle funds transfers long after it was known BCCI was "a fundamentally corrupt criminal enterprise."

Stephens was also closely linked to the Chinese-Indonesian Lippo Group banking empire run by the Riady family, whom the Stephens family invited in as co-owners of their Worthen Banking Corp. A US Senate investigation found the Riadys to have had long-standing close ties to Chinese intelligence. See "Hillary's lost memories" by Charles R. Smith, Newsmax.com, Mar. 5, 2007.

three cruise missiles. The White House blamed bad target data supplied by the intelligence community. But a published report later suggested China was using the site to relay Serbian army orders, and that Slobodan Milosevic had been expected to be in the building.[37]

Since then there has been a steady parade of aggressive US moves that could be interpreted as proactive efforts to head off Chinese economic growth and eventual power projection. These include the invasion of Afghanistan soon after the Sept. 11, 2001 terror attacks in the US, effectively taking the "high ground" of Central Asia and thwarting a likely Chinese push into oil-rich Kazakhstan and gas-laden Turkmenistan. The invasion of Iraq also certainly falls into this category, as we will see in Chapter 7. So does the rapid and broad-ranging détente which has emerged between the US and India, China's natural and longstanding rival in Asia and the developing world. The US has unleashed a relentless war of words, diplomacy, economic sanctions, and likely covert initiatives against all of China's would-be allies among such rogue states as Sudan, Syria, Yemen and Iran. And it has also put in the doghouse Venezuelan strongman Hugo Chavez, who has courted China as a possible taker of his heavy crude and as a counterweight to US influence in South America.

In every venue where China has attempted to acquire strategic resources or lay the foundations for client-state relationships that might enhance its ability to stand up to the US and its allies, China has been confronted with some form of resistance. In some cases that has shown up as "indigenous" militant groups (Southern Sudan, Ethiopia, Somalia and Nigeria), or elsewhere as well-orchestrated world media opprobrium (Sudan, Chad, Myanmar, Tibet and North Korea). Small wonder that the paranoia-prone Beijing elite feel convinced they are being targeted for containment by the US and its for-now oil ally Russia.

Domestically, around 1998 there began a series of odd US policy and market movements that wittingly or unwittingly set the stage for, and have since aided and abetted, the incredible surge of world oil prices.

Perhaps most notable in this regard was Washington's complete acquiescence in allowing a spate of oil industry mega-mergers in

---

37. Center for Research on Globalization, "US Air Strike on China's Embassy in Belgrade in 1999 was Deliberate," Dec. 29, 2005.

1998, which were a necessary precedent for the marked tightening-up of global crude oil production. Within the brief span of just 13 months, from mid-1998 to late 1999, four huge oil company mergers totaling a quarter of a trillion dollars in value dramatically consolidated the industry and recast its competitive landscape. The spree began with British Petroleum (BP) announcing a friendly $65 billion stock-swap takeover of Amoco in August 1998 (to make BP a mostly US-owned oil major). That was followed by Exxon's $86 billion (stock and debt) deal to buy Mobil in December. BP struck again in April 1999, acquiring debt-heavy Atlantic Richfield for about $33 billion to put it ahead of rival Royal Dutch Shell in market value. Meanwhile, in Europe, French major Total had gobbled up Belgium's Petrofina in December 1998 for $13 billion, and in July 1999 launched a successful hostile takeover of giant state rival Elf Aquitaine, for $70 billion.

In barely a year's time, the equity market value of the oil industry's top four players (now ExxonMobil, BP, Shell and Total) had swelled from less than half, or 46%, of overall industry market capitalization to almost two thirds, at 63%. It was an unprecedented orgy of oil mergers, which continued with Chevron acquiring Texaco a year later, Conoco and Phillips joining in 2001, and a spate of similar buyouts and mergers of other upstream and downstream independents.

Washington regulators, however, calmly treated the events as nothing unusual. They rationalized the rush to bigness as a logical move to help the majors compete with foreign state-owned oil companies. Aside from some token downstream refining and marketing assets that were required to be divested to resolve local monopoly issues (at huge gains in most cases), government scrutiny and opposition to the deals was almost non-existent. They sailed through with minimal public debate, far different than the political firestorm that was to greet Chinese attempts to buy much smaller Unocal a few years later.

In every case, proportionate capital spending of the combined companies fell. Their oil production has been flat or falling since the combinations, despite rosy assurances that the deals would make the majors more efficient and "competitive." Amazingly, the Western oil majors as a group have been stunningly unable (or unwilling) to respond to sharply higher oil prices with increased supply, despite torrents of cash flow and ever-improving technologies, as we shall see. Chinese oil majors, on the other hand, have shown consistent and substantial liquids volume growth, despite their relatively poor upstream properties and primitive technical base.

Another odd move by the US government around the time of the oil merger binge was to forge a new alliance of sorts with Saudi Arabia, which had seen worsening fiscal problems from low oil prices, and a shrinking of its international oil market share from 17% in 1990 to barely 12% in 1998. In an unusual meeting at the Saudi ambassador's residence near suburban Washington's Fort Marcy Park in September 1998, including Saudi Crown Prince Abdullah, Foreign Minister Saud al-Faisal and Oil Minister Ali Naimi, the Saudis dangled before the CEOs of the US majors the prospect of renewed foreign ownership of oil reserves there. But the Saudis warned they would drive world oil prices even lower unless non-OPEC producers curbed their output.[38]

Separately the Saudis met with Vice President Al Gore, and the Clinton Administration set in motion plans for a Saudi trip by then-Energy Secretary Bill Richardson. The US was clearly getting on board with the notion of oil market tightening and price support.[39] Undisclosed at the time but later reported by *Platts Oilgram News*, the Saudi crown price also met that day with former president Bush and his ex-National Security Advisor, Brent Scowcroft. The Saudi initiatives thus appeared to have the blessing, if not the impetus, of the US national security establishment.[40]

As if to demonstrate Saudi (and US) power to control the market, world oil prices plunged in the ensuing weeks from more than $16/barrel to under $11 by November 30. The oil world had been put on notice the game was changing, and the easy oil pricing of the prior 15 years was over. From that low ebb, oil prices in January 1999 began a relentless upward move that has since raised the price of crude more than 12-fold in barely nine years. Along the way,

---

38. Neil Fleming, ed., *Old Oil, New Rules: Strategies for the 21ˢᵗ Century*, Standard & Poor's, McGraw-Hill, 2000, pp. 84-85.

39. Ibid., p. 85.

40. "Saudi Arabia seen as common link in Exxon-Mobil merger talks, low crude prices," *Platts Oilgram News*, Vol. 76, No. 231, Dec. 1, 1998, p. 1.

Russia was brought into the price-support arrangement in a series of meetings in Moscow and Riyadh between 2001 and 2003. Since then the Kremlin has restrained crude exports to just under 4.5 million b/d or roughly half the Saudi market share. Naturally, China views this as US-led market intervention to raise prices.

After the terror incidents of 9/11, the Bush Administration ordered a massive increase in crude holdings of the US Strategic Petroleum Reserve, regardless of market prices. From about 560 million barrels in the SPR at that time, the Department of Energy added 40 million barrels in 2002 at prices ranging upwards of $30 per barrel, and was moving to reach the full authorization of 700 million barrels. Ignoring rising prices, it dropped a prior policy which would let oil companies delay their "in-kind" US crude royalty payments when futures became "backwardated," with near-term deliveries priced higher than future months.[41]

This volume of SPR buying is seemingly modest in relation to the 7.3 billion barrels consumed yearly by the US, and the roughly 5.5 billion barrels of crude and refined product it imports. But we will see that such buying of light, sweet crude can have a disproportionate upward impact on prices. It clearly helps tighten the market by absorbing surplus barrels that otherwise might go begging for a buyer and weaken the market. The US also leaned on other world governments (including China!) to establish or expand their own SPRs. This dubious strategic stockpiling could have accounted for all or more of the barely 1% increase in 2003 world oil consumption, to 78.4 million b/d.[42]

Another key move by the US government was passage of the Commodity Futures Modernization Act of 2000. That would eventually turn the oil futures market from mainly a zero-sum risk-hedging and price-discovery vehicle into a quasi-securities market. The ensuing flood of investment dollars into oil futures quickly swelled the paper demand for crude to many multiples of the physical crude market. But rather than a rising tide lifting all boats with real wealth

---

41. US Senate Committee on Governmental Affairs, Permanent Subcommittee on Investigations, Minority Staff report, "U.S. Strategic Petroleum Reserve: Recent Policy has Increased Costs to Consumers but not Overall U.S. Energy Security," Mar. 5, 2003, p. 24.

42. "Petrodollars," *Platts Oilgram News*, Vol. 81, No. 177, Sept. 15, 2003, p. 3.

creation, the torrent of presumably "smart" institutional money and non-industry hedge funds has created what amounts to a massive self-inflating Ponzi situation.

It is difficult to believe that US regulators at the Commodity Futures Trading Commission and the Securities and Exchange Commission, who have had to collaborate in regulating this new hybrid commodity-securities market, did not understand the price and risk ramifications of this action. Most glaring in this regard has been the CFTC's utter elimination of speculative position limits on the torrent of pension fund and other institutional investment money that has poured into the relatively small market for oil futures through so-called "swaps" dealers since 2003.[43]

Securitization of oil futures has encouraged the massive expansion of outside participation in oil markets by letting small investors, pension funds and other non-industry players buy futures indirectly through oil or commodity index ETFs (exchange-traded funds). Analysts calculate several hundred billion dollars of new investment money has thus been drawn into what would otherwise be a highly speculative and mostly loss-making futures market, mainly on the "long" side as buyers. As we shall see, these burgeoning derivative investment vehicles also create more opportunity for inconspicuous government market intervention to keep prices up.

One fateful aspect of that 2000 legislation was what came to be known as the "Enron Loophole." This allowed unregulated electronic trading of energy futures by large players and, as the name suggests, let Houston energy merchant Enron quickly engineer a runaway increase in US natural gas prices. As the CFTC seemingly stood by helplessly, NYMEX gas prices soared to an unheard-of level of nearly $10/Mcf in the last week of 2000, quadruple their price of a year earlier. Since just over 6 Mcf of gas has the Btu equivalent of a barrel of oil, the price of one commodity tends to affect the other. Suddenly, it appeared as if crude was worth $60 a barrel, when its actual price had just ebbed from $30 a barrel to barely $20. It soon rebounded to $25 and, after dipping in early 2002, began its relentless climb past $100 a barrel.

---

43. Michael W. Masters, prepared testimony to the Permanent Subcommittee on Investigations, Committee on Homeland Security and Governmental Affairs, US Senate, May 20, 2008, p. 7.

Price-reporting services like *Platts* were systematically conned by bogus trade information from market participants, which helped feed the gas price run-up. Though many of those traders were later prosecuted for misleading the price-reporting services, the damage had been done.

Little impact so far on China's economic growth

Whatever plan the US might have put in place to boost oil prices seems to have had little visible impact so far on China's breakneck growth spurt, and could take many years to make its toll felt. By itself, oil pricing would be unlikely to ever have the lethal effect on Beijing that it had on Moscow. Indeed, the Chinese regime has demonstrated resilience, advance planning and somewhat indifference to the threat of more-than-$100-a-barrel oil. It has acted to shield itself by recycling huge foreign currency inflows from booming exports into subsidies for oil refiners and consumers. Retail price controls have driven China's refining industry into the red as crude prices have risen, but that impact has been partly offset by subsidies to those companies, plus their upstream profits from expanding domestic crude production.

The oil subsidies have insulated Chinese motorists from the effect of rising crude prices, and until recently they were paying even less at the pump than US drivers. True, lower incomes in China make gasoline and diesel relatively more expensive for buyers there, and they face periodic scarcity and long lines for petrol due to the production disincentives of Chinese price controls. But despite all that, China's car count is on a sharp rise from about 24 per 1,000 population in 2006 to a projection of around 40 in 2010, or 55 million cars, according to China's National Development and Reform Commission.[44] Optimistically, the NDRC hopes to limit motor fuel demand growth to "no more than 50%" by 2010 with better motor fuel efficiency.

The PRC economy appears to be much stronger and better financed than was Moscow's in the 1980s. Along with a huge trade surplus, it has accumulated more than $1.5 trillion of dollar-denominated financial reserves. By cleverly mixing totalitarian control with capitalist profit motivation, the PRC has created a for-

44. "Every 1,000 Chinese to own 40 cars in 2010," *Shanghai Daily*, May 24, 2006.

midable growth machine increasingly self-funding and immune to the kind of credit rationing from Western banks that drove down the USSR.

In fact, the US would likely argue it was the Chinese who started the economic war. By methodically holding down the value of its currency and linking it closely to the dollar, using hefty subsidies to promote exports and imposing various taxes and non-tariff restraints on imports, the PRC has waged what amounts to a classic mercantilist trade war to gain strength at the expense of its primary foes: the US, India, Russia and Japan. With admission to the World Trade Organization, China has gained low-tariff access to OECD markets while maintaining the protective aura of its own developing-nation status. But rather than bring itself into conformity with world trade norms, critics say China has flouted the rules and grabbed leading world market shares in key strategic industries with below-market, or even predatory, pricing.

Critics argue China has, in effect, been dumping low-priced manufactured commodities on world markets at below their full cost in order to keep its people working and to utilize an industrial base over-built either due to poor planning or ambitions for world market domination. Its massive expansion of basic industrial capacity in steel, aluminum, alumina, copper and other materials has been financed heavily with foreign direct investment and unrestrained Chinese bank lending. That has positioned China to eventually dominate a range of other key strategic industries like shipbuilding, airframe manufacturing, automotive parts, heavy equipment and, yes, drilling rig manufacturing. Not to mention armaments, already a major Chinese export category.

The George W. Bush Administration has begun to bring legal challenges of Chinese trade practices, and threatens to file more such actions. It has launched cases over product piracy, limits on the sale of US books, music and movies, and has won out-of-court settlement of a dispute over manufacturing subsidies. In the words of US Trade Representative Susan Schwab: "Dialogue where possible and enforcement when necessary."[45] Congress had more than 100 China-trade related bills pending at the end of 2007, mostly aimed

45. Remarks by Susan C. Schwab, US Trade Representative, to a meeting of the US Chamber of Commerce in Washington, DC, Jan. 17, 2008.

at controlling imports and forcing up the value of China's currency, the renminbi.[46]

In February 2008 the WTO handed down its first condemnation of Chinese trade practices, backing European and North American carmakers in a case brought in 2006 over heavy taxation of auto parts entering China as if they were finished vehicles. That was seen as a ploy to boost and protect China's own fledgling auto parts industry and shift jobs from the US, Canada and Europe. In what the Associated Press called a sweeping preliminary decision, a WTO panel sided heavily against China, which had agreed not to treat parts as finished cars when it entered the WTO in 2001. Still, China can appeal the ruling, and then would still have "reasonable" time to change its tariffs. Much damage has been done already, and China's auto parts industry has gained a valuable boost into that high-value-added global manufacturing niche.

China insists it has made great progress in complying with WTO standards of behavior. But critics say it has dragged its feet in many ways, and flouted international trade protocols with rampant subsidies, non-tariff import barriers, dumping and other mercantilist trade tactics. A 2007 report by the US Chamber of Commerce on China's WTO compliance cited "increasingly sophisticated [anti-US] discriminatory investment practices, government procurement preferences, mandatory national standards and other tools of competitive advantage." It warned about "inadequate transparency and the lack of domestic legal and political accountability," as well as continuing "legacies to China's command economy."

Ominously, the Chamber noted, "The fires of Chinese nationalism are burning with more intensity in ways that are having an increasingly less subtle impact on American business in China."[47]

---

46. The US-China Business Council, 11th Congress, First Session Legislation Related to China, as of Dec. 20, 2007.

47. Myron Brilliant and Jeremie Waterman, US Chamber of Commerce, "Issues of Importance to American Business in the US-China Commercial Relationship," September 2007, p. 7.

5

China's Oil Response: The Home Front

Knowing it has faced serious vulnerability to crude oil supply and world prices, the PRC has undertaken a multi-pronged strategy to insulate and defend itself. Unfortunately, it is playing poker with a relatively weak hand as the stakes rise precipitously. Short on crude at home, it has been driven to seek foreign sourcing for either equity ownership of reserves or merchant barrels. Seldom has it found a great bargain. And wherever China goes for oil, trouble seems to follow.

Struggling to boost output at home

China's most obvious crude supply option would seem to be raising production at home. But this has been difficult and costly. At an estimated 3.7 million b/d, China already ranks as the world's sixth largest producer, with about 70% of US domestic crude output of 5.1 million b/d. But China's proved reserves of 12.8 billion barrels[1] are barely half those of the US, and only about 9.5 years of production at the current rate, versus more than 11 years for the US. It is already drawing hard on its known oil reserves.

With much cost and effort, China has managed to offset steep decline rates at existing fields, and actually increase the volume of its crude output in recent years at a rate of about 1.5% annually. But that has been far outstripped by the growth rate in China's oil consumption, which has been running at nearly 10% since 2003. It's demand rose more than 6% in third-quarter 2007 from a year earlier, to 7.69 million b/d.[2] As of mid-2008, the IEA was forecasting 5.5% petroleum demand growth in China for that year, to 8 million b/d.[3]

---

1. CIA, *The World Factbook*, China,
2. EIA, *International Petroleum Monthly*, April 2008, Table 2.4.
3. International Energy Agency, Oil Market Report, June 10, 2008, p. 15.

Various structural problems limit China's ability to meet its own petroleum needs internally. In particular, one-fourth of China's production, or some 900,000 b/d, comes from a single oil field, Daqing in northeast China's Heilongjiang province. First discovered in 1959, output from Daqing's 60,000 wells was maintained at 1 million b/d, or more than one-third of China's total, for 27 years until 2003. Given the relatively shallow depth, low pressure and complex geology, CNPC rates that performance a "miracle in the world petroleum industry."[4] Years of aggressive and reportedly wasteful[5] production at Daqing, however, have begun to show up in a worsening double-digit natural decline rate. This has been unable to be offset by heavy water-flooding and, since 1996, costly polymer floods that now account for one-fourth of Daqing oil production.[6] Water cuts there are now in the range of 90%, creating a massive fluid-handling task and pollution risks.

In 2004 CNPC trimmed Daqing output sharply to extend the field's life and improve ultimate recovery of the oil there, but Daqing's decline rate remains more than 5%, and by 2010 its output is expected to fall to about 500,000 b/d.[7] Similar aging onshore northeastern fields account for about 70% of CNPC oil production, and consume a large portion of its upstream investment funds to sustain output. Per-barrel production costs onshore China are said to be half-again higher than world averages.[8]

A glimpse of the sorry state of Chinese onshore oil operations can be seen in the dismal financial results of Ivanhoe Energy, one of a smattering of small and dubious but politically connected Western oil and gas companies that have been given concessions there. Since 1997 Vancouver-based Ivanhoe has had development rights

---

4. Xu Wenrong, CNPC assistant president, "Tapping the Potentials of Mature Oilfields: CNPC's Practices in China's Eastern Oilfields," Feb. 13, 2007, Houston presentation to CERAweek.
5. James Kynge, *China Shakes the World*, (New York: Houghton Mifflin), 2007, p. 136.
6. Gary A. Pope, *Overview of Chemical EOR*, University of Texas, Oct 26, 2007, p. 5.
7. B. Kong, US Department of Energy, Pacific Northwest National Laboratory, "An Anatomy of China's Energy Insecurity and Its Strategies," October 2005, p. 33.
8. Shaofen Chen, "Motivations behind China's Foreign Oil Quest: a Perspective from the Chinese Government and the Oil Companies." *Journal of Chinese Political Science*, Vol.13, No. 1, 2008, p. 92.

from CNPC on 22,400 gross acres in the Kongnan Block of China's venerable multi-billion-barrel Dagang oil field near Tianjin.

In 2004 Ivanhoe finally drilled its first development well there after the yo-yo sale and repurchase of part of its stake to Japan's Nippon Oil in 1999 and then to Chinese state investment bank CITIC in 2004. By the end of 2007 it had 40 wells in production, totaling a gross 1,900 b/d, or a net 888 b/d to Ivanhoe. That was barely more than the net 750 b/d Ivanhoe averaged in all of 2005 from 22 new wells and 13 re-stimulations that year. In 2005, Ivanhoe earned a net $11.93/bbl in China at an average sale price of just under $50/bbl. In 2006 its China net fell to under $1/bbl despite a price jump to more than $62/bbl, as field operating costs doubled to $14/bbl and China's windfall profits tax kicked in. In 2007 Ivanhoe actually lost $1.75/bbl in China despite an average sale price of almost $65/bbl, as field operating costs topped $18/bbl. The per-barrel loss was partly due to lower expected oil recovery, which forced Ivanhoe to spread remaining sunk costs over fewer barrels. That was even after writing off about 40% of the $86 million Ivanhoe had invested in China.

At the end of 2005 Ivanhoe slowed drilling for "detailed evaluation" of production results and decline rates. After adding another 17 wells in 2006, it persuaded CNPC to let it cut its planned development of 115 wells to only 44, or barely one-third what had been promised.[9] China, in short, has been an unmitigated disaster for Singapore-based Ivanhoe CEO Robert Friedlander. Lead director at Ivanhoe is retired banker A. Robert Abboud, whose First Chicago was the first US bank to open a China branch, in 1978.[10] CITIC made Ivanhoe buy back its nearly $30 million 40% stake at Kongnan, but most of the payment was in Ivanhoe shares then trading at $2.50 each. By early 2008 Ivanhoe had skidded to barely $1.20/share.

Tarim Basin's "Sea of Hope" and offshore oil

To augment the difficult life-extension of China's existing old oil fields, the PRC has pushed hard to find and develop more oil and natural gas reserves in the prolific Tarim Basin of far north-

---

9. Ivanhoe Energy, Form 10-K, Mar. 17, 2008.
10. Ivanhoe Energy, Form 8-K, May 19, 2006.

western Xinjiang province. But despite the highly promising reserve potential there, actual oil production growth has been slow, at less than 5% a year.[11] And even though Xinjiang could be producing 1 million b/d by 2010, the great distance of this "Sea of Hope" from China's coastal refining and consumption centers, and the lack of pipeline infrastructure, make that oil hardly more economical than foreign barrels. This is particularly true, from a Chinese corporate management perspective, after factoring in the up to 40% windfall profits tax Beijing imposes on domestic crude production at prices above $40 a barrel.

The third leg of China's domestic oil production push is offshore on its continental shelf. Though only about 500,000 b/d in 2007, Chinese offshore crude output has been growing at double digits, and has been targeted to double by 2010 to more than 1.3 million b/d. Traditionally the exclusive realm of China National Offshore Oil Corporation (CNOOC), rival majors CNPC and Sinopec have also been encouraged to explore and develop offshore fields. To tackle this much more complex and expensive type of drilling and production, Chinese firms realize they need foreign partners to share the risk and provide technology. In recent years, however, there has been a general exodus of US and other foreign companies from Chinese waters.

Disappointing exploration results, bureaucratic hassles, taxes, and onerous partnership rules that give the Chinese partner 51%, and up to 100% ownership after cost-recovery, put a damper on Western oil company interest there. That is not to mention the tacit geopolitical restrictions that may constrain US and other western firms from active Chinese exploration and production (E&P). There is also the risk of running afoul of the US Foreign Corrupt Practices Act in dealing with China's notoriously opaque politico-economic system. Distrustful of the US and international oil majors, which it regards as state enterprises, China has had instead a penchant for dealing with small, obscure and problematic independent Western operators and promoters. As with Ivanhoe, the results have been predictably poor.

Overall, despite a flurry of PR announcements over the years, US and other foreign upstream investment in China has been rather minimal and fraught with operational difficulty, and it has focused

11. Kong, p. 34.

mainly on natural gas rather than oil production. The US oil majors have been conspicuously absent there. Tellingly, US giant ExxonMobil has no reportable upstream involvement in China. It does have about $3 billion of refining, marketing and petrochemical assets in China, including 25% of a $5 billion Fujian refinery expansion now being built with Saudi Aramco (25%) and Sinopec (50%). But as previously noted, such downstream assets serve mainly to increase the Chinese need for high-cost crude.

Chevron in 2007 got a trivial 26,000 boe/d of upstream production from China, or 1% of its total, mainly from legacy properties acquired with Texaco in 2001. In December 2007 it did announce plans to take a 49% operated stake in the 2,000 square km Chuandongbei natural gas development area in central China, with an estimated 5 Tcf of possible resources. But whatever investment Chevron makes there will be dwarfed by its development efforts offshore Thailand and Australia, which will likely target expensive LNG exports to China.[12]

ConocoPhillips appears to have been perhaps the most active of the US majors in China, mainly offshore in partnership with CNOOC. But its experience there has been mixed. In 2007 output from the company's 24.5% stake at the Panyu oil field in the South China Sea, acquired with the purchase of Burlington Resources in 2006 and operated by CNOOC, rose slightly to 12,100 b/d. But its two nearby Xijiang fields, 80 miles offshore south of Hong Kong, had net crude production of only 7,900 b/d, down from 10,100 b/d in 2006.

In China's shallow Bohai Bay, ConocoPhillips operates the Peng Lai 19-3 field, found in 1999 on a vast 1.6-million-acre concession. It averaged a net 10,500 b/d in 2007, down from 13,800 b/d a year earlier. Phase II development at Pen Lai was approved in 2005 on reserves found in 2000. But the first of five more platforms was not installed until 2007, with first output not slated until 2009. It awaits arrival in 2008 of one of the world's largest floating production vessels.[13] That project appears to be running years behind schedule, and ConocoPhillips has reduced expected volumes from its 49% stake by about one-third, to 61,400 b/d.[14]

---

12. Chevron news releases, Dec. 18, 2007, and Mar. 11, 2008.

13. ConocoPhillips, Form 10-K, Feb. 22, 2008, p. 13.

14. *ConcoPhillips Factbook*, Asia Pacific, p. 36, as of June 30, 2007, and viewed in May 2008. In a 2006 China Business Unit report, however, the company said "We

Odd bedfellows

Another example of frustration for US companies in China involves Houston upstream independent Apache, which in 1994 was wooed into taking a non-operated minority stake in a shallow-water Bohai Bay concession called Zhao Dong, just offshore from the Dagang field. That block had been granted in 1993 to curious Louisiana exploration minnow XCL. How tiny XCL landed what was then China's first foreign "onshore" oil concession, while the US majors were champing at the bit for action there, has long been a mystery. The answer may have more to do with China's penchant for "relationship" business deals than any technical prowess by XCL. XCL had close ties to the regime of corrupt Louisiana Gov. Edwin Edwards and had on its board of directors a bevy of prominent politicos, including former US China Ambassador Arthur Hummel, noted UK diplomat Sir Arthur Michael Palliser and ex-Houston mayor Fred Hofheinz.[15] With odd ties as well to a post-Soviet Ukraine oil venture called Carpatsky Petroleum, XCL may well have been an intelligence front.[16]

After XCL claimed a phenomenal 15,000 b/d discovery well in 1995 (inflated with down-hole pumps, it turned out), Apache stepped up its ownership and took over as operator. When XCL failed to keep up its share of the $150 million development cost, Apache forced XCL-China into bankruptcy. The failed company was taken over in 2003 by bondholders led by Trust Company of the West. Field development was finally completed and Zhao Dong came on line in 2003, a full eight years after the discovery. CNPC then stepped in to claim 51% ownership by paying its share of sunk costs.

But production at Zhao Dong was far less than expected, and in 2006 Apache cashed out its 7,300 b/d share of output by selling its stake to Australia's ROC Oil for $260 million, at a gain of $173 million.[17] TCW then sold its matching XCL-China Zhao Dong stake

are targeting 190,000 barrels of oil every day at the plateau production of these projects by late 2008."

15. "Eight Years after Find, Apache, XCL near Production in China," *Platts Oilgram News*, Vol. 81, No. 30, Feb. 13, 2003, p. 4.

16. "Ukraine Producer Carpatsky, Pease Join," *Platts Oilgram News*, Vol. 77, No. 102, May 28, 1999, p. 3.

17. Apache, Form 10-Q, Nov. 8, 2006, p. 7.

for $228 million to emerging Chinese oil major Sinochem.[18] But by late 2007 ROC's Zhao Dong output was below 4,800 b/d, and it had taken a major reserve write-down there.[19] Costly further development to revive output has sapped cash.[20] ROC's stock price fell by half from late 2007 to early 2008, despite oil prices soaring past $100 a barrel and claims of a massive new oil reserve find nearby. By June ROC had sought a stock-swap combination with larger Australian independent Anzon Australia. Sinochem appears to have been stung as well at Zhao Dong, one of its first upstream equity ventures.

Another of the unlikely companies which emerged with notable China oil concessions was Canadian-listed Texas minnow Pendaries Petroleum, founded by former US Asia intelligence officer Robert Rigney. It was an ironic relationship, since Rigney had flown F-86 jets against Chinese MiGs in the Korean War. In 1964 he was posted to the US embassy in Jakarta as an intelligence officer during the overthrow of the Sukarno regime. During the US-China collaboration against the Soviets in the 1980s, Rigney began training oilfield workers for CNOOC. His marketing firm, Setsco, began selling Chinese-made Hughes Tool drill bits in the US. The bits were made in a Chinese plant set up by Hughes supposedly for use in China only. When Hughes found those cut-rate bits were showing up back in the US, it got a federal court injunction. The sales stopped, but Rigney's China ticket had been punched.[21]

In 1995 Rigney capitalized on his China connections to land a key Bohai Bay concession similar to XCL's for Oklahoma-based Kerr-McGee and partners Murphy Oil of Arkansas and Texas refiner Valero Energy, for whom Rigney had also arranged shipments of Chinese heavy crude. Rigney later bought out the Valero and Murphy Bohai Bay interests through Setsco, for the benefit of a private company called Sino-American Resources. Among Sino-American's directors was Rigney's friend and controversial former Texas

---

18. Sinochem press release, Feb. 8, 2007.
19. ROC Oil Co. Ltd., fourth-quarter 2007 report to shareholders, Jan. 31, 2008.
20. ROC Oil Co. Ltd., 2007 Annual Financial Report, Feb 28, 2008, p. 16. Cash from operations in 2007 was $138.1 million, less than ROC's $62.3 million of development and $82.4 million of exploration outlays. Zhao Dong was its biggest development project, accounting for more than half that spending.
21. "Tiny Pendaries Facing Huge Costs in Chinese Upstream," *Platts Oilgram News*, Vol. 76, No. 127, July 6, 1998, p. 1.

Lt. Gov. Ben Barnes. Sino-American was controlled by Pendaries, whose board included former chairman Guy Snowdon of Rhode Island-based state lottery operator GTECH, for whom Barnes had been a lucrative and controversial lobbyist.

In 2001 Pendaries was bought out by Denver upstream independent Ultra Petroleum for what was then about $50 million worth of Ultra stock, recently worth about $2.4 billion. In another sign of US frustration in China, Ultra sold all its China interests in September 2007 to a unit of Singapore Petroleum Co. for $223 million. It booked a pre-tax gain of $98 million, but at a cost in retrospect of billions of dollars of shareholder dilution.[22]

As with tiny XCL, Pendaries and Ivanhoe in oil, the Chinese have mostly shunned the international majors to deal with obscure US minnows in natural gas development. For instance, in 2004 state-controlled China United Coalbed Methane Co. Ltd. agreed to let Houston start-up Far East Energy Corp. take over as operator of two ConocoPhillips coalbed methane concessions totaling 1.3 million acres in Shanxi and Yunnan provinces. That made tiny FEEC the largest foreign holder of such CBM rights in the PRC. CEO of FEEC is Michael McElwrath, a senior Department of Energy official in the first Bush Administration who also served in the Reagan Interior Department. As of year-end 2007, FEEC had racked up $80 million of exploration costs in five years, with no gas production, no revenues and $49 million of accumulated losses.[23] Since mid-2007 its stock had lost two-thirds of its value by early 2008, at an equity market capitalization of about $75 million.

Similarly, CUCBM has granted 6,620 sq km of CBM concessions in five blocks with a net 920,000 acres to Green Dragon Gas, controlled by California heavy-oil refiner and producer Randeep Grewal. Though it had no revenues or gas production at mid-year 2007, and portions of Grewal's private US Greka Energy empire remain mired in a protracted New York bankruptcy case, Green Dragon claimed a market value of more than $600 million. That was based on Grewal's float of just 5% of Green Dragon's thinly-traded shares

---

22. Ultra Petroleum, Form 10-K, Feb. 26, 2008, p. 66. Ultra shares have soared since 2001 on its Rockies natural gas play, going from about $3 each to near $80 despite a 2:1 split in 2005. In retrospect it grossly overpaid for Pendaries.
23. Far East Energy Corp., Form 10-K, Mar. 13, 2008.

on London's Alternative Investment Market in 2006, to raise about $25 million after the World Bank's International Finance Corp. dropped plans in 2005 to lend Greka's China arm $20 million and infuse $10 million of equity.[24] Grewal himself has lent the company $18 million, and it has borrowed $50 million in other convertible notes. That has funded the drilling of just over 150 CBM wells and purchase of a Beijing gas utility stake. Green Dragon hopes to start some CBM sales in late 2008, but may have to truck compressed gas to urban markets due to lack of pipelines.[25]

CTL, ethanol and other alternatives

While short on oil, China has some of the world's largest coal reserves. Unfortunately, they tend to be deep and low-grade coals requiring costly underground mining, and are generally far from population and power centers. To make more valuable use of that resource, China has long dabbled with the idea of converting coal to liquids, as the Germans did during World War II. Though capital- and energy-intensive, the Fischer-Tropsch process is a proven way to make diesel-like liquid fuel from coal. Other products could be methanol or di-methyl ether (DME), an alternative fuel to costly propane.

For more than 20 years the PRC has struggled to come up with an economic way to do that CTL conversion, with apparently limited success. The costs of building a commercial-scale CTL plant using conventional Sasol or Shell technologies are massive, at around $5 billion each. The operations are complex, require vast amounts of water and are dogged by environmental issues, including the creation of prodigious amounts of carbon dioxide. China's first major CTL project, built in 1999 to convert 500,000 mt of coal a year at Pingdingshan in central China's Henan province, proved to be a costly failure when its local coal turned out to have too much sulfur and ash content.[26]

---

24. "California Producer, refiner Greka files for liquidation," *Platts Oilgram News*, Vol. 83, No. 233, Dec. 5, 2005, p. 1. Saba Enterprises Inc. Ch. 7 bankruptcy docket 05-60144, Southern District of New York.

25. Green Dragon press release, Mar 3, 2008; Interim Results 2007.

26. "Coal-to-Liquids Technology: China's Path to Commerciality," Platts.com, Dec. 19, 2006.

Undaunted, China's state planning agency, the NDRC, in 2004 told state coal mining giant Shenhua Group to build a coal liquefaction plant in remote Inner Mongolia. It is to be the world's first commercial-scale "direct liquefaction" CTL plant. The huge facility is designed to ultimately turn out the equivalent of 100,000 b/d of refined oil products. The first phase was pegged to cost about $3.3 billion for output of 20,000 b/d slated in 2007 with the rest due on line in 2010. But the project appears to be running behind schedule and above cost.[27] Startup was pushed back until late 2008, a year later than planned.[28] At least half a dozen more costly CTL projects are now under way in China. Dozens more are in the planning stages. But official statements that China expects to displace 10% of its oil imports with CTL by 2010 appear to be wildly optimistic.

Other would-be alternatives to imported crude for transport fuel are domestic biofuels such as ethanol. Chinese planners have set an ambitious goal of meeting 15% of the country's motor fuel needs by 2020 with such non-petroleum liquids. From about 1 million mt of bio-ethanol blended into fuels in 2005, China has been rapidly adding capacity. It had set a goal of doubling that volume by 2010 to 2 million mt/year, with a tenfold increase by 2020. Even so, 10 million mt/year of ethanol is equivalent to only a little more than 200,000 b/d of crude petroleum, or roughly the throughput of one mid-sized oil refinery.

As of late 2007 China already had 2.1 million mt/yr of ethanol plants operating, and another 2.5 million mt/year planned by 2010. But sharply rising grain prices and worries about keeping China's 1.3 billion people adequately fed due to drought and storm damage have prompted cutbacks in ethanol output. Existing plants have been running well below capacity as grain prices have skyrocketed. All new corn-based ethanol projects have been halted, and the nearly 2 million mt/year of current corn-based ethanol capacity is slated to be converted to less-efficient non-food grains and starch plants to be grown on scarce "marginal" land.[29] In a contest between using grain for food or fuel, the PRC has little choice but to feed its people first.

27. Kong, p. 37.
28. Reuters, "Shenhua says won't shift CTL plant to listed arm," Mar. 5, 2008.
29. Joshua Speckman, "Biofuel industry faces feedstock uncertainty," *Bioenergy Business*, Feb. 12, 2008.

Draconian efforts at fuel efficiency

D esperate to curb oil imports, China's other main line of defense is improved fuel efficiency. In mid-2005 China launched the first phase of new passenger car mileage standards, with requirements roughly 5% tougher than in the US. Phase II kicked in at the start of 2008, with a required 10% improvement.[30] As the world's No. 3 carmaker behind the US and Japan, and under authoritarian control, China is eager to rein in fuel use without driving up automobile costs and crimping growth of its burgeoning auto industry. In 2007 it produced some 9 million cars and trucks, up from less than 1.1 million in 1992, and domestic unit sales of 8.8 million cars were up 22% from 2006.[31] According to a *China Daily* report in early 2008, however, as crude topped $100 a barrel, rising pump prices for gasoline and diesel had prompted 80% of survey respondents to rethink plans to buy a car. More than one-third had decided to wait for lower fuel prices.[32]

The Chinese government has also stepped in to limit how warm buildings can be in winter, and how cool in summer. But its biggest energy efficiency problem is not so much with thermostats and passenger cars as with industrial fuel consumption. The PRC's determined effort to make itself into a powerhouse producer of basic commodities like steel, cement, glass and petrochemicals has forced up energy use even faster than its GDP growth. This is highly anomalous for modern economies, and the trend is aggravated by China's notorious habit of wasteful industrial-energy practices. For instance, Chinese plants used 41% more energy to make a ton of ethylene than those in Japan in 2000. Chinese steel output used 17% more energy per ton than in Japan that year, cement consumed 31% more, and even power generation itself used 18% more energy than in Japan. Compared to the US, China used 19% more energy to make a ton of urea, and 40% more gasoline per ton-mile of highway freight movement.[33]

---

30. Kong, p. 38.
31. "China auto production, sales hit record 8.8 mln units in 2007," Xinhua, Jan. 13, 2008.
32. APECC newsletter, Vol. V, Issue 2, February 2008, p. 14.
33. "An Unquenchable Thirst for Oil," Merrill Lynch, Global Securities Research & Economics Group, 2004, p. 9.

Chinese officials have been mandated by Beijing to boost the economy's overall energy efficiency per unit of GDP by 20% between 2006 and 2010. But instead of a targeted 4% annual improvement to reach that goal, energy efficiency actually fell 1.3% in 2006. Bureaucrats then managed only a 3% efficiency gain in 2007, when it took the equivalent of 1.17 mt of coal to generate each unit of GDP. Yearly improvement goals are no longer published.[34]

No matter how stingy the Chinese try to be with their energy use, their efforts are drowned out by the PRC's breakneck effort to build up power- and fuel-guzzling strategic industrial facilities for metals, mining and heavy manufacturing. As of 2005, industrial energy demand accounted for an astounding 70% of China's total consumption of about 1.5 billion mt of oil equivalent. Transportation was only 7%.[35] "For most of the country, conservation remains a low priority," notes China energy scholar Wenran Jiang. "The administrative announcements and measures are lost in the convoluted bureaucracy. Even for those local governments wanting to do more, concrete directions from the central government are unclear. Moreover, the market still favors traditional (and unclean) sources of energy, such as coal, and for many, achieving high GDP numbers through large-scale investments in energy, construction and other heavy industrial sectors remains the priority."[36]

China's continued inability to keep up with electricity demand, and the sorry state of its power grid reliability, drives not only huge inefficiencies and economic losses from blackouts and brownouts. It has also led to rampant, costly and wasteful consumption of diesel and fuel oil to run aging oil-fired power plants or small generators for private use. The year 2003 was a particularly bad one for Chinese brownouts, do to poor power planning in prior years. Fuel oil demand soared to feed obsolescent oil-fired generators, mainly in southern China, that had to be called into service. September 2003 imports were almost 60% higher than a year earlier, and year-to-date

34. Reuters, "China '07 energy efficiency improved by 3.27%," *The Economic Times*, Feb 27, 2008.
35. CEIC data from *China Energy Statistical Yearbook*, as cited by Rosen and Houser, p. 8.
36. Wenran Jiang, "China's Struggle for Energy Conservation and Diversification," *China Brief*, The Jamestown Foundation, Vol. 7, Issue 3, Feb. 7, 2007.

oil imports were running 30% ahead of 2002 against GDP growth of about 9%. Oil-fired power plants are less than 1% of official Chinese nameplate generating capacity, which is three-fourths coal-fired and one-fourth hydro, natural gas or nuclear. But unofficial oil-fired power-plant capacity is estimated at several times that volume, and they were probably running flat-out that year.[37]

Much worse power shortages staggered China's manufacturing hub of Guangdong province in January and February of 2008, when severe snow and ice storms toppled power lines and cut supplies from western provinces. Press reports said peak shortfalls were as much as 10 gigawatts, on Guangdong's own 38 GW of generating capacity, and went on for weeks. Local officials have asked Beijing to address what they say is a chronic and worsening 6 GW power shortfall there that could continue for two or three years, forcing closure of less efficient steel and other industrial plants. They have okayed continued operation of a number of inefficient or costly oil- and gas-fired power stations that were due to be phased out. That will boost demand for heavy fuel oil.[38]

Even before the devastating winter storms of early 2008 left large swaths of China dark and frigid for days and weeks, chronic power shortages have played havoc with industrial production and daily life. Though down by a half or two-thirds from 2003, electricity deficits in 2005 were still 15 to 20 million kWh, according to news reports. And since one kWh in Zhejiang province had been calculated to generate about $3 of industrial output, economic losses have been "gigantic," says a 2005 US Department of Energy study. With China's national economy missing about 70 cents of GDP on average for every foregone kWh, the cumulative drain on GDP for the five years from the start of 2000 through 2004 would have been more than $120 billion, or 10% of the PRC's 2001 GDP.[39]

Working against conservation efforts in China are the pervasive subsidies built in to industrial electricity rates, which run far below those in the US and other industrialized nations. Motor fuels are also subsidized, in effect, by capping the wholesale prices that can be charged by refiners and limiting retail profit margins. By adjust-

37. CS First Boston equity research, *China Oil & Gas Databook*, Oct. 30, 2003, p. 6.
38. Reuters, "China's Guangdong faces severe power shortage," Mar. 6, 2008.
39. Kong, p. 4.

ing those controlled prices only infrequently and passing on only a portion of world crude costs, the PRC has attempted to hold down apparent consumer inflation. As we have seen, state-owned refiners like Sinopec and CNPC are only partially made whole for their losses with subsidy payments.

While energy subsidies may mollify industry and consumers, such practices run counter to WTO notions of fair trade. So far, the subsidies have been an affordable cost of doing business for the PRC. But as China's currency is dragged down with its persisting *de facto* peg to the declining US dollar, any softening in Chinese export volumes and tax revenues could sorely test the PRC's ability to sustain its subsidy regime. If, say, it aimed to keep the effective cost of $100/bbl imported crude down to $40/bbl through retail price controls to sustain economic growth, the annual cost to Beijing would be a staggering $100 billion in refiner losses or cash outlays for subsidies. That would be only partly offset by about $25 billion in revenues from its windfall profits tax on domestic crude at $100/bbl. At higher prices the problem grows geometrically.

One way or another, Chinese industry and motorists are likely to face sharply rising fuel costs, along with inflation in food and other raw material prices.

De facto rationing and rising civil unrest

Even if China can hold down fuel-cost inflation, its populace feels the pain anyway. To maintain the appearance of price stability, China has opted to regulate its energy use through *de facto* rationing: brownouts, blackouts and long lines for diesel and gasoline.

In November 2007, as world crude prices pushed above $90/bbl, the PRC raised gasoline and diesel prices about 10% to curb demand, and ordered refiners to step up production and fuel imports to ease transport disruptions and long lines at service stations, sometimes resulting in deadly violence. Even with the hike, retail prices rose to only about $3.20/gal for gasoline and $2.69 for diesel.[40] That brought the price in line with US pump prices on gasoline, but to only three-fourths the cost of US diesel, and likely only break-even margins for Chinese refiners. The PRC vowed it would then hold

40. "China Hikes Fuel Prices Amid Shortages," AP, *International Herald Tribune*, Nov. 1, 2007.

the line on prices for the rest of 2008, even though crude priced soared to almost $140/bbl in May. By June, faced with worsening fuel outages and anger at long waiting lines for petrol, it allowed another price hike of almost 20%. Though steep, that covered less than half the rise in crude prices. Compared to most other countries, Chinese prices for gasoline and diesel remain a bargain.

Combined with overall inflation running at a worrisome annual rate of almost 10% in early 2008, and other social discontents, political pressure is building from public unrest in China. Declining levels of social services and rapidly rising inequality between rich and poor and between urban and rural dwellers, in a culture that had prided itself until recently as the world's most egalitarian, have bred simmering civil discontent.

In March 2008 that caldron boiled over into deadly mass rioting in suppressed Tibet, and prompting deployment of troops to China's restive western provinces. According to press reports, hundreds of Tibetans and ethnic Han Chinese immigrants died in the March 2008 rioting in Lhasa and other parts of Tibet, amid a brutal crackdown by Chinese troops and armed police. Though blocked in China, worldwide Internet scenes of Tibet violence began to spark talk in Europe and elsewhere of Olympic boycotts, which would be a severe blow to both the image and economic standing of the PRC.

The Tibet uprising was not a unique or isolated incident, however. In addition to deploying army units to Tibet in March 2008, the PRC stepped up security in far northwestern Xinjiang province for fear of an outbreak of violence there by the Muslim Uighur community. Two Uighurs died and six were injured the prior month in a police raid on an alleged "terrorist gang" in Urumqi. According to China's Xinhua news service, they were believed to have been collaborating with the East Turkestan Islamic Movement to stage terror attacks, possibly around the Beijing Olympics in summer 2008. Oil-rich Xinjiang has been the scene of frequent clashes between the Islamic Uighurs and PRC authorities.

All across China there has been a rising tide of social unrest. Government statistics in early 2006 listed 87,000 "public order disturbances" in 2005, up 50% in two years. That included a December 2005 mass uprising near Guangdong's Shanwei city over land seizures for a power plant, in which up to 20 people died. A 2006 report by the US Congressional Research Service cites China's "wide and growing income gap, unmitigated by a reliable social safety net. Official corruption and the lack of political power among average citizens further stoke the anger of the aggrieved."[41]

While it can be argued that on average the Chinese population is docile and accepting of the status quo, clearly the PRC leadership has been preoccupied with the threat of civil uprisings, both rural and urban. If consumer price inflation and worsening fuel and power shortages persist, China's elite will need to be all the more wary.

---

41. Congressional Research Service, "Social Unrest in China," May 8, 2006, p. 4.

6

"Going Out," and Trouble Follows

Frustrated in trying to grow its own oil output at home, and nervous about relying on what it sees as a US-dominated international crude market, China has told its major oil companies to "go out" to acquire foreign equity oil holdings. That has been the PRC's chief means to achieve oil security since it became a net importer in 1993. It became its official strategy in 2000 after the 15th Party Congress.

Just how successful this strategy has been remains a matter of debate within the Chinese leadership. One thing seems certain: Wherever the Chinese have gone looking for oil in the ground, trouble has never been far behind. From Sudan, Syria and Yemen to Venezuela and Iran, China's overseas oil acquisition campaign since the mid-1990s has been dogged by geopolitical strife and contention.

The West would argue the PRC has made its own headaches by choosing to deal mainly with renegade states. The Chinese, however, would say those are the only places they can get a fair deal, being welcomed as the main alternative to Western oil majors. When PRC companies venture into other venues, like Nigeria and Kazakhstan, China sees the US or Russia plotting to throw up political and operational roadblocks at every turn.

Since China began its overseas equity oil acquisition campaign in earnest in the mid-1990s, the PRC had garnered about 850,000 b/d of net foreign production as of early 2008. That amounted to just over 10% of China's overall crude consumption, and about 20% of its import needs. It is up from less than 300,000 b/d of foreign equity production, or 8.5% of Chinese imports, as recently as mid-2005.[1]

---

1. EIA, "Country Analysis Briefs: China, Oil" August 2006.

Of course little of that crude actually has made its way to China. Of some 690,000 b/d of foreign equity oil production in 2006 by China's three majors, customs data suggest no more than 250,000 b/d actually arrived in the PRC, or only about 7% of PRC crude imports that year.[2] The bulk of those foreign barrels are sold or swapped abroad to avoid costly transport to China, where they might not fit with PRC refinery capacity anyway. In Sudan, where CNPC is the largest producer with around 200,000 b/d of equity crude in 2006, arch-rival Japan actually imported more Sudanese crude that year than did China. They bought it from CNPC.[3]

In theory, revenues from the sale of China's foreign production could be used to offset the cost of an equivalent amount of Chinese crude imports. But the actual economics of that trade may be questionable. China's new overseas oil production tends to be relatively expensive, and therefore less profitable than the average barrels produced by Western oil majors. Indeed, China's huge cash outlays in recent years to buy, explore and develop foreign oil fields that may not be on production for many years, if ever, probably makes its "going out" effort a net cash drain for now, even at very high oil prices. Whether those long-term investments could pay off at much lower oil prices is questionable.

Details on the costs and profitability of Chinese overseas oil production are limited, since most of it occurs within private (unlisted) state parent companies CNPC, Sinopec Group and CNOOC. Their listed subsidiaries, particularly PetroChina and Sinopec, are subject to US and international financial disclosures, and are generally used to hold no-growth onshore China assets. The foreign oil growth mostly shows up in the secretive state parents, with little disclosure on costs or profits. This strategy is presumably aimed at shielding the public subsidiary stocks trading in New York and London from being battered by political backlash from "going out" moves into the wrong neighborhoods. It also spares the Chinese from having to disclose the often murky commercial terms of these foreign oil deals.

Just what the Chinese have really paid for foreign oil and gas assets in recent years in total is almost impossible to quantify. In many cases the deals were cemented for CNPC, Sinopec or CNOOC by

2. Houser testimony, p. 89.
3. Ibid., p. 90.

visits from top PRC officials, with lavish promises of sidedeals for Chinese state-to-state economic support in the form of loans, infrastructure projects or perhaps arms or other security arrangements. Limited transparency in many of the Chinese foreign upstream deals also raises the specter of kickback side-arrangements to benefit foreign government leaders personally.

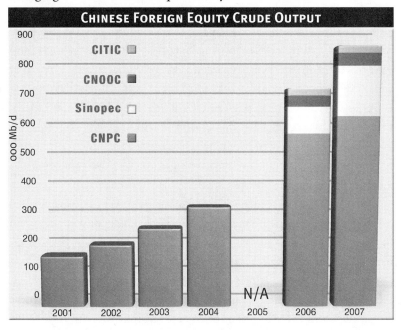

Clearly, however, the Chinese outlays and future spending commitments have been in the multiple tens of billions of dollars. A rough tally of the reported figures suggests the total could run well over $50 billion. Some of that has been forcibly refunded to PRC companies in the form of mandated sell-downs of their foreign acquisitions in Kazakhstan, Russia and other countries wary of Chinese dominance in such strategic assets. But by any measure, China's foreign oil shopping spree has been an expensive one. And it does not appear to have been all that cost-effective. PRC firms have had to pay top dollar for what the industry has considered mostly marginal assets. And despite costly efforts to boost production from these properties, the limited added oil volumes certainly have had no impact on holding down soaring world oil prices. In fact, it could be argued that by "going out" for equity oil, rather than just relying on market purchases, China has actually hurt itself by triggering US reaction that has engendered the world oil price run-up.

There are a number of reasons why China's "going out" foray for oil has likely been a disappointing economic bargain. Most notably, it has been faced with stiff bidding competition just about everywhere it goes for foreign oil concessions. Its perennial nemesis has been India, whose companies probably have been tacitly encouraged (if not financially supported) by the US to bid up the price on nearly every big Chinese foreign deal. Secondly, the assets which have tended to be on auction have been relatively unattractive: heavy or sour oil prospects in hard-to-develop reservoirs. Third, they tend to be remote venues, lacking pipelines and other infrastructure. Finally, when the Chinese do score an economic win, much of the "upside" in their deals has been taken back by host governments or other partners who cash in on preemptive rights to buy their shares of the assets at a similar or even lower price.

Given the small return of physical crude to China from all this foreign activity, some elements in the PRC leadership have begun to question the viability of "going out" for equity oil. The critics, particularly in China's Ministry of Foreign Affairs, note the strategy tends to enrich China's oil majors, and thus empower their executives. But the benefits may be only trickling through to Chinese consumers and the PRC economy, at what may be a high political cost being paid to gain and sustain foreign footholds. "Is it really worthwhile to lend diplomatic support to these projects," observed China analyst Trevor Houser in mid-2007 Washington hearings, "if all [it is] doing is putting money in the pockets of the [Chinese] oil companies and not actually getting any degree of oil security?"[4]

Houser notes, "This is creating a little bit of heartburn in Beijing." PRC diplomats end up expending goodwill and political capital when they "have to go clean up the mess" created by oil dealings in problematic countries. He also cites the risk of asset expropriation in the sorts of corrupt, dictatorial states where, ironically, the Chinese have chosen to invest perhaps *because* of those characteristics. "China is new to foreign investment in this way and hasn't had to endure regime change where their assets were nationalized. Once that happens, and it will happen sooner or later, the thinking

4. Ibid., p. 90.

is going to change pretty fundamentally about whether you should start applying some [transparency] conditions on your companies and [directing] where they invest."[5] Perhaps reflecting these doubts about "going out" for oil, the PRC has now moved to set up a National Energy Commission to oversee oil policy, rather than leave that to the state-owned Chinese majors. It is formulating a delayed new energy law.[6] It also plans to re-create a national energy ministry, perhaps in 2009.[7]

Chinese boots in Sudan

The clearest illustration of these "going out" problems may be in Sudan. That is where China made its real debut on the international oil stage in 1996 when CNPC stepped in to take a 40% interest in a foundering oil venture controlled by dodgy Canadian upstream independent Arakis Energy. Pressed for cash after having shelled out upwards of $200 million to buy and develop that former Shell and Chevron concession, Arakis had put a non-operated 75% of its Sudan play up for sale. Various US companies were rumored to have looked at buying in, including Occidental Petroleum, despite the high cost of having to drill many wells to tap what was thought to be the highly fragmented reservoir there. But the Sudan government, then under terrorism sanctions by the Clinton Administration, dictated no US buyers would be allowed.

That opened the door for CNPC (40%) and Malaysian state oil partner Petronas (30%) to pick up the next $750 million or so of Arakis' investment in what would be called the Greater Nile Petroleum Exploration Company. That would include much of the cost of building a 1,500 km pipeline to the Red Sea, symptomatic of the geographically "challenged" deals China would acquire. That pipe was completed in 1999 to deliver 250,000 b/d, employing thousands of Chinese laborers. Arakis kept 25% and operatorship of the concession and pipeline. Sudan's state-owned oil company Sudapet got a 5% equity cut. "There was a significant political component in

---

5. Ibid.
6. "China set to finalize new energy policy plan," *Platts Oilgram News*, Vol. 86, No. 52, Mar. 13, 2008, p. 4.
7. "New China Energy ministry unlikely in 2008," *Platts Oilgram News*, Vol. 86, No. 23, Feb. 1, 2008, p. 5.

the decision" by Sudan to go with the CNPC/Petronas deal, Arakis CEO John McLeod told *Platts* at the time.[8]

With the pipeline still not finished and Arakis facing cash calls, it sold the rest of its Sudan stake and operator rights to big Canadian independent Talisman Energy in 1998 for $200 million in stock. Talisman, whose share price was then battered by human rights protests, exited in 2003 by selling the interest to India's ONGC. Operatorship effectively then went to CNPC. Politics apparently played heavily in deciding who the buyer would be in that deal as well. CNPC and Petronas reportedly had been eager to get the rest of the Arakis interest in the Greater Nile blocks 1, 2 and 4, including the 150,000 b/d Heglig field, and were confident they would win. But Sudan, either wary of too much Chinese presence in its oil industry or under pressure from the US, apparently directed the sale to India.[9] Soon afterwards, progress emerged in peace talks to end Sudan's 20-year north-south civil war, leading to a treaty in 2005 splitting the country's oil revenues 50:50 between the factions.

Since 1998 CNPC is reported to have invested upwards of $8 billion in Sudan, including a second major pipeline to deliver 150,000 b/d of oil to the Red Sea from a sizeable oil find in 2002 at the Palogue field on Block 7E, where it has a 41% stake. It also built a pipeline from CNPC's wholly owned 40,000 b/d Fula field on Block 6 to a refinery it rebuilt at Khartoum. Overall China's net interest in Sudan crude is about 200,000 b/d, or nearly half of Sudan's total output and two-thirds of its exports.[10] But very little of this crude goes to China. In fact, the bulk goes to rival Japan, which can pay a better price for Sudan crude than Chinese refiners.[11]

The all-in cost of China's Sudan play may be vastly greater than the reported numbers suggest, however. By becoming a mainstay support of the pariah Khartoum government, the PRC has been tarred with international opprobrium. It has been widely associated with the starvation and genocide in Darfur, where estimates are that

---

8. "Arakis Pulls In Two Hefty Partners for Sudan Work," *Platts Oilgram News*, Vol. 74, No. 238, Dec. 9, 1996, p 1.

9. Based on comments from a senior industry executive familiar with Sudan. See also "Petrodollars," *Platts Oilgram News*, Vol. 81, No. 75, Apr. 21, 2003, p. 3.

10. EIA, "Country Analysis Brief, Sudan," April 2007. CNPC website, "CNPC in Sudan," Mar. 20, 2007.

11. Rosen and Houser, "China Energy: A Guide for the Perplexed," p. 33.

some 200,000 to 400,000 people have died, and 2 million made refugees, in recent years. Critics charge China has fueled the slaughter there with arms shipments, in defiance of a UN embargo, and has set up weapons plants in Sudan. The PRC notes it has made modest donations of humanitarian aid to Darfur, but critics note this is less than the PRC gave to build a palace for Sudan's government.[12] A raft of human rights groups have emerged to hammer the PRC on its Sudan links, pressuring western shareholders of PetroChina like Warren Buffett to divest, and urging boycotts. Among the notables to yank their backing of the 2008 Beijing Olympics over Darfur abuses was Hollywood director Steven Spielberg, who in February 2008 withdrew as artistic director of the games.[13]

Hollow victory in Russia, Paying up in Angola

Chinese oil major Sinopec Group appeared to have scored a coup in 2006 by beating out Indian rivals for the right to buy Russian oil producer Udmurtneft for $3.5 billion from TNK-BP. That would have given Sinopec 120,000 b/d of equity crude production, and China's first major upstream property in Russia. But before the ink was dry on the deal, Russian state-owned major Rosneft stepped in to take 51% of Udmurtneft and wrest operating control from Sinopec. Clearly, the Chinese would not have been allowed to own even that minor Russian producer without taking on state Rosneft as operating partner.[14] The sale was no doubt aimed at relieving the appearance in Beijing that Moscow was systematically excluding Chinese purchases of Russian oil assets, which it clearly had. CNPC had previously tried to buy all or part of Russian producers Slavneft, in 2002, and Yuganskneftegaz, in 2004, and had been summarily rebuffed. In July 2006 CNPC was allocated $500 million worth of shares in the Rosneft IPO, a fraction of the $3 billion it had sought.

Little of Udmurtneft's crude is likely to reach China any time soon, however. Its high sulfur content makes it unable to be shipped via the Russian pipeline system, or processed by most Chinese refin-

12. SaveDarfur.Org, "China and Sudan Fact Sheet.".
13. "Spielberg in Darfur snub to China," BBC News, Feb. 13, 2008.
14. Eurasia Group, "China's overseas investments in oil and gas production," prepared for the US-China Economic and Security Review Commission, Oct. 16 2006, p. 14.

eries. Whatever does make it to China will have to move by rail.[15] The rest gets sold in Russia at a discount. Sinopec may book nominal profits on the deal, but it appears to have overpaid for a doggy asset that offers little or no relief to China in terms of crude oil supply.

About the same time Sinopec Group bought Udmurtneft, it put up $2.2 billion in signature bonuses to win rights to parts of three Angolan offshore exploration blocks, partnered with Angolan state oil company Sonangol (25%). Their Sonangol Sinopec International (SSI) had already stepped in to take a 40% stake in BP's Block 18 there in 2004, which includes the Greater Plutonio field development that came on line in late 2007 and is slated to produce upwards of 200,000 b/d at its peak. SSI had grabbed that former Shell stake away from a negotiated sale to Indian buyers in 2004 by having Sonangol exercise its preemptive right. That followed soon after a timely offer of $2 billion in oil-backed loans to Angola by China's Export-Import Bank. Chinese companies have since been busy building schools, hospitals, bridges, railroads and military communications in Angola.[16] SSI was also given a deal to build a $3 billion, 240,000 b/d "Sonaref" refinery in Angola, but by mid-2007 Sinopec had been dropped as a participant in that project.[17]

Kazakhstan pipe dreams

Similarly, much has been made of Chinese upstream inroads in Kazakhstan, particularly CNPC's 2005 purchase of Canadian-listed PetroKazakhstan (PKZ) for a rich $4.2 billion. That deal was won, like Udmurtneft, in the face of concerted Indian opposition from ONGC Videsh Ltd. (OVL) and steelmaker Mittal Group, which had bid up the price. Based on PKZ's prior share price, analysts thought the deal to be perhaps $1 billion overvalued for PKZ's roughly 150,000 b/d of mostly heavy crude from central Kazakhstan's Kumkol field. The Kazakh government held up the sale until CNPC agreed to on-sell one-third of PKZ's equity and a half-in-

15. "Energy to top Russia-China summit agenda," *Platts Oilgram News*, Vol. 85, No. 61, Mar. 27, 2007, p. 2.

16. Paul Hare, "China in Angola: An Emerging Energy Partnership," The Jamestown Foundation, *China Brief*, Vol. 6, Issue 22, Nov. 8, 2006.

17. "Angola's Sonangol targets refinery startup in 2013," *Platts Oilgram News*, Vol. 85, No. 176, Sept. 6, 2007.

terest in PKZ's Shymkent refinery for a less-than-proportional $1.4 billion to state-owned KazMunaiGaz. Russia's LUKoil also insisted on its preemptive right as partner to buy out PKZ's 50% stake in adjacent Turgai Petroleum, with its 68,000 b/d of output. LUKoil won an arbitration case allowing it to buy Turgai at a (presumably lower) negotiated or appraised price. The net effect was to deprive CNPC of PKZ's most attractive growth prospects.

The logic behind CNPC's purchase of PKZ was that those Kumkol barrels could be moved via a new 200,000 b/d oil pipeline, which was to be built at great expense, to the northwestern Chinese refining center at Alashankou. In theory, that would cut CNPC's cost of crude imports and boost the value of PKZ's oil. Plans for the pipeline, which had been shelved due to high costs in the mid-1990s, were quickly revived and the Chinese set about to build the 613-mile pipe at a breakneck pace.

But the very heavy Kumkol crude requires it to be mixed with lighter Kazakh or Russian barrels to allow year-round pipeline shipment. A dearth of nearby light Kazakh crude and tight limits on Russian oil flows through Kazakhstan have played havoc with that plan. The costly new pipeline joint venture of CNPC and KazTransOil, which went into service in mid-2006, has limped along at less than half its capacity. The US EIA has reported Kazakh crude flows through that line were only 85,000 b/d in 2007, plus only 12,000 b/d of Russian crude.[18] At that rate, the line is unlikely to be boosted to its designed capability of 400,000 b/d with added pump stations, making the existing pipeline an under-used and expensive boondoggle for the Chinese. The bulk of what had been PKZ's crude appears to still be headed west or north, or shipped to China in costly railcars.

At the end of 2006 CNPC sold its PKZ stake to public affiliate PetroChina for $2.8 billion, or roughly its net cost in the 2005 deal, despite a doubling of oil prices and substantial further capital investment there in PKZ and the pipeline. That either means PetroChina got a windfall gift from parent CNPC, or else the economic value of PKZ went nowhere despite two years of soaring oil prices. For all of 2007, PetroChina has reported its 67% of PKZ netted it more than $600 million under IFRS on about $1.7 billion of revenues. That is

18. EIA, "Country Analysis Briefs: Kazakhstan."

impressive, but may include an unspecified one-time gain on selling its 50% of Turgai, skewed transfer pricing, or other anomalies.[19]

In the same way CNPC was forced to sell down its PKZ stake, Chinese investment house CITIC Group had to on-sell to KazMunaiGaz at no gain a half-interest in Canadian-based Nations Energy in 2007. CITIC had bought that 39,000 b/d Kazakh heavy oil producer in December 2006 for $1.9 billion from Indonesian tycoon Hashim Djojohadikusumo.

PKZ and Nations are symptomatic of a series of expensive investments Chinese companies have made in next-door Kazakhstan which have now totaled about 200,000 b/d of equity oil production but pitifully little importable crude. Kazakh strongman Nursultan Nazarbayev appears to have skillfully played off China against Russia and the West to divvy up and cash in on Kazakh oil resources without allowing any one outside faction to dominate. He has cautiously limited Chinese oil ownership in Kazakhstan, but has not been squeamish about using the threat of Chinese takeovers to try and prod foot-dragging Western majors to step up production at their large Kazakh oil projects and thus more promptly turn Nazarbayev's oil reserves into cash.

Clash over Kashagan

A good example of this was the tug of war over Kashagan, a mythic-scale oil find in the shallow northern Caspian Sea. Identified as a huge prospect in Soviet times, but not actually drilled until 2000, the massive subterranean Kashagan oil structure is officially estimated to have recoverable reserves of more than 20 billion barrels. Some sources who have seen the geological data, however, say the oil in place could be several hundred billion barrels, with a high ultimate recovery, comparable to Saudi Arabia's Ghawar field.[20] Kashagan occupies an underground mountain or "reef" of oil-bearing rock sprawling over 3,000 sq km: 125 km long by 25 km wide.

In 2003, CNOOC and Sinopec fought hard for the right to buy a one-seventh stake at Kashagan from UK seller BG Group for $1.23 billion. That would have locked in enough proved reserves to justify reversing or building more than 1,000 miles of new pipelines

19. PetroChina, Form 6-F, Mar. 21, 2008, p. 126.
20. "Petrodollars," *Platts Oilgram News,* Mar. 12, 2001.

all the way across Kazakhstan to China. Nazarbayev appeared to be pushing for Chinese participation there to speed development and start turning that oil into cash.[21] After intense political wrangling, the other Western majors controlling Kashagan (at that point Eni as operator, ExxonMobil, Shell, Total, ConocoPhillips and Japan's Inpex) preempted the Chinese purchase, but agreed to on-sell half that stake to the Kazakh government at no gain.

Despite persistent prodding by the Kazakhs, however, the Kashagan majors have repeatedly pushed back the expected start-up date for that huge development. It was originally hoped to begin output in 2005, but the partners eventually promised a 2008 production launch. That has now been delayed to 2012-13, and development costs have soared to more than $19 billion. Eni has cited problems in handling the high-pressure hydrogen sulfide gas that will have to be reinjected at Kashagan. Frustrated Kazakh officials have demanded and won a doubling of their stake in the venture to an equal 16.81%, for a cost of just $1.8 billion.[22] Still, for the Western majors, giving up some equity at Kashagan may be a small price to pay for keeping Kashagan's planned 1.5 million b/d of production off the market a few more years, and thus protecting world crude prices. The freezing out of Chinese interests at Kashagan and that project's interminable delays are a major blow to PRC oil procurement dreams. This has convinced the Beijing leadership the US is actively thwarting their oil acquisition efforts. They've got that right.

Murky deals

China's defeat at Kashagan may be doubly frustrating in light of the extensive efforts it has made to curry favor with the Nazarbayev regime. A particularly odd transaction in that regard may have occurred in 2005, when CNPC's Hong Kong affiliate paid $140 million to buy out the indirect 5% stake held by a murky British Virgin Islands (BVI) firm in Kazakh oil producer AktobeMunaiGaz. The rich buyout came right about the time CNPC emerged

21. "Kazakhstan blocks BG's sale of Kashagan," *Platts Oilgram News*, Vol. 82, June 15, 2004, p. 1.

22. "Eni Delays May Lead to New Fines," Wall Street Journal Online, May 13, 2008, p. B4. Eni, Form 6-K, "Material Developments Relating to the Kashagan Field Development Project," Feb. 18, 2008.

as the winning bidder for PetroKazakhstan.[23] Perhaps coincidentally, mainly BVI entities were allegedly used by indicted American deal-maker James Giffen to funnel kickbacks from Western oil majors on Kashagan and other Kazakh oil plays to key officials of the Kazakh government, including Nazarbayev's family.[24]

Ownership behind that BVI company, Darley Investment Services, was never disclosed, nor how it came to own 20% of CNPC International (Caspian) Ltd. (the other 80% of which was owned by CNPC or its Hong Kong unit). But CNPC International (Caspian) turned up as owner of a 25.12% stake in CNPC-AktobeMunaiGaz soon after the Kazakh government sold its remaining equity there, in exactly that amount, on the Kazakh stock exchange in 2003 for $150 million.[25] Thus, in just two years, whoever owned Darley appears to have reaped a nearly five-fold return on investment, assuming CNPC International (Caspian) bought the Kazakh shares directly in 2003, and Darley put up its share of the purchase price. If Darley didn't actually have to put up cash, then its return verges on the infinite. If it was a bribe conduit, the Darly deal would have dwarfed the $30 million or so of western oil company kickbacks allegedly arranged through Giffen.

AktobeMunaiGaz was one of CNPC's first major foreign investment plays. It outbid Western majors like Amoco, Texaco and Unocal in 1997 to snare 67% voting control of that Kazakh state-owned production company, then pumping about 50,000 b/d from the Kenkiyak and Zhanazhol fields in Kazakhstan's northwestern Aktyubinsk area. CNPC paid $325 million and committed to spend another $4 billion over 20 years for development and pipelines. It was part of a total $9.5 billion of commitments made there that year by the PRC, including rehabilitation of the aging Uzen oilfield.

Much of that promised Chinese spending in Kazakhstan has been deferred or reneged on. But CNPC is reported to have since plowed some $2.5 billion into AktobeMunaiGaz. It more than

---

23. "CNPC pays $140-mil for control of Caspian unit," *Platts Oilgram News*, Vol. 83, No. 198, Oct. 13, 2005, p. 2.

24. United States of America v. James H. Giffen, S1 03 Cr. 404, Indictment, Southern District of New York.

25. "Kazakh government sells 25.12% stake in CNPC-AktobeMunaiGaz," *Platts Oilgram News*, Vol. 81, No. 104, June 2, 2003, p. 6.

doubled output there to more than 120,000 b/d by 2005, the year CNPC upped its voting control to 95% with the Darley deal.[26] Still, that is a very large investment for modest incremental production. And nearly all of it flows west or to Russia for processing, being sold at a considerable discount to the Persian Gulf crude needed for Chinese refineries.

In other Kazakh plays, CNPC in June and August 2003 bought out Saudi Arabia's private Nimir Petroleum (35%) and the US' ChevronTexaco (65%) stakes in the 1.5 billion barrel North Buzachi heavy oil field for curiously undisclosed terms. It then on-sold a half-interest to Canadian-based Nelson Resources. But when LUKoil took over Nelson in 2005 for $2 billion, CNPC found it was unable to use preemptive rights to recoup that interest. Now, after having tripled North Buzachi's output since 2003 to 27,000 b/d, CNPC must share the field with the rival Russians.[27]

In 2004 Sinopec closed the purchase of private Houston-based First International Oil Corp. for $153 million, getting undisclosed but apparently small reserves and production on large but scattered and unexplored acreage in Kazakhstan.[28] The industry calls that land "goat pasture." The main beneficiaries in that deal may have been Bush and Oppenheimer family interests invested quietly in FIOC.[29]

Bad deals in the wrong places with odd partners

PRC "going out" efforts farther afield than Central Asia are looking even more costly and counter-productive, returning only minimal barrels to mainland China so far, often at hefty financial and political costs. China's first such foray is a case in point. In 1993 CNPC farmed in for 50% of Peru's aging onshore Talara oilfield, with 1,800 abandoned oil wells. After many millions of dollars invested and thousands of new wells drilled, CNPC was able to book only modest added production at Talara.[30] It has since expanded that

26. "The Oil Sector, Part. 2," *Oil & Gas Vertical Analytical Service*.
27. CNPC Web site, "CNPC in Kazakhstan," Mar. 19, 2007.
28. "Chinese interest in Kazakh operators attracting others," *Platts Oilgram News*, Vol. 83, No. 125, June 30, 2005, p. 1.
29. "Russia & the Republics," *Platts Oilgram News*, Vol. 75, No. 208; Oct. 27, 1997, p. 3.
30. Kong, p. 40.

operation in 2003 by taking 45% in a venture with Peru's Pluspetrol, netting CNPC about 20,000 b/d of crude after a 96% water cut.[31]

Elsewhere in South America, the PRC has cut a series of oil deals with maverick Venezuelan strongman Hugo Chavez. But only a trickle, if any, of the Chinese crude produced there finds its way to the PRC. And the ventures have faced the same kind of expropriation and punitive tax moves Chavez has imposed on other foreign oil majors. In 2006, CNPC's 100% service contract for the Intercampo oil field on Lake Maracaibo and Caracoles in the eastern Venezuela Basin, which had been generating 21,000 b/d for CNPC, were converted on orders from the Caracas government to a joint venture, with CNPC owning only 25%. CNPC's 2004 deal for the Zumano field was also ordered recast as a JV in 2006, cutting its share of the field's 19,000 b/d output to 40%.

Similarly, Venezuela decided in 2006 to shut down its ill-fated Orimulsion project to blend bitumen with water to make boiler fuel, leaving 70% owner CNPC holding the bag after completing the 70,000 b/d MPE-3 extra heavy oil field and 130,000 b/d emulsification plant.[32]

Various schemes have since been proposed by the Venezuelans whereby CNPC or Sinopec would make huge investments in Venezuela's upstream and downstream oil operations, including a purported $10 billion plan floated in 2007 to produce an eventual 800,000 b/d of heavy oil for China.[33] But these have remained mostly just talk, and Venezuelan claims that it would be exporting 300,000 b/d to China by the end of 2007 have remained a pipedream. Almost no Venezuelan oil actually makes the nearly 14,000 km trip to China, since the natural market for that crude is the US Gulf Coast, at one-fifth the distance.[34] Shallow ports in Venezuela and the narrow Panama Canal limit tanker loadings to about 55,000 dwt, when the nearly 50-day round trip would require at least a 200,000 dwt

31. CNPC website, "CNPC in Peru," n.d.

32. CNPC website, "CNPC in Venezuela," Mar. 20, 2007

33. "PdVSA, CNPC set target of 800,000 b/d at Orinoco," *Platts Oilgram News*, Vol. 85, No. 62, Mar. 28, 2007.

34. Rosen & Houser, p. 33. Though Chinese customs figures for 2006 show 84,000 b/d of imports from Venezuela, "industry sources confirm that due to a total lack of appropriate refining capacity, all of this oil was traded out in favor of more suitable crudes."

supertanker.[35] China could use shuttles and supertankers if it could reverse the 800,000 b/d Panama pipeline, built to handle Alaska North Slope crude. But that now moves about 100,000 b/d of Ecuadorian crude west to east. Chances of building an alternate line across Colombia from Venezuela are slim, given the often near-war status of their relations.

Transport and access problems dog many other Chinese foreign oil investments. For instance in Sudan-neighbor Chad, CNPC and Chinese state investment bank CITIC each bought 25% in 2003 of Friedhelm Eronat's private Swiss-based Cliveden Petroleum Ltd., which had 50% of Chad's 440,000 sq km Permit H.[36] Operator EnCana of Canada had recently discovered upwards of 100 million barrels of heavy oil on that former ExxonMobil concession. But with no pipeline to get the oil to market, EnCana in 2006 agreed to sell its 50% of that non-producing concession for $202 million to CNPC.[37] CNPC also bought out CITIC for undisclosed terms, and then sold half of Permit H to affiliate PetroChina, which now rates it "one of our most important overseas exploration blocks."[38] To help create a market for that oil, CNPC last year offered to build

---

35. Roy Neresian, "The Economics of Shipping Venezuela Crude to China," Touch Briefings, Exploration & Production: *The Oil & Gas Review 2005,* Issue 2, Dec. 2005.

36. Cliveden obtained the Chad concession through a Chapter 11 proceeding in the Southern District of Texas involving Trinity Gas Resources, Case No. 03-31453-H3-11. Eronat is a former business partner of Mobil dealmaker J. Bryan Williams, who was indicted along with James Giffen in relation to the Kazakh bribe laundering and was sentenced to 46 months in prison after pleading guilty in 2003 to tax evasion (Case No. 03-cr-00406-HB-1, Southern District of NY).

Eronat is identified anonymously in the Giffin indictment as a co-conspirator but was able to thwart extradition from the UK to face charges in the US, according to his then-attorney, Peter Felter. Eronat's "assetless shell company," Vaeko, played a key role in Mobil's scheming to obtain an interest in Kazakhstan's giant Tengiz field, according to the Giffen indictment. See "Federal Indictments Reveal Inner Workings of Kazakh Deals," *Platts Oilgram News,* Vol 81, No. 65, Apr. 4, 2003.

A Cliveden affiliate also reportedly showed up with Chinese participants in a 2003 Sudan oil concession near Darfur, but through a lawyer Eronat denied involvement there, according to a June 10, 2005, story in the UK *Guardian* newspaper by Adrian Gatton.

37. EnCana press release, "EnCana sells all of its interests in Chad," Jan. 12, 2007.

38. PetroChina, Form 20-F, May 11, 2007, p. 19.

Chad a refinery.[39] As part of the deal, China agreed to give Chad preferential loans and infrastructure for water and power.[40] When that oil will finally reach a market, at what price, in what volumes and at what all-in cost is a matter of conjecture. But little of it is likely to reach China, and at a doubtful bargain for the PRC.

Next door to Chad, CNPC is heavily invested in another large but landlocked and non-producing oil play in Niger, believed to hold up to 3 billion barrels of oil in an extension of the Chad-Sudan oil trend. It farmed in for 80% of the 17.3 million acre Ténéré Block won in 1997 by Canadian minor TG World Energy. CNPC agreed to fund $105 million of exploration and three wells through 2007. But the first two were non-commercial or dry, and then the Niger government halted work under a security alert due to Tuareg rebel attacks.[41]

Perhaps in a bid to commercialize CNPC's would-be Chad and Niger crude reserves, the Chinese government in early 2006 offered $102 million to buy and a further $2 billion to rebuild the burned-out remains of Nigeria's defunct 110,000 b/d inland Kaduna refinery.[42] It was part of a package of Nigerian deals unveiled after a 2006 visit there by PRC President Hu Jintao. For $16 million and unspecified spending commitments CNPC got the rights to four exploration blocks: two in the Niger Delta (one onshore, one off-shore) and two inland in the Chad Basin.[43] CNPC lost out on the Kaduna refinery to politically-connected Nigerian rival Blue Star Oil, which bought 51% for $160 million. But in early 2008 CNPC was still offering to invest in the plant.

About the same time as CNPC's 2006 Nigeria deal, CNOOC Ltd. emerged as the buyer of a 45% stake in Nigeria's deepwater OML 130 Akpo field, under development by France's Total. CNOOC outbid the Indians by paying a hefty $2.7 billion to the seller: former Nigerian defense minister Theophilus Danjuma's SAPETRO. The Indian government had nixed ONGC's earlier winning bid because

39. "CNPC invests in oil refinery in Chad," Chinadaily.com, Oct 7, 2007.
40. Reuters: "Key facts about Chad," Feb. 3, 2008.
41. TG World Energy, "Niger Project Update," Jan. 31, 2008.
42. "CNPC Wins Four Nigerian Exploration Licenses," AfricanOilJournal.com, May 19, 2006.
43. CNPC website, "CNPC in Nigeria," Sept. 29, 2007.

dealing with Danjuma was "too risky," according to Indian press reports.[44] CNOOC was undeterred.

Partly as a result of the desultory competitive bidding between Chinese and Indian companies for upstream deals, the two countries attempted to form a joint acquisition effort in 2006. That led to combined ventures in Syria and Colombia, along with the Indian participation in Sudan. But their rivalry outweighs their cooperation. There have been no further joint Chinese-Indian upstream deals, and their partnerships are said to be generally contentious.

Chinese firms have a raft of other foreign ventures, totaling well over 100 by early 2008, but most are not yet producing oil or gas, and will require substantial capital investment and time to become economic. The following are among the more notable, and pricey, overseas oil and gas deals signed by Chinese companies in recent years:

April 2002: PetroChina pays Devon Energy $262 million for former Santa Fe Snyder Indonesian properties with net production of 17,100 boe/d.[45]

April 2002: CNOOC Ltd. buys interests in five aging Indonesia oil and gas fields from Repsol YPF for $585 million.[46]

January 2003: CNOOC Ltd. buys a 44% stake in Indonesia's offshore Muturi PSC and 42.4% of the Wiriagar PSC for $275 million. In May 2004 it buys another 21% at Muturi for $105 million. Even with its prior purchases there, however, CNOOC reports 2006 Indonesian output of only 40,000 boe/d, mostly natural gas.

May 2003: CNOOC Ltd. pays $348 million to buy a 5.3% stake in Australia's North West Shelf project.

June 2005: Sinopec pays $84 million to buy a 40% stake in Canada's Northern Lights oil sands project, from 60% operator Synenco Energy. But two years later Synenco scraps plans for a 100,000 b/d syncrude upgrader there, as costs tripled to some C$6.3 billion. In

---

44. "CNOOC to buy Nigeria block for $2.27-bil," *Platts Oilgram News*, Vol. 84, No. 6, Jan. 10, 2006.

45. Robin Pagnamenta, "State Administration of Foreign Exchange (SAFE) Chinese fund builds €1.8bn stake in Total, *Times* (of London), Apr. 4, 2008.

46. "BP says Chinese state fund buying its shares," *Platts Oilgram News*, Vol. 86, No. 68, Apr. 7, 2008, p. 2.

March 2008 Synenco lets go most of its 100 employees, and indefinitely deferred plans to mine bitumen by 2011.[47]

February 2006: CNPC and India's ONGC jointly buy Petro-Canada's net 22,200 b/d of non-operated Syrian production from 36 fields for $580 million.[48]

February 2006: CNPC and Sinopec Group, through their Andes Petroleum consortium, pay $1.42 billion for the Ecuador assets of Canada's EnCana. They take a big hit just a few months later, because almost half of the 72,500 b/d of net production there is from a 40% stake in Occidental Petroleum's nearby Block 15, seized by Ecuador's government in May 2006 in a tax dispute. Andes unsuccessfully demands a refund of its purchase price from EnCana, but gets back only $256 million.[49] Since then Ecuador has upped its windfall profits tax on oil to 99%.

August 2006: Sinopec Group and ONGC together pay $850 million for the 20,000 b/d Colombian arm of US-based Omimex Resources, with plans to invest another $1 billion there.[50]

April 2007: CNOOC Ltd. pays C$120 million to boost its holding to 14.6% in Canadian oil sands developer MEG Energy, after paying C$150 million for an initial stake in 2005.[51]

December 2007: Sinopec Group agrees to invest $2 billion in a "buyback" deal to develop Iran's Yadavaran oil field, expected to eventually produce 300,000 b/d. Sinopec would get a 14.98% rate of return. But work there awaits mine-clearing. The deal omitted earlier plans for China to also buy Iranian LNG.

February 2008: Chinese state oil trader Sinochem agrees to pay London-listed Soco International $465 million for its 16.8% stake in Yemen's 40,000 b/d East Shabwa development.[52]

March 2008: Sinopec Group agrees to pay struggling Australian independent AED Oil Ltd. about A$600 million ($540 million) to

47. "Oil sands startup makes effort to right itself," *Platts Oilgram News*, Vol. 86, No. 53, Mar. 14, 2008, p. 6.

48. "Sinochem buys Soco's Yemen assets for $465 mln," Reuters.com, Feb. 4, 2008.

49. CNOOC Web site, "Cooperation worldwide."

50. "China-India venture to invest in Colombia," *Platts Oilgram News*, Vol. 84, No. 184, Sept. 26, 2006. p. 3.

51. EnCana, Annual Information Form, Feb. 22, 2008, p.5.

52. "China, India team to buy Syria assets from Petro-Canada," *Platts Oilgram News*, Vol. 83, No. 245, Dec. 21, 2005, p. 1.

take an operated 60% equity stake in AED's Puffin oilfield and un-developed Talbot find offshore northwestern Australia in the Timor Sea. Sinopec apparently outbid Apache of the US and Canada's Talisman Energy. Touted as expected to produce 25,000 b/d, the $100 million Puffin development came on stream late in October 2007 at a disappointing 10,000 b/d, and in first-quarter 2008 averaged only 2,500 b/d.[53]

April 2008: France's Total and BP disclose that Chinese state investment funds have been acquiring shares in the open market and may have reached the range of around 1% of their outstanding stock. China's State Administration of Foreign Exchange paid about $2.8 billion for 1.6% of Total, equivalent to about 38,000 boe/d, 63% oil.[54] BP said an unidentified Chinese state fund had recently bought between 0.5 and 0.75% of its shares, which would equate to a value of about $1 billion to $1.5 billion, and imply an equivalent of 19,000 to 28,500 boe/d.[55] That is a costly way to buy oil, with only dividends for cash flow and no operating control, but may be a bargain compared to other recent hard-asset Chinese foreign oil deals.

June 2008: Hong Kong-listed PRC property firm and upstream independent United Energy Group Ltd. agrees to pay $212 million for a 60% stake in troubled Houston-based Transmeridian Exploration, which had faced de-listing in the US after racking up almost $200 million of losses while trying to develop Kazakhstan's South Alibek field.

53. AED Oil Ltd. ASX statement of half-year results to Dec 31, 2007, Mar 13, 2008. Nigel Wilson, "BHP shores up dwindling oil," *Australian*, July 5, 2007.
54. CNOOC Ltd., Form 6-K, press release: "CNOOC Limited Closes Repsol YPF Deal," Apr. 19, 2002.
55. "PetroChina Agrees to Buy Devon's Indonesia Assets," *Platts Oilgram News*, Vol. 80, No. 72, Apr. 16, 2002, p. 1.

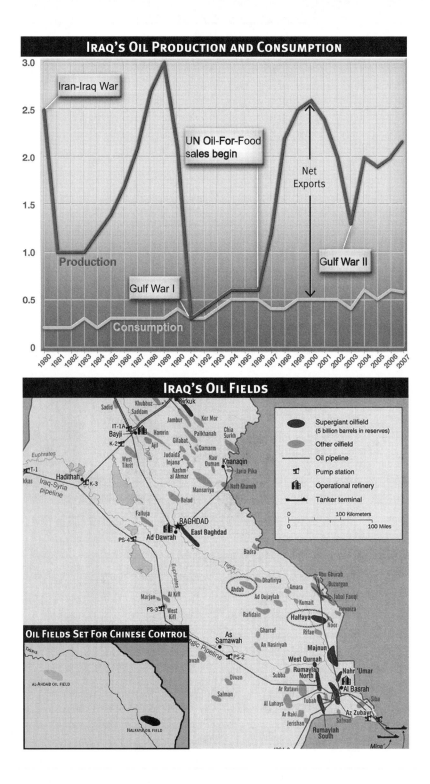

IRAQ'S OIL PRODUCTION AND CONSUMPTION

3.0
2.5
2.0
1.5
1.0
0.5
0

Iran-Iraq War

UN Oil-For-Food sales begin

Net Exports

Production

Gulf War I

Gulf War II

Consumption

1980 1981 1982 1983 1984 1985 1986 1987 1988 1989 1990 1991 1992 1993 1994 1995 1996 1997 1998 1999 2000 2001 2002 2003 2004 2005 2006 2007

IRAQ'S OIL FIELDS

Khubbuz
Sadid
Saddam
Kirkuk
Jambur
Kor Mor
IT-1A
Bayji
Hamrin
Palkhanah
Chia Surkh
K-2
Gilabat
Qamarm
Euphrates
West Tikrit
Judaida
Nau
Duman
Khanaqin
IT-1
Injana
Hadithah
K-3
Kashm al Ahmar
Jaria Pika
kkas
Iraq-Syria pipeline
Mansuriya
Naft Khaneh
Balad
Falluja
BAGHDAD
East Baghdad
PS-4
Ad Dawrah
Badra
Tigris
Euphrates
Dhafiriya
Abu Ghurab
Buzurgan
Ahdab
Amara
Jabal Fauqi
Marjan
Al Kifl
Ad Dujaylah
Kumait
Bawaiza
PS-3
West Kifl
Rafidain
Halfaya
Noor
Gharraf
Rifae
As Samawah
An Nasiriyah
Majnun
PS-2
West Qurnah
Diwan
Rumaylah North
Nahr 'Umar
Subba
Al Basrah
Salman
Ar Ratawi
Siba
Al Luhays
Tubah
Az Zubayr
Ar Raki
Jerishan
Safwan
Rumaylah South
Mina'

Supergiant oilfield
(5 billion barrels in reserves)
Other oilfield
Oil pipeline
Pump station
Operational refinery
Tanker terminal

0   100 Kilometers
0   100 Miles

OIL FIELDS SET FOR CHINESE CONTROL

TIGRIS

AL-AHDAB OIL FIELD

HALFAYA OIL FIELD

7

Saddam Crosses
the Line

I am saddened that it is politically inconvenient to acknowledge what every-one knows: the Iraq war is largely about oil.

— Alan Greenspan[1]

Let our position be absolutely clear: An attempt by any outside force to gain control of the Persian Gulf region will be regarded as an assault on the vital interests of the United States. It will be repelled by the use of any means necessary, including military force.

—President Jimmy Carter, 1980 State of the Union address

There has never been a good official explanation for why the US and its allies invaded and occupied Iraq in March 2003. At the time, President George W. Bush declared the reason for sending waves of bombers and some 170,000 allied troops into that country to unseat the Saddam Hussein regime was to prevent development of weapons of mass destruction. But no evidence was ever found of any nuclear, biological or chemical weapons program in Iraq which could have possibly justified such blatant aggression against an otherwise peaceful—indeed, crippled—sovereign state.[2]

A fall-back explanation for the invasion, occupation and regime change was that Saddam had been covertly scheming with Al Qaeda. That murky Islamist guerrilla and terror group, the global US nemesis, is blamed for the 9/11 attacks on New York's World Trade Center and the Pentagon outside Washington, DC in 2001. This explanation of the Iraq invasion has been equally unpersuasive. There must have been some very serious, but unmentionable, reason

---

1. Bob Woodward, "Greenspan Is Critical Of Bush in Memoir," *Washington Post*, Sept. 16, 2007.
2. "CIA's final report: No WMD found in Iraq," AP via MSNBC, April 25, 2005.

for committing US troops to that long and costly engagement. And there was: Oil.

Yes, Virginia, the 2003 Iraq war was about oil. But not in the way most people suspect.[3] Popular opinion holds that the US moved in both to settle Bush family unfinished "bidness" with Saddam and to grab Iraq's vast oil reserves. That presumably would benefit US oil companies, or service giants like Halliburton, thus rewarding interests viewed as connected to the Bush Administration.[4] True, Halliburton's KBR unit became a major US contractor in post-war Iraq. But since the war, no major oil or oilfield service companies from the US, or anywhere else, have been allowed to take over operation, revitalization or exploration of Iraqi oil assets. In June 2008, at long last, Iraq began the process of awarding limited service contracts there to some US oil majors. But production results from those contracts could be many months or years away and would not involve equity oil interests. For now, nobody's making much of a profit off Iraq oil. (Instead, the industry has been making a killing on everybody-*but*-Iraq's oil.)

Five years after the war, Iraq oil production continues to limp along at barely 2 million b/d, well below the 2.5 million b/d rate just before the 2003 invasion. Exports have been running about 1.5 million b/d, mainly headed east through the Persian Gulf, since Iraq's 600-mile pipeline to the Turkish port of Ceyhan remains a target for supposed insurgent bomb attacks and is often out of service. Iraq's oil infrastructure, though suffering minimal direct damage in

3. "Petrodollars," *Platts Oilgram News*, April 21, 2003
4. George W. Bush's vice president, Dick Cheney, had been CEO of Halliburton in 1997 and 1998 and had presided over what turned out to be its disastrous merger with Dresser Industries. Bush's father George H.W. Bush had been given his first oilpatch job at Dresser in 1948 after attending Yale by then-CEO Henry Neil Mallon. Mallon had been a close friend of Bush's father, Connecticut Sen. Prescott Bush, who sat on Dresser's board. George H.W. Bush named one of his own sons Neil Mallon Bush.

Unfortunately for Halliburton, Dresser brought with it a heap of unappreciated asbestos liability claims which in 2003 prompted Halliburton to put much of its operations through a "pre-packaged" Chapter 11 bankruptcy reorganization to fund a $4 billion payout to asbestos claimants. In 2006 it sold to the public a minority stake in its KBR (Kellog Brown & Root) construction and government services arm, which had managed about $10 billion of Iraq contracts for the Pentagon. The rest of KBR was exchanged in 2007 for Halliburton shares.

the 2003 war, remains in a rusty shambles. It is mostly functioning with the same old dilapidated pipes, pumps and creaky refineries that strained to move and process Iraqi crude in the cash-strapped Saddam era.

Post-war drilling activity, using aging state-run rigs and lacking modern well technologies, has been minimal and stunningly inefficient. Typical was a report in *Platts Oilgram* describing the state of affairs more than two years after the war. It noted that during all of 2005 in Northern Iraq, except for a small work area run by US contractor Parsons, "essential field maintenance, reservoir management, well-drilling and workovers fell far short of required levels. The only rig operator at work was the Iraqi Drilling Company (IDC). Its two workover rigs recompleted just six wells and its five drilling rigs completed only 13 new wells. Oil ministry officials say that met only 40% of their goal."[5] Operations elsewhere around the country were similarly abysmal and remain so, despite the granting of a modest number of contracts to begin looking at rehabilitation of some Iraq fields.

In short, post-war Iraqi oil operations have been a joke. This is despite the fact it is one of the lowest-cost places in the world to add incremental oil production. According to the US EIA in 2006, the cost of adding a million barrels per day of production at Iraq's giant Kirkuk field was as little at $750 million. At that rate, the investment would be paid back, at $100/barrel, *in about one week.* Another million barrels per day of capacity at the Rumalia field would cost only about $3 billion, for a payback in one month. The EIA notes only 17 of Iraq's 80 discovered fields have been developed, with little deep drilling and a total of only 2,300 wells in the whole country, of which only 1,600 were producing in 2006.

With or without security risks there, it strains credulity that the Iraq government, the US Department of Energy, the Pentagon and the entire roster of international oil majors would just ignore the massive and easy-to-get oil potential of Iraq as market prices screamed past $100 a barrel.

What if the 2003 war had not occurred and the Saddam Hussein regime had been freed of UN sanctions as expected later that year? Iraq's oil ministry had confidently predicted in 1997 it would

---

5. "Iraq oil output fails to live up to 2005 targets," *Platts Oilgram News*, Vol. 84, No. 1, Jan 3, 2006, p. 1.

be producing 3 million b/d within one year of exiting UN sanctions, which had been in place since Iraq's 1990 invasion of Kuwait. Iraq had planned to boost its output to 6 million b/d in less than 10 years after sanctions.[6] And that was not an unreasonable goal, given the fact Iraq is second only to Saudi Arabia in found oil reserves with more than 100 billion barrels, and likely double that in probable reserves. Moreover, only about one-third of Iraq has even been explored for oil. It is possible Iraq could hold more than Saudi Arabia's 250 billion barrels of proved oil reserves.

At 6 million b/d, Iraq output would merely match Saudi Arabia's ratio of reserves to production. No major new discoveries would be required. All it would take would be money invested, and existing technologies applied, to flood the market with Iraqi oil. Needless to say, that did not happen. And it likely won't, even though various non-US oil majors and a smattering of independents have been eagerly waiting to gain access there, regardless of the security risks. In a triumph of lethargy that can only be interpreted as intentional, the US has allowed Iraq's oilfields to lie fallow and, through Iraq's disheveled post-war occupation government, has blocked any move by outsiders to "make hay while the sun shines."

Saddam's Iraq had good reason to be confident it could, indeed, muster the needed investment and rapidly push ahead to that production target of 6 million b/d. It had already found "deep pockets" to foot the bill. Rather than rely on its own bumbling and cash-strapped oil ministry, in a significant departure from past practice, Iraq planned to farm out the work to foreign companies. While UN sanctions were still in place in the late 1990s, Iraq began lining up international majors and state oil companies to undertake that development as soon as permitted to work there after UN sanctions were lifted. The format would be standard industry production sharing agreements (PSAs) that would give the operators an equity interest in the reserves they developed. This was unusual for the Middle East, where the big reserve holders like Saudi Arabia, Kuwait, Iran and Iraq had generally banned foreign equity oil ownership since

---

6. Saddam was being conservative. Ahmad Chalabi, leader of the opposition Iraqi National Congress, told the daily *Asharq al-Awsat* in December 2002 that a post-Saddam Iraq would target 6 million b/d of output in just two or three years, with investment of around $38 billion.

their expropriation of those interests in the 1960s and '70s. Saddam was offering a major enticement, and most of the world's oil majors queued up to bid for a piece of the Iraq action, including such US firms as Conoco and Arco.

This was happening while UN sanctions banning such foreign oil investment were still in place, and with no timetable for them to be lifted. The negotiations went on outside the reach of the UN Oil-For-Food Program, which had begun to allow about 2 million b/d of Iraq oil exports in late 1996. Saddam's regime skillfully dangled the prospects of dozens of known, multi-billion-barrel oil fields, and exploration rights to vast tracts of Iraq's unexplored Western Desert, in front of the foreigners. But it was particularly keen on spreading those deals around among companies from nations represented on the UN Security Council, and thus wielding clout in getting the sanctions lifted. Russian, French and Chinese companies thus were most favored, much to the ire of US officials.

The first and largest of these tentative Iraq PSA deals was signed in 1997 with the Chinese. State major China National Petroleum Corp partnered with PRC arms-maker Norinco in a venture called al-Waha, which was given development rights to 50% of the huge al-Ahdab field in eastern Iraq, covering some 250 sq km near the city of Al Kut. They were to invest $1.3-billion over 23 years and could expect to get 100,000 b/d from that 1.4 billion barrel proved oil reserve.

In addition, CNPC was in line to be granted rights to the "super-giant" Halfayah field with 5.5 billion barrels of recoverable reserves, and possible production of 360,000 b/d. The status of the Halfayah deal remained murky, however, and it apparently still had not been finalized at the time of the 2003 war. CNPC was also reported to be dickering for rights to Iraq's Subba-Luhais fields, with 1.3 billion barrels of proved reserves and expected capacity of 240,000 b/d of crude.[7]

The only other pre-war Iraq production sharing agreement formally signed, also in 1997, was with a group led by Russian major LUKoil for the West Qurna field in Southern Iraq, with 6 billion barrels of proved reserves and 15 billion barrels in place. LUKoil was obligated at that time to invest $3.7 billion over 23 years to rehabili-

7. Haider A. Khan, *China's Energy Dilemma*, University of Denver, 2005, p.10.   127

tate and develop that field for what was expected to be potential cumulative output of 4.8 billion barrels by 2020. But Baghdad declared LUKoil's 68.5% interest there void in late 2002, on the verge of war, after it was learned the Russian firm had gone to Washington to secure continued rights to the field after any US-led regime change in Iraq.[8] Allowed to keep their separate 3.25% West Qurna stakes were Iraq-friendly Russian oil firms Zarubezhneft and Machinoimport.[9] The Iraqi Oil and Gas Ministry held the other 25%. Since the war, LUKoil has partnered with now-merged ConocoPhillips to try and win renewed development rights at West Qurna. Five years after the war, West Qurna's fate remains in limbo, with no near-term development of that oil in sight.

Pre-war UN sanctions banned any foreign companies from actively drilling or otherwise developing Iraqi oil properties. But UN rules did allow for non-production-related seismic and other geophysical evaluation activities. Some level of work was undertaken, and CNPC was able to deploy various teams of supposed oilfield technicians to Iraq in the months and years before 2003. How many and for what true purpose is not known. Whatever was going on, Baghdad reportedly became frustrated that CNPC and LUKoil were not more active with such preliminary work.

What has been reported, however, are the activities of other Chinese firms involved in breaching UN sanctions by delivering unapproved communications and other high-tech gear to Iraq. Of particular note in that regard is Chinese telecom major Huawei Technologies, founded in 1988 by a former PLA officer and now China's largest telecom systems provider. In 2001 Huawei was identified as the contractor building an upgraded fiber-optics communications network in Iraq, which critics warned could let Saddam integrate his air defense network. China denied Huawei was do-

---

8. Middle East Economic Survey, Vol. XLV, No 51/52, Dec. 23-30, 2002.

9. State-owned Russian oil company Zarubezhneft by itself was the largest single recipient of Iraq oil allocations under the UN Oil-For-Food Program at 183 million barrels or 4% of total allocations. It actually lifted 168 million barrels or 5% of the volumes actually sold under OFFP, according to the UN Independent Inquiry Committee headed by Paul Volcker. Machinoimport was identified by the IIC, along with LUKoil Asia Pacific, as helping to front for 62 million barrels of under-priced Iraq oil allocated under OFFP to Vladimir Zhirinovsky, head of the ultra-nationalist Liberal Democratic Party of Russia.

ing Iraqi defense work, but admitted it was one of three Chinese telecom firms which violated UN sanctions by installing fiber-optic cable systems without UN approval.[10] China claimed it ordered the work stopped. But published reports in the Indian press, hotly denied by the Chinese, noted Huawei had also been involved in building fiber-optic communications and surveillance systems for the Taliban regime before the US-led invasion there.[11] The systems in Iraq were said to be among the earliest targets of US and allied warplanes in the 2003 war.

What was China offering to Saddam to lock up equity reserves that would either supply China's growing oil thirst or hedge its cost of buying barrels elsewhere? That remains a mystery. But clearly from the viewpoint of US defense planners, Chinese inroads with Saddam were seen as eventually creating a client-state relationship similar to Beijing's grip on Sudan. Therein was cause for severe heartburn. Saddam had crossed the line.

A new American century

By early 1998, even while beleaguered Bill Clinton was still president, the US national security policy apparatus had shifted from a posture of Iraq containment to one of regime change. That was epitomized by an open letter sent to Clinton in January of that year by the "Project for a New American Century," an "educational organization whose goal is to promote American global leadership." It was heavily focused on countering Chinese expansionism. Formed in early 1997, PNAC was headed by neoconservative editor William Kristol of the *Weekly Standard*, and listed a Who's Who of influential figures connected to the US national security establishment. Signatories to the Iraq letter included Elliott Abrams, Richard Armitage, William Bennett, John Bolton, Zalmay Khalilzad, Richard Perle, Donald Rumsfeld, Vin Weber, Paul Wolfowitz, James Woolsey and Robert Zoellick.

The PNAC letter ominously warned US Iraq policy was "not succeeding," and that "we may soon face a threat in the Middle East more serious than any we have known since the end of the Cold

10. John Gershman, "Arms Sales to Taiwan: A Flashpoint Issue," International Relations Center, Foreign Policy in Focus, March 2001.
11. "Chinese IT firm denies 'Taleban link'," BBC News, Dec. 10, 2001.

War." It further stated, "Given the magnitude of the threat … The only acceptable strategy is one that eliminates the possibility that Iraq will be able to use or threaten to use weapons of mass destruction. In the near term, this means a willingness to undertake military action as diplomacy is clearly failing. In the long term, it means removing Saddam Hussein and his regime from power. That now needs to become the aim of American foreign policy."[12]

In September 1998, Congress passed an "Iraq Liberation Act," signed into law by President Clinton in October.[13] By November, Clinton had launched a bombing campaign against Iraq, which was called off at the last moment when Iraq seemed to relent on giving UN arms inspectors access to restricted sites there. But a month later, in December 1998, as Clinton was about to face impeachment hearings, he ordered a four-day aerial attack called "Operation Desert Fox." It used cruise missiles, carrier-based aircraft and B-1 bombers to attack purported WMD sites, as well as Iraqi air defense installations. The proximate cause for the attacks was supposedly Iraq's interference with UN weapons inspectors, and failure to disarm and to repudiate Saddam's alleged weapons of mass destruction. "Mark my words," Clinton warned in a televised speech, "he will develop weapons of mass destruction. He will deploy them, and he will use them."[14]

Ironically, Swedish diplomat Rolf Ekeus, who headed the UN inspection effort for Iraqi WMDs, called the UN Special Commission (UNSCOM), was just at that time "getting close to certifying that Iraq was in compliance" with UN Resolution 687 ordering it to disarm its WMD effort.[15] The bombing seemed to be an overblown reaction to what had been a long pattern of Iraqi cat-and-mouse games with weapons inspectors. It sparked a wave of criticism that Clinton had launched the attack to deflect attention from his own political woes. Later, the CIA was accused of having infiltrated UNSCOM to provoke a pretext for the air assault that could even target

12. "Open letter to President Clinton regarding Iraq," Project for the New American Century, Jan. 26, 1998.
13. Public Law 105–338, Oct. 31, 1998.
14. "Transcript: President Clinton explains Iraq strike," CNN.com, Dec. 16, 1998.
15. Andrew Cockburn, "Why Clinton is Culpable: Iraq's WMD Myth," *Counter-Punch*, Sept 29-30, 2007.

Saddam for assassination by bombing.[16] And former UN weapons inspector Scott Ritter, a former US Marine Corps intelligence officer, later alleged a UK intelligence unit called Operation Rockingham had been used to help generate misleading reports of Iraqi WMDs to provide a pretext for military action.[17] Clearly, something besides the threat of WMDs was driving a fundamental and urgent policy change toward finally removing the dictator who for more then two decades had been a US bulwark and foil against Iran.

In response to that 1998 bombing effort, France, backed by Russia and the PRC, formally proposed that the UN Security Council lift the Iraq oil embargo in place since 1990.[18] That effort gained gradual momentum and by late 2002, after years of relentless pressure and revelations of scandalous mismanagement of its Oil-for-Food Program, the UN appeared headed toward a lifting of Iraq sanctions. The oil embargo was expected to be over by the end of 2003. That would allow unrestricted development and sales of Iraq crude. It would also mean a surge of Chinese "oilfield workers," who could effectively garrison al-Ahdab, Halfayah and other key Iraq oil fields. Once ensconced, as in Sudan, they might never be removed without provoking direct military conflict between the US and China. Washington was indeed facing a national security nightmare that would dwarf the problem created by armed Chinese presence in Sudan. PNAC's warnings to Clinton were coming true.

The erosion of international support for Iraq sanctions, and the looming threat of Chinese boots on the ground there by late 2003, put the Bush Administration under a severe time squeeze. To avert Chinese occupation of the Iraq fields, the US would have little choice but to invade the country and occupy it, with or without allies or UN support. Moreover, that would have to happen before the summer of 2003 to avoid military operations during the desert summer. With no clear pretext for launching such an obvious war of aggression, Washington policymakers were under the gun to find an issue, any issue, which might justify an invasion. They again turned

---

16. Mark Tran, Ian Black, "US 'Spied on Iraq,'" *Guardian*, Jan. 7, 1999.

17. Neil Mackay, "Revealed: the secret cabal which spun for Blair," *Sunday Herald* (UK), June 8, 2003.

18. Sen. Frank Murkowski, "Our Toothless Policy on Iraq," *Washington Post*, Jan. 25, 1999; p A21.

to bogus but useful claims of secret Iraqi efforts to build weapons of mass destruction. This message was delivered in dramatic form by Secretary of State Colin Powell to the UN General Assembly on Feb. 5, 2003.[19]

Powell recited a litany of circumstantial evidence and secretive reports of Iraqi WMDs. Though later found to be dubious or outright fabrications, they laid the foundation for a US-led ground attack. "We know that Saddam Hussein is determined to keep his weapons of mass destruction," Powell told the General Assembly. "He's determined to make more. Given Saddam Hussein's history of aggression, given what we know of his grandiose plans, given what we know of his terrorist associations and given his determination to exact revenge on those who oppose him, should we take the risk that he will not some day use these weapons at a time and the place and in the manner of his choosing at a time when the world is in a much weaker position to respond? The United States will not and cannot run that risk to the American people. Leaving Saddam Hussein in possession of weapons of mass destruction for a few more months or years is not an option, not in a post-September 11th world."

The UN Security Council eventually passed Resolution 1441 in November of 2002, finding Iraq in "material breech" of UN sanctions. That document gave no particular order or permission for military action against Iraq. But it noted a prior Iraq-related resolution of 1990, authorizing member states to "to use all necessary means to uphold and implement ... all relevant resolutions ... and to restore international peace and security in the area." [20] Bush thus had what Washington would claim to be legitimate international authority to conduct its own invasion of Iraq.

At home, the Bush Administration won lopsided passage of a Congressional "Joint Resolution to Authorize the Use of United States Armed Forces Against Iraq" in October 2002.[21] Its sweeping powers gave Bush permission to wage war "as he determines to be necessary and appropriate" to defend the US from "the continuing threat posed by Iraq," and to "enforce all relevant United Nations

---

19. US Secretary of State Colin Powell, address to the UN Security Council, "Iraq: Denial and Deception," Feb. 5, 2003.
20. Text of UN Security Council Resolution on Iraq, Nov. 8, 2002.
21. Public Law 107–243, Oct. 16, 2002.

Security Council Resolutions regarding Iraq." It passed overwhelmingly: 296-133 in the House and 77-23 in the Senate. As with Clinton's 1998 bombing campaign, the public debate revolved around WMDs and Saddam's alleged links to terrorist activities. And all those claims were later found to be groundless.

Indeed, the alleged cooking of intelligence data to support the 2003 Iraq invasion spawned an ongoing political storm for George W. Bush and then-Prime Minister Tony Blair in the UK, where a now-infamous "Downing Street memo" surfaced in 2005. Those notes from a pre-war 2002 briefing had Blair Foreign Secretary Jack Straw stating Bush had "made up his mind" to attack Iraq but "the case was thin" on WMD/terror grounds. The memo further quoted Sir Richard Dearlove, head of Britain's Secret Intelligence Service, stating that US "intelligence and facts were being fixed around the policy" of Iraq regime change.

Never was China overtly mentioned as a factor in the decision-making.

The ghost of presidents past

Curiously missing from the Congressional debate about authorizing the invasion of Iraq was one key item of US international policy which ought to have been invoked by the looming Chinese presence in Iraq: the Carter Doctrine. Crafted by National Security Advisor Zbigniew Brzezinski, it was first enunciated by President Jimmy Carter in his 1980 State of the Union address in response to the Soviet invasion of Afghanistan. It stated flatly, "Let our position be absolutely clear: An attempt by any outside force to gain control of the Persian Gulf region will be regarded as an assault on the vital interests of the United States. It will be repelled by the use of any means necessary, including military force."

In 1981 President Reagan expanded that doctrine to include the defense of Saudi Arabia with what was termed the "Reagan Corollary." Together, these basic statements of US policy laid the groundwork for the 1991 invasion of Iraq.

And, though tacit, they would have to have been key factors in authorizing the 2003 war. It seems clear the threat of Chinese occupation of key Iraq oil fields by armed security forces, as had occurred in Sudan, would have set off all sorts of alarm bells under the Carter Doctrine and Reagan Corollary. Policy-wise, the invasion of Iraq in 2003 had ample rationale in established US doctrine, based simply upon the imminent threat of Chinese oilfield occupation. The fact no one could dare mention that consideration at the time is one more of those "dog that didn't bark" moments in playing the *The Oil Card.*

Since the 2003 war, China has been all but frozen out of any involvement in Iraq. The status of its al-Ahdab claim is highly doubtful. In June 2003 CNPC challenged a statement by Iraq's then-oil minister Thamir Ghadban that its al-Ahdab development deal was now "void by mutual agreement."[22] But any Chinese development of the field will apparently require the issuance of new approvals by Iraq. Meanwhile, China has let it be known it would challenge any other development effort there.

Some talks have reportedly continued in Baghdad and Beijing over renewal of some form of PSA at al-Ahdab, but nothing has been concluded and would have to await final implementation of a long-delayed Iraq hydrocarbons law.[23] As part of the bargain, China has reportedly agreed to forgive "a large margin" of the $10 billion debt it claims is still owed by Iraq from Saddam's regime. However, as the *Financial Times* has noted, that may be only a token gesture, since the debt is all but uncollectible anyway. Don't hold your breath waiting for Chinese oil production in Iraq.

Since the 2003 US-led invasion of Iraq, allied combat deaths have grown to more than 4,000, despite only 140 in the initial assault and capture of Baghdad. Estimates of Iraqi civilian deaths have ranged from under 100,000 to more than 1.2 million.[24] The financial costs will total between $1 trillion and $2 trillion.[25]

As horrific as those statistics are, and however mismanaged and brutal the Iraq occupation has been, the lingering question is what the costs and casualties might have been by now if the US and

22. EIA, "Country Analysis Brief: Iraq," August 2007.

23. "CNPC seen regaining oil exploration rights to Iraq's al-Ahdab field," AFX News Ltd, Mar. 9, 2007.

24. "Update on Iraqi Casualty Data," Opinion Research Business, January 2008.

25. Linda Bilmes and Joseph Stiglitz, *The Economic Cost of the Iraq War: An Appraisal Three Years After the Beginning of the Conflict*, National Bureau of Economic Research, February 2006.

China had been drawn into a direct military confrontation. By that measure, it is not far-fetched to argue the 2003 Iraq war would have been a bargain at twice the price. Far from being a capricious, vindictive and wanton exercise of US military might, as critics around the world proclaim, the war may have been both an entirely rational enterprise and the lesser evil. Unfortunately, if this thesis is correct, the promulgators of this bloody adventure would be bound under national security law from making that case in public, and must simply take their lumps. And they certainly have.

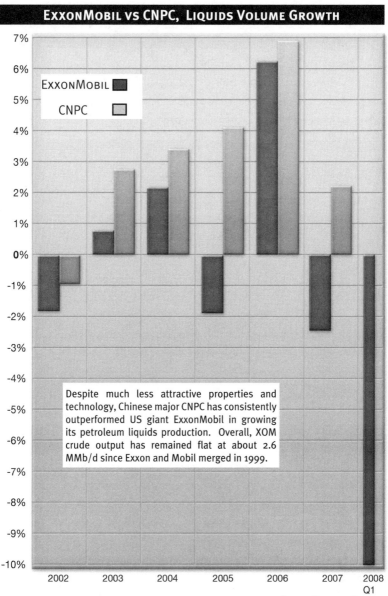

EXXONMOBIL VS CNPC, LIQUIDS VOLUME GROWTH

ExxonMobil ■
CNPC □

Despite much less attractive properties and technology, Chinese major CNPC has consistently outperformed US giant ExxonMobil in growing its petroleum liquids production. Overall, XOM crude output has remained flat at about 2.6 MMb/d since Exxon and Mobil merged in 1999.

Source: Company Reports

—8—

The Role of
the Oil Majors

I've said for more than two years that the fundamentals do not support the price of crude oil. It is other issues, largely geopolitical...
— ExxonMobil CEO Lee R. Raymond[1]

A company should repurchase its shares only when its stock is trading below its expected value and when no better investment opportunities are available.
— The Golden Rule of Share Buybacks[2]

Among the telltale bits of circumstantial evidence that oil prices are being controlled upward to restrict Chinese economic growth is the odd behavior of the major Western integrated oil companies in recent years. Particularly when contrasted with their operating and investment policies during the 1980s, when the US was aggressively waging a successful economic war on the Soviets, the financial posture of Big Oil raises a host of questions.

The most glaring of these curiosities is why the majors, with their decks awash in cash from sky-high oil prices, have pursued such miserly reinvestment plans lately to bring more oil supply on stream and reap even more gargantuan profits. At $100/barrel, the profit margin on US oil production for a company like ExxonMobil had to be more than $50/barrel, even after corporate income taxes. Foreign barrels are usually less profitable, due to sliding-scale tax and royalty regimes, but still offer great returns and rapid recovery of capital outlays. In a logical world and a free market, oil companies would be "making hay while the sun shines," frantically putting profits back

---

1. Lee R. Raymond interview with Maria Bartiromo, CNBC, Nov. 8, 2005.
2. Michael J. Mauboussin, "Clear thinking about Share Repurchase," Legg Mason Capital Management, Jan. 10, 2006, p. 5.

to work in the business to capture profits and grow. Instead, since at least the late 1990s, the Western majors have scrimped on reinvestment in their basic business in favor of such low-return financial alternatives as paying down low-cost debt and buying back their own pricey shares. As most corporate leaders would admit, large share buyback programs like those of the oil majors usually imply a sick business: declining enterprises generating more cash than there are ongoing business opportunities for them to invest in.[3]

Let's look at ExxonMobil, by far the largest and arguably best-managed of all the major integrated oil companies. More than any other single company, ExxonMobil tends to epitomize the US oil business, and it sets the pace, if not the agenda, for the rest of the world oil majors. With an equity market value now of more than $500 billion, bolstered by about 40% from its 1999 stock-swap take-over of Mobil, it stands head and shoulders above its nearest rivals. It has about twice the market value of second- and third-ranked Royal Dutch Shell and BP. US rivals Chevron and ConocoPhillips trail at about 40% and 30% of ExxonMobil's value.

With the Mobil deal, Exxon alone accounted for almost one-fourth of the entire market value of traded Western oil companies in 1999. And with the flurry of oil mega-mergers in the late 1990s, the top four majors (ExxonMobil, Shell, BP and France's Total) had climbed from 46% of total industry public valuation to 63%. The top 10 rose from 73% to 86% of the value and the top 15 rose from 80% to 90%.[4] Their capital spending accounted for similar shares of the industry's total outlays. All the hundreds of lesser independent companies, frankly, didn't amount to much in terms of relative market value or spending clout. Moreover, the majors overwhelmingly control access to the most favorable exploration opportunities and enjoy the newest and best technologies, either developed in-house or with major oilfield service companies. The playing field has changed some since 1999, as Russia's LUKoil and China's three major oil companies have emerged as large public companies. Other state-run oil companies also have been developing into full-fledged international majors, like Petrobras in Brazil. But even so, oil industry capital spending, technology and

---

3. Ibid., p. 6.
4. Fleming, pp. 77-86.

market value remain dominated by ExxonMobil and the public Western majors.

A popular perception is that the US and other western governments are somehow corrupted, controlled or held hostage by the money and political power of Big Oil: that it is the oil companies which, one way or another, dictate public policy. But to whatever extent the oil industry may exert influence, ultimately it is these companies, no matter how large, which end up at the mercy of government. The reality is that the oil majors, even if widely held and publicly traded, often operate abroad as *de facto* extensions of their home governments. Indeed, it is interesting to note that for policy purposes Chinese military and political analysts regard ExxonMobil and other foreign oil majors as if they were, in fact, state-owned enterprises. Of course Western oil executives would likely chortle at that suggestion and take great umbrage at the notion they are somehow doing the bidding of state controllers. But the national security linkages between governments and the oil majors run very deep and at many levels. Though rarely discussed, there can be no doubt oil companies often provide the "cover" for intelligence operatives, carry the flag to foreign shores, and can be used to wield great influence abroad. Key among their attributes in this regard is their ability to create oil wealth, and spread it around with easily mis-priced deals.

That was then ...

There is little outward evidence of any direct US state control of ExxonMobil or other US oil companies. But an analysis of the company's odd investment behavior over the past several decades seems at least to raise the possibility its spending activities have been skewed by Washington's geopolitical objectives. In particular in the 1980s, when the Reagan Administration and the US national security establishment were trying to bankrupt the Soviets with cheap oil, pre-merger Exxon seemed to be embarked on a crazy, spendthrift, devil-may-care oil investment binge in the face of weak and falling commodity prices. It was exactly the kind of behavior the company had long eschewed, and has since renounced.

Under CEO Clifton Garvin, Exxon in the '80s seemed to go against all the characteristic behavioral patterns expected of a cartel-supporting oligopolist in a weak pricing environment. As US and world oil demand was falling sharply in 1982, due to new car mileage rules and the phase-out of oil-fired US power plants, the normally tightly disciplined Exxon strangely went wild with exploration and drilling outlays. It scrambled to boost oil production, even though the market was becoming glutted and prices were falling off a cliff. Its mantra at the time was the standard rationale of corporate growth: more volume, more market share. Nonsense, said industry veterans at the time, who were puzzled by what seemed to be truly reckless, needless overproduction sure to further weaken oil prices and cripple the industry.

In 1982, for instance, the year in which Ronald Reagan signed NSDD-66 to declare economic war on the Soviets, Exxon boosted its upstream capital spending about 2%, to a record $6.94 billion. That was even though its profits from oil and gas production fell by a sharp 17% to $3.43 billion as its realized crude price averaged just $27.66/barrel, down 7% that year. Including exploration expense, Exxon's upstream outlays of $7.3 billion to find and develop oil and gas reserves jumped to far more than the roughly $6.4 billion of cash it was generating in that business through earnings plus non-cash charges like depreciation, depletion and amortization. The company did not disclose its upstream cash flow from deferred taxes, but it still appears its 1982 upstream outlays exceeded its overall upstream cash flow – an incredible spurt of over-spending by current standards. To fund that investment and still pay its dividend, giant Exxon had to draw down cash and boost debt levels that year. Mighty Exxon was, in effect, borrowing money to drill exploration wells and speed up production in an already glutted market.[5]

Exxon's upstream reinvestment continued at near 100% of its upstream cash flow through 1985, excluding un-quantified upstream deferred taxes. Its exploration spending alone jumped to 33% of upstream cash flow in 1982 and remained in the 20% range for several years. How well-spent was that money? Hard to tell. Despite its much-vaunted technical prowess, Exxon's exploration dry-hole rate of 57% climbed to almost 74% in 1986. The total number of net wells it drilled, including production wells, surged to 1,565 in 1983 and then on to almost 2,500 in 1985, before receding to a

5. Exxon Corp., 1983 Form 10-K, p. 7; 1983 Annual Report to Shareholders, pp. 1, 27.

more normal 1,111 in 1986. The company's current financial disclosures reveal it cost an average of almost $4 just to *find* a barrel of reserves in the 1980s, not counting development costs. Compare that to ExxonMobil's current "finding cost" per barrel of under $1, in much-inflated dollars.[6]

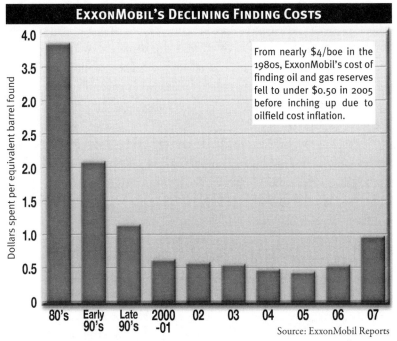

ExxonMobil's Declining Finding Costs

From nearly $4/boe in the 1980s, ExxonMobil's cost of finding oil and gas reserves fell to under $0.50 in 2005 before inching up due to oilfield cost inflation.

Dollars spent per equivalent barrel found

80's · Early 90's · Late 90's · 2000 -01 · 02 · 03 · 04 · 05 · 06 · 07

Source: ExxonMobil Reports

The breakneck 1980s drilling effort, heavily geared to what was then the company's relatively high-tax US properties, smacked of some kind of desperate bid to boost production. And that it did. In 1983, the first year after Reagan signed NSDD-66, giant Exxon's output of crude oil and natural gas liquids jumped an incredible 12%, to 1.58 million b/d. It kept up a brisk 5% growth pace in those liquids volumes through 1987, when they averaged 1.84 million b/d, even though Exxon's realized crude and liquids price fell by half in that period, to under $13 a barrel in 1986. That year, upstream net from its own production, not counting equity interests in other companies' ventures, had ebbed to just $1.6 billion, from $3.8 billion in 1984.[7]

Were it not for Exxon's sheer size, global scope, integration, deep pockets and invulnerability to raiders, that big-spender

6. ExxonMobil, 2006 Financial & Operating Review, p. 25.
7. Exxon Corp., 1987 ARS, p. 37; 1985 ARS, p. 39.

strategy in the face of low oil prices would have been a sure road to ruin if it persisted for very long. Except for yield-hungry individual investors and retirees, Wall Street soured on Exxon. The company's split-adjusted share price fell by 56% from late 1980 to mid-1982, and took two years to recover. Despite high dividends and stock buybacks, it was overtaken in 1993 by General Electric as the most valuable US industrial corporation, at $90 billion. Though it has now regained the top spot, with an equity market capitalization of more than half a trillion dollars on the oil price run-up, the oil giant still has the lowest institutional ownership percentage of any of its US peers. The "smart money" remains wary of ExxonMobil.

Fortunately for Exxon, the spending spree abated by the late 1980s before it did severe damage to the company, while leaving deep scars on lesser rivals who were trying to follow the same paradigm. In fact, Exxon emerged an extraordinarily lean and efficient company as a result of all the cutting of superfluous costs required to fund that heavy upstream reinvestment in the 1980s. By contrast, No. 2 Texaco went through Chapter 11 bankruptcy reorganization in the 1980s, after losing a Texas court case over snatching Getty Oil away from Pennzoil. Chevron was hobbled for years after buying Gulf Oil in 1984 for what then seemed like a rich $13.1 billion. Phillips Petroleum and Unocal had to take on big debts to fend off raiders. The 1980s were a mighty rough decade for oilmen trying to make a buck.

Indeed, any major US oil company that tried to respond rationally to low oil prices in the 1980s by cutting high-cost exploration work, and just letting reserves decline until costs ebbed and prices recovered, was sure to be pounced upon by the new breed of stock market raiders who materialized almost out of nowhere. Small-time Amarillo wildcatter T. Boone Pickens Jr. for instance, backed by Drexel Burnham Lambert junk bond financier Michael Milken, was able to make much of Gulf's poor reserve replacement record in the early 1980s, and castigated Gulf for falling into what Pickens called self-liquidation mode. His tiny Mesa Petroleum was able to gain a stock foothold and stage a proxy fight that ultimately put Gulf in play to be bought by another major, Chevron.

Curiously, some top Gulf managers at the time told me they were nervous that somehow the US government itself was behind the Pickens/Milken raid. Could such an out-of-the-blue takeover threat have been used by national security interests to enforce a mandate to boost oil production, no matter the near-term economic sense? Aside from the fact one less-than-fully-credible former CIA "asset" has claimed to me that he and other government operatives were assigned to travel with and assist Pickens, there is no evidence of such a diabolical and coercive plot. But the theoretical possibility certainly exists, maybe even without Pickens' awareness, and poses an intriguing object for retrospection. It would explain a lot.

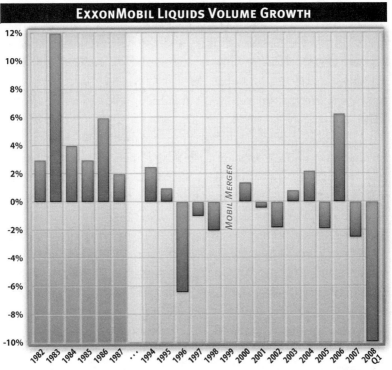

Source: ExxonMobil Reports

This is now

Now let's compare Exxon's aggressive spending and oil production growth in those key years of the 1980s, when low oil prices were strangling the Soviet economy, with the company's behavior since the late 1990s. Under the demanding, gruff and seemingly miserly command of former downstream manager Lee Raymond as CEO, the company took a markedly opposite tack. From peak liquids production of 1.84 million b/d in 1987, Exxon's output was allowed to gradually ebb and remain flat for the next decade of relatively low oil prices, which bumped along in the range of about $20 per barrel. In 1993, the year China became a net crude importer, Exxon's liquids output was 1.67 million b/d, and varied little until 1999, when it swallowed Mobil. That merger bumped up the combined company's liquids output to 2.52 million b/d that year, which held uncannily steady for the next six years, until a slight rise in 2006 to 2.68 million b/d. It fell again in 2007 to 2.62 million b/d and dipped in first-quarter 2008 to 2.47 million b/d, down 10% from a year earlier.

Thus, at a time when crude oil prices were rising more than 10-fold from late 1998, amid worsening fears of a looming world oil shortage and rising Chinese demand, the richest and most capable oil explorer of all proved utterly unable, or unwilling, to raise its liquids production. So much for "make hay while the sun shines."

Raymond cut the company's upstream reinvestment rate. From nearly 100% upstream cash flow reinvestment into oil and gas production in the mid-1980s, Exxon's reinvestment rate on upstream cash eased to about 70% in the low-price mid-1990s after the collapse of the Soviet Union. That is to say, on upstream profits of about $3 billion a year and non-cash expense of about $3 billion a year from 1993 to 1998 (for cash flow of about $6 billion a year), Exxon was spending about $4.5 billion a year on upstream capital outlays and exploration. That was generally more than enough to fully replace all its oil and gas production volumes with new "proved" reserves in those years. And it was doing so quite profitably: Exxon's disclosed cost of replacing its produced volumes with new oil and gas reserves (its "reserve replacement cost" for both finding and development) averaged about $4 per barrel equivalent. That was well under the market price, and less than half its cost in the grow-grow 1980s. Even at modest prices, the 1990s appear to have been a much better time to invest in oil and gas exploration and production than the 1980s, but Raymond held back.

Its reinvestment pattern got even more tight-fisted after the Mobil merger. Upstream capital and exploration outlays for the merged company rose about 40% in 1999 to $8.4 billion, or 77% of upstream cash flow, in line with its proportionate enlargement with Mobil. But within one year that spending had been slashed 12% to $6.9 billion in 2000, or just 39% of upstream cash flow, despite a clear upturn in crude prices. Upstream investment spending then recovered, and roughly doubled over the next five years to around $15 billion annually. But it has grown far slower than oil prices and profits. ExxonMobil upstream spending as a percent of upstream cash flow has fallen to below 50%, from nearly 100% in the mid-1980s and 70% through most of the 1990s.

The falloff in purely exploration spending by ExxonMobil has been even more dramatic. From outlays routinely running around 30% of upstream cash flow in the mid-1980s, exploration was cut to half that rate in the 1990s, fell to under 10% after the Mobil merger, and in the past two years was a paltry 3%. In absolute dollar terms, the company's exploration spending in 2006 of $2 billion was barely higher than the $1.9 billion incurred in 1999 after the Mobil merger, and much less if adjusted for inflation.

Where has all that extra cash been going? Raymond led Exxon-Mobil on a massive stock buy-back effort, which has roughly matched the company's upstream reinvestment spending. From the end of 2002 through 2007, ExxonMobil has spent a prodigious $80 billion to repurchase 20% of its own shares in the market. Some of those have been redistributed in the company's generous stock awards program for top mangers, but most have been simply squirreled away as treasury shares for possible use in a major acquisition. The stock price has tripled from about $30 a share in mid-2002 to around $90 in early 2008, as oil prices have soared and the buyback buoyed demand for the stock. So ExxonMobil is sitting on a large paper profit on its repurchased shares. But when its stock price was languishing in the $40 range, and then skidded briefly in 2002, the buybacks looked like a marginal or bad investment, reaping perhaps only about a 5% annual cash return on the dividends saved. Since early 2007 ExxonMobil has been trapped in a flat trading range of about $90/share despite a near-tripling of oil prices and in mid-2008 had fallen to under $85.

By contrast, based on ExxonMobil's own disclosed costs of finding new reserves to replace what it has pumped, the discounted present value of future cash flows created from upstream reinvestment appears to be many, many times greater than the funds expended. In other words, even though ExxonMobil's cost of replacing its reserves rose to $7/barrel in 2006, that was a fraction of the after-tax value that would be created by putting the money back into finding and developing new reserves, even if their ultimate cash flows were discounted at 10% a year to reflect time required to eventually get the oil and gas out of the ground.

Compared to a static, no-growth financial strategy like buying back stock, upstream reinvestment would seem to be a no-brainer for ExxonMobil, as they say. There are signs that new CEO Rex Tillerson, an upstream veteran who replaced Raymond in 2006, may be moving to increase exploration and production spending. But as a percentage of the company's ever-rising oil and gas cash flows, those outlays are likely to remain no better than 50%.

It gets worse. Given the astoundingly attractive economics of finding and producing new oil, it would make sense to prudently use some debt financing at ExxonMobil's Triple-A borrowing rate of less than 6% interest to fund more upstream activity. Instead, ExxonMobil has used its torrent of unspent incoming cash to pay down debt to negligible levels and to build up a breathtaking cash hoard of some $35 billion at year-end 2007. Minimizing debt is laudable and almost always a good investment. But for a company which claims to be growing, and obsessed with earning a return on assets of well over 20% a year, the minimal interest yield on those amassed funds and lack of debt leverage is clearly a drag on performance. Especially compared to what ought to be easy money from more oil investment. What can these guys possibly be thinking?

Speculation is that ExxonMobil will eventually use its mountain of cash and treasury shares to make a major acquisition. That would make up for years of ExxonMobil's own flat oil volume trend. But at current reinvestment rates it would likely signal a killing-off of production growth in any acquired company, as happened with Mobil. That occurred as well with Chevron's 2005 takeover of Unocal and ConocoPhillips' 2006 purchase of Burlington Resources, two big independents which were poised to grow their production at double-digit rates. It is interesting to note the last major acquisition reportedly eyed by ExxonMobil was that of wayward Russian major Yukos, whose CEO Mikhail Khodorkovsky was brashly planning to ignore Kremlin instructions and build Yukos' own 600,000 b/d crude oil pipeline into China. Before ExxonMobil could seal a deal, Russian tax authorities began a stunning assault on Yukos to dismember the company. Khodorkovsky is now in a Russian prison. Had ExxonMobil prevailed in obtaining a controlling stake in Yukos, it is reasonable to postulate the Russian firm's upstream reinvestment, production growth and certainly its China export plans would have all taken a dive.

There is something seriously wrong with this picture of ExxonMobil's stewardship of its wealth in oil and cash. It seems as if the company has to work hard at doing so little with its financial, geological and technical resources. Its success, driven by the wild rise of crude oil prices on fears of world scarcity, has to be chalked up as a triumph of lethargy.

To justify its paltry reinvestment efforts, ExxonMobil has wielded a variety of arguments. One is that it has shifted over the years to a different way of measuring its financial performance. Instead of profit growth, margins on sales, or return on equity, it has insisted that analysts apply the inherently conservative yardstick of "return on average capital employed." ROACE measures profits (plus interest expense) as a percent of total debt and equity. It is a particularly favorable way of looking at an old-line, low-growth industrial company like ExxonMobil which is under-investing for the future.

Business planners know that running an enterprise to maximize ROACE is a sure-fire way to kill off growth. The reason is that new investment gets booked as an asset. That increases the denominator in the calculation and decreases the numerator, since the investment has to be depreciated or expensed. New capital spending is thus discouraged even if it promises large, ongoing profits far down the road.

The irony in this is the more-than-20% ROACE rates ExxonMobil and other oil majors have been able to boast in recent years largely come from long-since amortized or depreciated upstream projects still in production, which are now gushing profits at phenomenal rates. In fact in the oil business, the *less* you invest, the higher your apparent ROACE is likely to be, in the near term. By scrimping especially on its US upstream reinvestment, ExxonMobil has seen its ROACE here soar to around a 50% return on capital. But its US oil volumes have plunged.

Another way ExxonMobil can justify its low reinvestment efforts, and tacitly encourage other companies to follow suit, is through its annual outlook for global oil and gas supply and demand. Consistently, ExxonMobil has stated the world is at no dire risk of running out of liquid hydrocarbons any time soon. So it asserts a more normalized commodity price is more like $35 per barrel, which would require a much more conservative investment approach than at current market prices.

Pay no mind to $100 oil, says ExxonMobil, the people who should know.

Meanwhile, in China ...

The relatively stand-pat spending and production pattern of ExxonMobil and its Western peers in recent years is in sharp contrast to the aggressive volume growth efforts of the crude-short Chinese. Though presumably driven by the same profit-making objectives as their Western counterparts, the Chinese have pursued a fundamentally different strategy. They have gone for increased crude volume, plowing back all or more of the cash they generate to find and develop additional oil and gas reserves.

The key player in this regard is CNPC, China National Petroleum Corporation. This state-owned giant is China's upstream equivalent of ExxonMobil, producing almost 60% of that country's 3 million b/d or so of crude oil. The rest of China's oil output comes mainly from downstream major Sinopec, which now has its own growing upstream operations, and from offshore operator CNOOC, or China National Offshore Oil Corporation.

About 84% of CNPC's 2.75 million b/d of crude output in 2007 was attributed to PetroChina, a publicly-traded affiliate floated in 2000, listed in New York and Hong Kong, but still 86% owned by CNPC. State-owned Sinopec and CNOOC also have similar list-

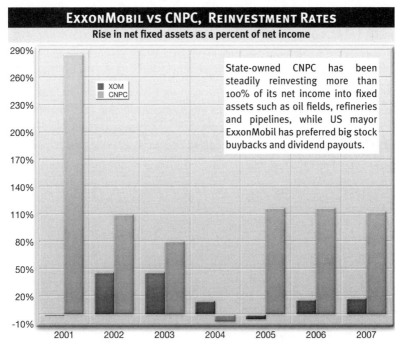

EXXONMOBIL VS CNPC, REINVESTMENT RATES

Rise in net fixed assets as a percent of net income

State-owned CNPC has been steadily reinvesting more than 100% of its net income into fixed assets such as oil fields, refineries and pipelines, while US mayor ExxonMobil has preferred big stock buybacks and dividend payouts.

ed, but almost wholly-owned, public subsidiaries. Financial data on parent CNPC is very limited, but PetroChina (NYSE: PTR) files US-style disclosures with the Securities and Exchange Commission. From these two sets of data, a picture emerges of very high reinvestment levels and a relentless push for more volumes both at home and abroad. Most of the growth is coming at the private state parent, while PetroChina struggles to offset the decline of its single largest producing field, Daqing, where output fell 4% in 2007.

From PetroChina SEC filings, it appears that company has been routinely plowing back roughly the same percentage of its upstream cash flow as ExxonMobil, and getting similar or better gains in oil production.

But instead of buying back stock like ExxonMobil, PetroChina has been issuing new shares, including a float of 4 billion shares, or 2.5% of its equity in Shanghai, to raise some $9 billion in November 2007. That momentarily gave the company a theoretical equity market value of more than $1 trillion in Shanghai, more than double that of ExxonMobil. Amid that hysteria, US investor Warren Buffet took some profits and sold down his PetroChina stake slightly, to under 10%. It was a shrewd move because the price spike was short-lived (see chart). Still, PetroChina's more representative New York-traded ADRs have outperformed ExxonMobil (XOM) more than five-fold since 2003 and at more than $250 billion have an equity value more than half that of XOM. Investing money back into the oil business certainly seems to beat stock buybacks in terms of stock market appreciation.

EXXONMOBIL VS PETROCHINA STOCK PRICE

PetroChina's dividend payout rate is comparable to ExxonMobil's, at about 40% of net income. But 86% of that goes to parent CNPC, which does *not* pay a dividend to its owner, the Chinese government. That lets CNPC reinvest significantly more of its cash flow back into the business. CNPC does not disclose its capital spending levels. But a fair approximation of its relative reinvestment rate to ExxonMobil can be seen in the growth of net fixed assets compared to reported net income. Except for 2004, CNPC has been routinely boosting its property, plant and equipment (PP&E) by more than 100% of its earnings. Besides reinvesting its profits and dividends from PetroChina, CNPC has also been building up its own sizeable cash hoard of about $27 billion at year-end 2007, net of debt.

ExxonMobil's PP&E account, which includes both upstream and downstream (refining) assets, has grown at only a fraction of its bottom-line earnings. In some recent years its PP&E has even declined as company-wide depreciation, write-offs and asset sales have exceeded new investment. Were it not for its build-up of cash and treasury shares, ExxonMobil's balance sheet would show little or no growth, and would actually be shrinking at times.

CNPC and the other Chinese oil majors have a big incentive to reinvest. Since until recently they have not been required to pay dividends to the Chinese government, they have been able to build up large cash balances. That money earns minimal interest in Chinese banks, so upstream oil investments look attractive, even at hurdle rates far less than the mid-teens returns being sought by Western oil majors.

Where is all that CNPC investment going? Much of it remains in China, and is spent via PetroChina in trying to maintain production at the aging Daqing field. But most of CNPC's own incremental spending appears to be going into foreign upstream ventures, not involving publicly traded (and scrutinized) PetroChina. That has fueled a much higher oil output growth rate for parent CNPC than for PTR. In 2007 CNPC reported net non-China oil output of 600,000, up 7% from the prior year and triple the level in 2002. Its overseas proved oil reserves surged 26% to more than 8.1 billion barrels, double its 2002 foreign liquids reserves.[8]

While CNPC, Sinopec and CNOOC are growing their foreign production, this output may actually reinforce Chinese suspicions that oil markets are being manipulated upward against them. Their contribution of more than 700,000 b/d of world crude supply, and more than 1 million b/d counting their partners' shares, has been enough to cover at least half the roughly 1.5 million b/d increase in total world oil demand since 2005, to around 85 million b/d. But instead of easing, crude prices have gone wild on the upside. China's ardent quest for foreign equity oil may actually be proving counterproductive.

8. CNPC 2007 annual report, pp. 9-10.

PROPOSED FAR EAST ASIA PIPELINES

Siberia

Okha

PROSPECTIVE REGION
PRODUCING REGION

R u s s i a

Tynda

Komsomol'sk

Skovorodino

(PHASE TWO)

Amur

EAST SIBERIA-PACIFIC
OCEAN PIPELINE

(CHINA SPUR)

Lake
Baikal

Chita

Irkutsk

Daqing

Vladivostok

Nakhodka

ILL-FATED YUKOS
PIPELINE PLAN

Sea of
Japan

Mongolia

China

North
Korea

PYONGYANG

SEOUL

BEIJING

South

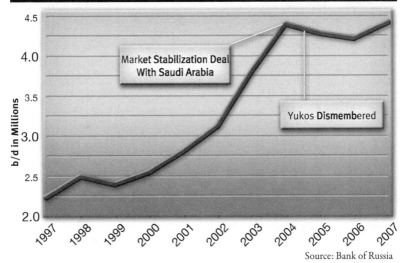

RUSSIAN CRUDE OIL EXPORTS

Market Stabilization Deal
With Saudi Arabia

Yukos Dismembered

b/d in Millions

4.5
4.0
3.5
3.0
2.5
2.0

1997 1998 1999 2000 2001 2002 2003 2004 2005 2006 2007

Source: Bank of Russia

—9—

Russia, and "Comrade Wolf"

The only item in (President Vladimir) Putin's geopolitical agenda is high oil prices. That's how his regime survives in Russia. That's why he is always playing a game of keeping the tension high, especially in the Middle East.
— Chess champion and Russian opposition candidate Garry Kasparov[1]

No effort to push up and sustain world oil prices would be possible without the knowing and active participation of the Russian Federation. And under its leadership since the end of 1999 by former KGB man Vladimir Putin, Russia has been a key and faithful US ally in that regard. Whatever other public differences may appear to bubble up from time to time between Washington and Moscow, the two powers have been marching in lock-step toward a shared goal of reining in Chinese economic ascendancy by raising the cost of, and limiting access to, foreign oil and other critical raw materials.

For Moscow this is a win-win proposition. It is rapidly replenishing its own depleted financial coffers while inflicting maximum possible non-military pain on its chief and longstanding geopolitical foe, China. Earnings from oil exports have let Russia boost its reserves of foreign-currency assets from $12 billion in 1999 to the world's third largest, at some $470 billion by year-end 2007.[2] Its federal budget has run in the black since 2001, and ended 2007 with a surplus of 3% of GDP. Economic growth has averaged 7% a year since the financial crisis of 1998, and Russian GDP on a purchasing power parity basis neared $2.1 trillion in 2007 ($1.3 trillion at the official exchange rate), up more than 8% that year.[3]

---

1. Kasparov interview on *Hardball with Chris Matthews*, MSNBC, Oct. 24, 2007.
2. CIA, *The World Factbook*: Russia
3. Ibid.

Still, it has at times been a very challenging game for Putin and the Kremlin's new guard. He has had to maintain cordial relations with Beijing while at the same time constricting Russian oil exports, especially via a long-promised eastward pipeline. And he has had to employ sometimes draconian measures against Russia's greedy new oligarchs bent on ramping up oil production to cash in on rising prices. But Putin has played his cards well. He completed his official rule as president in early 2008 having skillfully managed relations with both the US and China, at least outwardly. He greatly restored Russian financial strength and embarked on badly needed defense modernization. Along the way, he became *Time* magazine's "Person of the Year" in 2007, and may have "effectively" become one of the world's richest men, managing a fortune of some $40 billion.[4]

Of course no one in the Kremlin would be likely to confirm Moscow has been on board with a program to jack up world oil markets in cahoots with the US. But the numbers speak for themselves. A chart of Russian oil export volumes shows a sharp and steady ramp-up of Russian crude exports of more than 80% from 1999 to 2003, to about 4.5 million b/d. Then that volume magically flattened out, as Russia appears to have hit its agreed market share limit at roughly half the exports of US ally Saudi Arabia.

There would seem to be little or no basis for Russian claims that it suddenly reached the physical limits of its export potential. As of 2001, Russia has more than 40 billion barrels of proved and audited reserves in just its top four oil companies, and more than 80 billion barrels in its top 10. Adding in half their "probable" reserves pushed that number to 93 billion barrels. That is a reserve-to-production ratio of some 25 years; double that of most Western oil majors. Capital spending required to bring those barrels into production was running at under $10,000 per daily barrel, or half the cost of western production adds. The only constraint on continued steady output growth would seem to be pipeline capacity for getting the crude to export locations.[5]

---

4. Luke Harding, "Putin, the Kremlin power struggle and the $40bn fortune," *Guardian* (UK), Dec. 21, 2007.

5. Mikhail Khodorkovsky, "Russia, the Persian Gulf and World Oil Supply," Yukos Washington presentation, Feb. 7, 2003, p. 9.

Rather like the Saudis, the Russians have been religiously sticking to their presumed (non-OPEC) quota limits to tighten the physical world market for crude oil. The goal is to avoid even the kind of small wet-barrel surpluses that can send prices skidding as physical sellers go begging for buyers.

The critical discussions in bringing Russia into the world oil price support system appear to have occurred soon after the 9/11 terror incidents in 2001, when Saudi oil minister Ali Naimi traveled to Moscow to secure some level of production cuts. At the time, crude prices had plunged from the mid-$20 range to the mid-teens as the world economy reeled from what was expected to be a global economic slowdown. OPEC was "inviting" non-member producing states like Mexico, Norway and Oman to achieve some 500,000 b/d of output cuts alongside a reduction of 1.5 million b/d by OPEC itself. Russia was being asked to be a major contributor to that goal, but at the time came up with a commitment to cut a mere 30,000 b/d. "That disappoints anybody. The Russians know that," Naimi reportedly commented.[6] Added Nigerian oil minister Rilwanu Lukman: "We are asking them to help a little bit. They share the benefits so why can't they share the burden."[7]

Clearly, Putin was first determined to revive Russia's severely crippled oil production capacity and re-establish its export market share before agreeing to any such restrictions. As the world's No. 2 oil producer behind only Saudi Arabia, Russia felt entitled to a more appropriate market share than the roughly 2 million b/d to which its foreign sales had ebbed.

Saudi-Russian negotiations continued over the next two years as Russian output and exports grew. In March of 2003, with Russian crude exports running at more than 4 million b/d, and another 2 to 3 million b/d of Russian fuel oil and other refined product being exported, oil minister Naimi traveled to Moscow for high-level talks. The subject was "to stabilize world oil markets," according to a spokesman for Russian Energy Minister Igor Yusufov.[8] Oil prices were still hovering at that time in the range of $20 to $30/bbl.

---

6. "Market drops on OPEC's unusual deal," *Platts Oilgram News*, Vol. 79, No. 222, Nov. 15, 2001, p. 1.

7. Ibid.

8. "Saudi, Russian oil ministers to discuss markets," *Platts Oilgram News*, Vol. 81, No. 49, Mar. 13, 2003, p. 6.

Those Saudi-Russian talks eventually led to a formal but secretive agreement in September 2003, unveiled during a rare Moscow visit by Saudi Crown Prince Abdullah. Without revealing the details, Russian prime minister Mikhail Kasyanov declared the accord would "promote stability" in world oil prices and supply. "To a great extent the stability of world markets depends on the predictability of our policies," Kasyanov said.[9]

It was at that point in 2003 Russia ceased its breakneck pace of production and export growth. It has bumped along at essentially those same levels ever since. Overall Russian oil production has leveled off at just below 10 million b/d. In early 2008 it was actually running slightly behind 2007 levels, despite the obvious production incentive of world prices that had soared to more than $100/bbl. This is remarkable discipline and can only be understood in the context of geopolitical priorities far exceeding immediate profit goals.

The fall of Yukos

It was around the time of the ramp-up in Russo-Saudi market "stabilization" talks in early 2003 that the Kremlin began its all-out assault on upstart oil oligarch Mikhail Khodorkovsky and his fast-growing Yukos empire. Press reports at the time tended to attribute the gathering brouhaha to Khodorkovsky's political ambitions and a festering personal rivalry with Putin. The numbers, however, suggest a bigger and more fundamental state security problem: Yukos planned aggressive oil production increases and Khodorkovsky had unveiled a scheme, in late 2002, to build a 600,000 b/d oil pipeline all the way into China.

Despite Kremlin warnings, Khodorkovsky remained adamant on building his own private line from Angarsk, near Lake Baikal, to the Chinese refining center at Daqing. Running for 1,600 km south and east from Lake Baikal through the Chita region, it would enter China near the Mongolian border and then run 800 km to Daqing. It was planned to be under construction by 2003, cost only about $1.7 billion to build, and be in operation by 2005. Initial throughput would be 400,000 b/d but would rise to 600,000 b/d in 2010.[10]

9. "Saudi Arabia-Russia oil pact to promote stability: Kasyanov," *Platts Oilgram News*, Vol. 81, No. 170, Sept. 4, 2003, p. 2.

10. Khodorkovsky, p. 12.

It would be a private venture, and thus outside the control of state pipeline monopoly Transneft. Like Saddam Hussein in his Chinese equity oil deals, Mikhail Khodorkovsky had crossed an invisible line in the sand, and had sealed his own doom. [11]

By building his own pipeline, Khodorkovsky also threatened to undermine separate plans by Transneft to build a major crude export line to Russia's Far East coast at Nakhodka near Vladivostok. The Transneft pipe would circumvent China, except for a possible low-volume spur to Daqing. Its main aim was to feed the crude-hungry refining market in Japan, which was offering enticing financing and long-term off-take commitments, likely with US encouragement. The Yukos pipe would sap the available crude flows and wreck the economics of the Transneft project, while offering a torrent of badly needed crude to the PRC. It would also give Yukos a leg up against state-favored rival LUKoil, state gas giant Gazprom, or emerging state-owned oil major Rosneft in developing the vast but unbooked potential of Eastern Siberia's stranded reserves of oil and gas.

Yukos was paying no heed to the Russian-Saudi market control imperatives coming to a head in 2003. Instead of starting to rein in its crude production and exports, Yukos was on a rampage to expand output. Its production had been rising at a remarkable pace of almost 20% a year for the prior decade, and at the end of 2002 had actually surpassed LUKoil at 1.7 million boe/d. There were no signs Khodorkovsky was even contemplating a slowdown of growth. In fact, in April 2003 Yukos had arranged a stock-swap merger with similarly fast-growing Sibneft, controlled by fellow oligarch Roman Abramovich. That would have given Yukos a combined 2.3 million boe/d of oil and gas output, heavily weighted toward crude. [12]

Before the Sibneft deal was even finalized, however, there was a flurry of interest from US majors ExxonMobil and Chevron about buying 25% or more of YukosSibneft. [13] Given the track record of squelching production growth in the other recent takeovers of Mo-

---

11. Charles A. Kolhaas, "Pipedreams: Khodorkovsky vs. Putin," *In the National Interest*, Nov. 19, 2003. "With this action," noted oil consultant Kolhaas, "Khodorkovsky had moved from involvement in domestic politics to international relations and foreign policy as well."

12. "Russian oil firms to create super-major," *Platts Oilgram News*, Vol. 81, No. 77, Apr. 23, 2003, p. 1.

13. "Petrodollars," *Platts Oilgram News*, Vol. 81, No. 197, Oct. 13, 2003, p. 3.

bil and Texaco, it is reasonable to speculate the main purpose in such an acquisition might have been to curb Yukos' crude output, along with a bargain-priced purchase of Russian oil reserves. Perhaps coincidentally, the reported US company interest in Yukos came amidst a Moscow visit by former US president George H.W. Bush in September 2003. Before any deal could be reached with the US companies, though, a devastating whirlwind of Russian government suppression, dismemberment and confiscation descended upon Yukos.

Mainly under the guise of tax claims and alleged fraud, the Kremlin moved dramatically in 2003 to obliterate Yukos. In July, key shareholder and Bank Menatep chairman Platon Lebedev was arrested and Yukos' Moscow offices were raided. In October Menatep's offices were raided, 44% of Yukos shares were frozen, and Khodorkovsky was arrested at gunpoint at a Siberian airfield. He would eventually be sentenced to nine years in prison for fraud and tax evasion.[14] In March 2004 UK lawyer Stephen Curtis, then head of dominant Yukos shareholder Group Menatep Trustees, died in a helicopter crash soon after he stated his life could be in danger and that any fatal mishap "would not be an accident."[15]

By mid-2004 Yukos was swamped with billions of dollars of Russian back tax claims, loan defaults, criminal investigations and state harassment. By year-end its 76.8% ownership of main production arm Yuganskneftegas had been auctioned off in a forced tax sale for $9.35 billion—a third of its appraised value—to a front for state oil major Rosneft. After a futile bid to seek bankruptcy protection in the US, Yukos was finally put into a Moscow receivership and was effectively liquidated by late 2006. Its demise coincides well with the leveling off of Russian crude output.[16]

Various media reports at the time attributed the Kremlin's crackdown on Yukos to Khodorkovsky's political ambitions or to the threat of more US ownership of Russian oil assets. But Khodorkovsky's political activities had been well-known for many years. And

14. A Timeline of Events can be found at www.khodorkovsky.info, the official website of the "press centre for defense attorneys of Mikhail Khodorkovsky and Platon Lebedev."

15. "CEO says Yukos profitable, able to pay debts to Russia," *Platts Oilgram News*, Dec. 2, 2005.

16. "Why did production in Russia stop growing?" Institute of Energy Policy, June 2005.

other Western investments in Russian oil had been proceeding. BP in mid-2003 was allowed to acquire half of TNK by swapping cash and BP's existing 25% of Russian producer Sidanco. ConocoPhillips would later be allowed to take a 20% equity stake, with key veto power, in oil major LUKoil. The most compelling argument for dismembering Yukos, but never mentioned by the Kremlin, would have been to achieve the broader economic and political goal of reducing production growth and thwarting pipeline sales to China. "I've heard that mentioned," allowed later Yukos CEO Steven Theede in a New York interview with *Platts* in late 2005.

Pipeline politics

With Yukos died Khodorkovsky's dream of a direct mainline crude link to China. The rival Transneft project, dubbed the ESPO (East Siberia-Pacific Ocean) Pipeline, has limped forward slowly. But it has been fraught with interminable delays, cost over-runs and re-routing due to alleged environmental threats. The latest push-back was announced in March 2008, when the Russian Industry and Energy Ministry officially approved a one-year postponement in commissioning the new line until fourth-quarter 2009 at the earliest. Transneft had hinted of a likely delay in late 2007 when construction of the initial section began running seriously behind schedule, allegedly due to a lack of qualified workers and difficult terrain.[17] There is continuing doubt about when there will be a working ESPO spur to Daqing.

Work on the ESPO line began in April 2006, five months late, and costs have spiraled. In late 2007 Transneft had to seek a hefty 20% increase in its already high pipeline tariff for the line. Transneft CEO Nikolai Tokarev told reporters the first-phase cost of the line had swelled to Rb300 billion ($12.2 billion), double the company's original estimate, and up from a revised budget of $11.5 billion in March 2007.[18]

The first stage of the ESPO pipeline involves a 2,694 km link that would move 600,000 b/d from East Siberian fields near Taishet

---

17. "Russia approves delay to ESPO startup until end-2009," *Platts Oilgram News*, Vol. 86, No. 60, Mar. 26, 2008, p. 5

18. "Transneft requests one year delay for ESPO startup," *Platts Oilgram News*, Vol. 85, No. 246, Dec. 13, 2007, p. 5.

to Skovorodino in Russia's Far East, near the Chinese border. But it is mainly designed to send crude to the Pacific and from there to Japan and beyond. Phase one also includes construction of a new export terminal near the port of Nakhodka, costing an added $2.8 billion or so. It would initially be fed by rail from Skovorodino. Eventually the pipeline would be extended the remaining 3,000 km to the port in a second phase, and its capacity boosted to handle 1.6 million b/d of new East Siberian crude slated to be developed.

China would get a relative dribble of that oil. A 100 km link from Skovorodino is to be built to the Chinese border with capacity to handle a modest 280,000 b/d, less than 7% of current Chinese crude imports, and less than half the volume in Yukos' doomed pipeline plan. That would be only about enough oil to feed one mid-sized refinery, and at far higher delivery fees than the Yukos plan. China would pay for the link to the border, and then pay to extend the pipe another 900 km to the refining center at Daqing.

Even if Phase One is commissioned on its new, delayed schedule, fill-time on the line would make it likely well into 2010 before exportable crude reaches Skovorodino by pipe, with Daqing many months later. Meanwhile, the Russian Government has said initial portions of the pipeline may be used instead to move East Siberian crude westward, to feed into the existing Transneft system serving Russian and European refineries.[19] China might see no oil from the new pipeline for years. A parallel natural gas pipeline will not be in operation before 2011, even if the two countries can agree on gas prices. When the ESPO oil does arrive, the transport tariffs are likely to approach $10/bbl. Despite that high rate, some estimates are the ESPO might not recover its huge investment costs for up to 40 years.

So just as the Reagan NSC conspired to delay and confound Russia's Yamal natural gas pipeline to Europe in the 1980s, the ESPO delay seems to figure heavily in US-Russian efforts to constrain crude oil supplies flowing to China.

In the interim, Russian oil continues to move to China via railcar, a slow and expensive way to ship oil that can be easily halted without leaving a costly pipe sitting idle. In 2007 Russia's East Siberia Railway moved a modest 180,000 b/d of oil into China, down

19. Ibid.

more than 12% from the prior year, and less than two-thirds of what had earlier been projected by the Russians.[20]

Wary neighbors

Russia's half-hearted arrangement to sell oil to China from its Siberian pipeline project is understandable. The two countries have been wary neighbors, or bloody enemies, ever since the post-World War II alliance forged by Josef Stalin and Mao Zedong fell apart acrimoniously in the 1959 Sino-Soviet split. China still refuses to recognize the legitimacy of treaties signed in the late 1800s by a weakened Qing dynasty, which ceded to the Tsars large swaths of Siberia. In 1968 the two countries moved more than a million soldiers to their frontier amidst worsening tensions and in 1969 fought a series of border engagements. Tensions eased, but the Soviets maintained a large military presence along the China border until 1985, when Mikhail Gorbachev's cash-strained Kremlin moved to normalize relations with China. By then China was busily helping the US defeat the Soviets in Afghanistan.

Since the Soviet collapse, Russia has been on the defensive against China as it struggles to rebuild its economy. Putin has made frequent forays to Beijing to try and smooth relations. Along with promises of the eventual oil pipeline, he signed a secretive deal in May 2007 to end one long-running border dispute and cede 120 sq km to China along their 4,300 km boundary. Rather than mark a fundamental warming of Sino-Russian relations, the boundary deal may be only a Band-Aid to defer outright conflict.

Trade tensions are growing between the two quarrelsome neighbors. Though cross-border trade jumped 44% in 2007 to $48 billion, and is expected to hit $60 billion in 2010, China reaped a more than $7 billion surplus on that volume.[21] Like the US, Putin has chided the Chinese for their lopsided trade practices: Some 90% of Chinese imports from Russia are in oil and natural resources. Instead of buying Russian machinery as they used to, the Chinese are exporting it to Russia. Chinese purchases of Russian arms, formerly running at $1.5 billion a year as Russia's biggest single customer, have reportedly eased.

20. "East Siberian Railway reduced oil transportation to China by 12.4% in 2007," *Interfax*, Jan. 24, 2008.
21. "China to import Russian high technologies," Xinhua, Jan. 27, 2008.

Meanwhile, as noted previously, Putin has blocked or neutered attempts by Chinese companies to buy into Russian oil reserves. Sinopec got only a minority stake in Udmurtneft, at great expense. CNPC's 2002 attempt to bid at auction for Moscow's 75% stake in producer Slavneft was thwarted by the Russian Duma, even though CNPC had been willing to pay a 75% premium, or $1.3 billion more than the eventually winning bid of $1.86 billion from TNK and Sibneft.[22] CNPC was allocated only an inconsequential 4% stake in Russian state-owned oil major Rosneft's July 2006 IPO, for a hefty $500 million. And though CNPC later formed a joint venture with Rosneft, called Vostok Energy, to develop East Siberian reserves, it has only minority control and those properties are not likely to generate exportable oil for many years. Russian oilfield services also appear to be off-limits for the Chinese: In February 2008 Putin blocked offshore driller China Oilfield Services Ltd. from taking a majority stake in TNK-BP services arm STU for $10 million, even though the deal had been cleared by Russia's energy ministry.[23]

China's threat to Siberia

Russian vulnerability in mineral- and oil-rich Siberia is palpable. With roughly the same land area as China, at just under 10 million sq km, Siberia's population of around 40 million is only about two or three percent of China's 1.3 to 1.5 billion people and is concentrated mainly between Omsk and Irkutsk. From Lake Baikal eastward, stretching more than 4,000 km and five time zones to Alaska, there are only about 5 million Russians: half the population of Moscow.

Undocumented Chinese migration to the region is estimated to be running in the hundreds of thousands per year, and could total well into the millions. This has raised concerns by Siberian leaders about "Finlandization" of the region by ethnic Chinese, despite Russian pogroms and resettlements in the 1930s aimed at reducing that threat. Some Western analysts have speculated this flood of Chinese immigration is no coincidence and may be a long-term plan

22. Kim Iskyan, "Selling Off Siberia: Why China should purchase the Russian Far East," *Slate,* July 28, 2003.

23. BBC News, "Russian president rejects Chinese bid for oil firm," Feb. 4, 2008.

by Beijing.[24] Russian NATO envoy Dmitry Rogozin, former head of the anti-immigration Rodina ("Motherland") party, has accused China of plotting a creeping demographic takeover of Siberia, if not an outright military conquest. While a lawmaker in the Duma, he proposed legislation to curb the inflow of Chinese immigrants and urged Russian resettlements to border regions to counter the Chinese "threat to Mother Russia."[25]

The Siberian economy is already subservient to Chinese trade and heavily oriented southward for both goods and income. "Everything we have comes from China—our dishes, leather goods, even the meat we eat is from China," observed one city official in Novosobirsk: "Siberia is becoming Chinese."[26] In the nearby town of Akademgorodok, home to 52 Soviet-era scientific institutes, an estimated 80% of income derives from the PRC, as the 18,000 scientists there happily take up research and technical work on Chinese projects from DNA to electron accelerators. "The West is wary of selling their technologies to the Chinese, so they come here," one Siberian official of the Russian Academy of Sciences told *Newsweek*: "Our own government doesn't give much importance to science. We need China's money."[27]

Indeed, Siberia has been far down the priority list for Moscow as it struggles to rebuild its economy. An only half-joking *Slate* commentary in 2003 suggested Russia should just sell Siberia to the Chinese, who have 150 million or so people living cheek to jowl just across the border and itching for *lebensraum*.[28] Otherwise, the Chinese could simply take it themselves. Would the Kremlin risk Moscow in a thermonuclear exchange to retain ownership of a forlorn and frozen wasteland it cannot afford to develop, let alone defend? The options are gloomy. "Fortunately for Moscow, Beijing is preoccupied with Taiwan, the US, Japan, and even domestic unrest," notes Mark Katz, a professor at George Mason University. "But if China ever decided to take measures that

24. "Russia-China Security Cooperation," *Power and Interest News Report*, Nov. 27, 2006.

25. Owen Matthews and Anna Nemtsova, "Fear and Loathing in Siberia," *Newsweek*, Mar. 27, 2006.

26. Ibid.

27. Ibid.

28. Iskyan.

Russia found threatening, Moscow could find fending it off to be extremely difficult—if not impossible."[29]

Ominously, in September 2006 China's PLA held a large-scale 10-day military exercise not far from Russia's far-eastern border. A "Red" mechanized infantry brigade from the Shenyang command advanced more than 1,000 km to "attack" a "Blue" armored brigade from the Beijing command.[30] "The nature of the exercise tells us that it is in preparation for war with Russia and, moreover, that what is being planned is not defense but attack," observed Andrei Piontkovsky, executive director of Moscow's Strategic Studies Center.[31]

The overall level of Russian military awareness of Chinese capabilities and intentions has been on a sharp upswing, particularly since the Chinese shoot-down of an obsolete weather satellite in low earth orbit in January 2007. Russia's own aging observation satellite network, on which it is heavily reliant for Far East surveillance, resides mainly at similar heights. It was rendered vulnerable by the Chinese technical demonstration. The rapid build-up and modernization of Chinese forces has also not been lost on the Russians, who have seen their own sales of military hardware to the PRC sag in recent years as the Chinese have developed more of their own sophisticated weaponry.

With this backdrop of growing Russian exposure in the East, the PRC invited Russian forces to participate in their first joint military exercises in 40 years in August 2005. Beijing is even believed to have picked up most of the tab. The "Peace Mission 2005" war games were supposedly geared to fight terrorism and separatist movements, but were really conventional, large-scale exercises including long-range bombers, neutralization of anti-aircraft defenses and air assault. Many commentators saw this as an ominous rekindling of Sino-Russian military relations. But more likely, it was designed to impress the Russians with China's growing might, discourage miscalculation, and send a veiled warning. While landing a big purchase

29. Mark N. Katz, "Russia's Security Challenges," *Eager eyes fixed on Eurasia. Vol.1. Russia and its neighbors in crisis*, ed. Iwashita Akihiro, (Sapporo: Slavic Research Center, Hokkaido University, 2007), p. 142-147.

30. "China's six most prominent key military maneuvers in 2006," People's Daily Online, Dec. 31, 2006.

31. Andrei Piontkovsky, "Moscow is squaring off with the wrong enemy," *Globe and Mail*, Dec. 20, 2007.

order for transport aircraft, the Russians got a look at what they eventually could be up against.[32]

In March 2006, on one of Putin's several Beijing trips, Chinese President Hu Jintao proclaimed 2006 as "The Year of Russia," and they agreed to hold eight military events in 2007.[33] Russia also hosted military exercises in the Ural Mountains with China and other Central Asian states in the China-instigated Shanghai Cooperation Organization. Formed in 2001 from an earlier 1996 grouping aimed at controlling "terrorism, separatism and extremism," the SCO includes the PRC, Russia, Kazakhstan, Kyrgyzstan, Tajikistan and Uzbekistan. While also seen as useful in thwarting US inroads there, Moscow likely views its SCO involvement as a way to keep in check Chinese ambitions for Central Asia, rather than as *rapprochement* with Beijing.

It is in that cautious light that one must understand Putin's cryptic and seemingly critical, but ultimately very revealing, comments about the US in his 2006 annual state-of-the-nation address. Drawing on an old Russian expression, Putin alluded to the US as "Comrade Wolf," who "knows who to eat." That is from one of Krylov's Fables about a wolf, a fox and a hare who fall into the same pit. Eventually the wolf asks "who shall we eat?" The fox looks at the hare and says: "Comrade Wolf knows whom to eat."

Putin's jibe came a week after US Vice President Dick Cheney had chided Russia for rolling back democracy and for coddling Iran in its effort to develop nuclear technology with weapons potential. "Where is all this pathos about protecting human rights and democracy when it comes to the need to pursue their own interests?" Putin asked, daring to lift the skirts on much bigger world conflicts in progress. "Here, it seems, everything is allowed; there are no restrictions whatsoever. We are aware what is going on in the world. Comrade Wolf knows whom to eat."[34] Then Putin alluded to a pet cat (Vas'ka) who "eats without listening, and he's clearly not going to listen to anyone."

---

32. "The Significance of Sino-Russian Military Exercises," *Power and Interest News Report*, Sept. 14, 2005.

33. DoD, "Military Power of the People's Republic of China 2007," p. 1.

34. "Putin hits out at Washington as Iran dispute intensifies," *Guardian* (UK), May 10, 2006.

In this nightmarish fable, Russia and China may be taking turns as Comrade Fox and Comrade Hare. Even combined, their efforts would be unlikely to prevail against Comrade Wolf. For at least temporary self-preservation, and maybe a free meal, it might well serve Comrade Fox if the wolf concentrates on the hare for a while. But the longer-term implications of Putin's metaphor are also instructive.

If oil-rich Russia were to align again with China, or otherwise pose a geopolitical threat to the US, crude pricing could again be driven down as in the 1980s. Moscow's hard-won (or fortuitous) economic gains could evaporate in a few years. Putin's fox remains just as vulnerable as the PRC hare to protracted economic warfare waged through basic commodity pricing and financial markets. And all too intimately aware of its effects.

10

The Saudi Role

Oil is an important and strategic resource for the world economy. It must not be used as a weapon.... Playing with this resource [will cause] the developing countries to become victims, as the wealthy countries can always find their ways to obtain supplies.

— Saudi Arabian Foreign Minister Saud al-Faisal bin Abdul Aziz [1]

How odd to hear the Saudis, kingpins of the 1970s Arab oil embargo, complain about the use of oil as a weapon. And how strange to accuse its customers: the developed nations. But that was the clear intent of remarks in February 2008 by Saudi Prince Saud al-Faisal at a meeting of fellow foreign ministers in Argentina. The speech got little play in the US, the presumed target of the criticism, but was quickly picked up by China's Xinhua news service.

Taken together with Russian President Vladimir Putin's "Comrade Wolf" remark in 2006, the Saudi admonition is a revealing confirmation of the central thesis of this book. Namely, that the US has brought its substantial financial, diplomatic and military powers to bear to force up the price of oil and other commodities in what amounts to economic warfare. Like the Russians, the Saudis find themselves as key *de facto* co-conspirators in this effort, with apparently little choice but to go along.

While they may be somewhat reluctant participants, however, the Saudis have been whining all the way to the bank with the Russians. From the late 1990s through the end of 2007, Saudi Arabia and other Middle East oil exporters amassed an astounding $30 trillion in wealth, tripling the region's financial reserves to nearly $770 billion. Stacked as $1 bills, that pile of money would reach to the moon.[2]

---

1. Xinhua, "Saudi Arabia urges rich countries not to use oil as weapon," People's Daily Online, Feb, 22, 2008, reporting comments at an Argentina meeting of South American and Arab foreign ministers.
2. Dr. Nasser Saidi, chief economist of the Dubai International Financial Centre, as quoted by Karen Remo-Listana in "Region's oil wealth soars to $30trn," *Emir-*

In a normally functioning oil market, it would be the Saudis calling the shots on oil pricing. They are by far the world's largest crude exporter, at around 10 million b/d, or 12% of total world demand. They hold a quarter of world proved oil reserves at more than a quarter of a trillion barrels: more than double those of No. 2 Iraq. Saudi Arabia is the only producing country with any substantial surplus oil capacity, at about 2 million b/d. And it is investing tens of billions of dollars to double that capacity cushion by 2009, while extending the life of existing fields in defiance of "Peak Oil" doomsayers. Except for the 1970s Arab oil embargo, it has never failed to make available whatever physical supply of oil the world needed, at the market cost, and has shown a periodic penchant in the past for driving down prices to enforce OPEC discipline. That should make it the world's arbiter of oil prices, raising or lowering output as required to stabilize prices. Instead, since at least 2003, it has been a seemingly ineffectual bystander as runaway oil prices have soared to previously unimaginable levels.

In September 2007 OPEC and the Saudis boosted output by a strong 500,000 b/d, with no noticeable affect in slowing oil's upward march past $100/bbl. In mid-June 2008, under dubious PR pressure from Washington, they announced plans to add another 200,000 b/d of output to quell what King Abdullah called "abnormally high" prices caused by "speculative factors and some other national government policies."[3] But the NYMEX responded that day by spiking more than $6/bb to a new intra-day record of almost $140 before closing down just a few cents.

As with China's efforts to boost world oil production by investing in overseas projects, the Saudis and other OPEC producers have come to realize that trying to constrain oil prices with more output is futile in the face of relentless buying pressure on the NYMEX. "We would be lying," admitted OPEC president and Algerian oil minister Chakib Khelil, "if we say to the world, 'well, if we increase oil production, the price will go down.'"[4]

---

ates Business 24/7, Mar. 31, 2008.

3. Abdullah's cryptic comments were relayed to the AFP wire service and no doubt sanitized by UN Secretary General Ban Ki-moon, who had been in talks that day (June 15) with the king and Saudi oil minister Ali Naimi.

4. Natalie Obiko Pearson, "OPEC Pres: Oil Prices High Because Of Weak Dollar," Dow Jones Newswires, Apr. 14, 2008.

To save face and retain some appearance of market leadership, Saudi officials led by oil minister Ali Naimi have had to rationalize ever-higher prices as being normal and justifiable to assure supply. When pressed about why oil rose to $50, then $70, then $90 and then well past $100/bbl, however, they resort to vague rhetoric about "speculators." OPEC head Khelil, a former World Bank economist, has tried to blame the price rise on the falling dollar.[5] But from the end of 2004 to April 2008, the US Dollar Index declined only about 12% while oil prices almost tripled from under $42/bbl.

The embarrassing reality is that neither the Saudis nor anybody else (besides Goldman Sachs, apparently) seems to have any clue as to how high oil prices will rise, why they need to go there, and how soon they will arrive.

Busting the Soviets

As we have seen, the US Reagan-era effort to weaken the Soviet economy by driving down oil prices would never have succeeded without the crucial support of Saudi Arabia. In 1985, then-Saudi oil minister Ahmad Zaki Yamani triggered a sharp collapse in world oil prices when he launched the kingdom on "netback" pricing to regain crude market share (see Chapter 1). By early 1986 world crude prices had tumbled from the high $20s to as low as $10/bbl, and bumped along near those levels until the Soviet Union officially disappeared in 1991.

Commentators rationalized the Saudi move to open the spigots and flood the market with cheap oil in 1985 as a desperate but necessary action to re-establish discipline among OPEC producer countries. Yamani claimed low oil prices were in the interest of Saudi Arabia, since they would discourage alternative energy investments, thus depleting its rivals long before the 200-year's worth of Saudi oil would be exhausted. But if that were really so, how much more urgent would it be to quell $100/bbl oil prices that have been spurring development of tar sands, coal-to-liquids and other alternative fuels? As we have noted, the Saudi decision to boost output in 1985 came only after protracted arm-twisting by top US national security staff and a key Washington meeting between President Reagan and King Fahd. In that summit, Reagan reiterated the US promise to de-

---

5. Ibid.

fend Saudi Arabia in the event of military threats, such as an attack by price "hawk" Iran on Saudi ports or shipping.

Ever since the US first recognized the kingdom of British-backed Arab warlord Ibn Saud in 1930, and Standard Oil of California's first sizable oil find there in 1935, US-Saudi relations have been intimate and their interests intertwined. Franklin Roosevelt pledged to defend the Saudis during World War II and in 1951 the US signed a far-reaching security pact with the kingdom. When the British withdrew their forces from east of Suez after Indian independence, the US became the great protector of the Saudi regime. It has remained so for the past 40 years, through constant tumult in the region. Whatever surface disagreements might bubble up from time to time between Washington and Riyadh, the underlying security arrangements, economic interests and foreign policy stance of the two countries have been closely aligned. Washington has few allies in the world who have proven as staunch (even if reluctantly so) as the Saudis. As a reward, the tenuous Saudi regime has been able to enjoy unmatched security in a very rough neighborhood. Even the nationalization of US company interests in Aramco in the 1970s was shrugged off as a necessary political reality.[6]

The new foe: China

The US-Saudi relationship entered a new phase in 1998. Impoverished from fifteen years of low oil prices, the Saudis were looking for financial relief. The US national security apparatus, meanwhile, had turned from regarding China as a potential "strategic partner" to instead viewing Beijing as a "strategic competitor."[7]

---

6. It has been argued that Exxon, Mobil, Chevron and Texaco suffered minimally from the paid-for expropriation of their equity stakes in Aramco. So long as they were still able to obtain the crude and pass the cost along to customers, company managers testified they were generally indifferent to who owned it. This came out in 1974 hearings by the Senate Foreign Relations Committee on "Multinational Petroleum Corporations and Foreign Policy." Relevant portions are cited by Blair, pp. 270-272. That point is also made by Christopher T. Rand's 1975 book, *Making Democracy Safe for Oil: Oilmen and the Islamic East*, Atlantic Monthly Press, pp. 303-305.

7. After his 1997 summit with Jiang Zemin, Bill Clinton had floated the idea of a "strategic partnership" with the PRC. That idea went nowhere, however, and by the time George W. Bush was elected in 2000, the official view on China was that

of "strategic competitor."

The economic war was about to begin. Whether by coincidence or coercion, both the Saudis and the US were getting interested in ramping up the price of oil.

This confluence of interest became manifest in September 1998 when a Saudi entourage led by no less than Crown Prince Abdullah trekked to Washington for an unusual gathering on September 26 at the residence of the Saudi ambassador, Prince Bandar. Officially, the meeting was called to invite the CEOs of the four former Aramco partners (Chevron, Texaco, Exxon and Mobil) and three other US majors (Phillips, Conoco and Arco) to participate in an unprecedented and long-sought opening of new Saudi oil and gas prospects for foreign exploration and ownership.

But as noted previously, it was also intended to lay out initial plans for a global rise in oil prices.[8] As reported by *Platts*, the Saudis delivered a *de facto* ultimatum that would bring the era of low oil prices to an end and start them on their upward journey. Unless the rest of the world, including the western oil majors, reined in crude production, the Saudis were prepared to drive prices down to levels where nobody but they could cover even operating costs. In return, the Saudis were offering the majors a crack at renewed equity interests in the desert kingdom's presumably vast, but undiscovered and untapped, natural gas resources.

Adding a geopolitical air to the gathering was a separate meeting with Vice President Al Gore. That teed up a trip to Saudi Arabia soon after by Clinton Energy Secretary Bill Richardson, who on Jan. 11, 1999 announced plans by the Department of Energy to begin refilling the Strategic Petroleum Reserve to its prior level of 600 million bbl.[9] The reserve had been drawn down in a series of SPR crude auctions by the Clinton Administration in 1996 and early 1997 as a budget-balancing move, raising $545 million for 28.1 million bbls, at an average of under $20/bbl.[10] Now DoE would acquire the oil by

---

8. "Saudi Arabia seen as common link in ExxonMobil merger talks, low crude prices," *Platts Oilgram News*, Vol. 76, No. 231, Dec. 1, 1998, p. 1.

9. US Department of Energy press release, "Richardson Announces Plan to Re-Fill the Strategic Petroleum Reserve," Jan. 11, 1999.

10. US Congress, minority staff report, Permanent Subcommittee on Investigations, Senate Committee on Governmental Affairs, "U.S. Strategic Petroleum Reserve: Recent policy has increased costs to consumers but not overall U.S. energy security," 108th Cong., 1st Sess., p. 13.

diverting barrels received under the Department of Interior's royalty-in-kind program, rather than sell that oil into the market for cash. There clearly had been a sudden sea-change in US oil stockpiling and pricing policies.

Undisclosed at the time of the 1998 Saudi gathering in Washington, but later reported by *Platts*, Abdullah also met that day with former president George H.W. Bush and his ex-National Security Advisor, Brent Scowcroft. At least one CEO at the event told a source he viewed Bush's presence as an official endorsement of the Saudi position. The former president later insisted to *Platts* his private meeting with Abdullah was just a friendly lunch, separate from the CEO gathering. But he did confirm a "brief encounter" with the oil executives as he was leaving, and that he was accompanied by Scowcroft.[11]

If the elder Bush was privy then to plans for a major upward move in crude prices, it would have been sweet revenge for his chagrin in the 1980s. As Reagan's vice president and himself a veteran of the Texas oil patch, Bush had been tasked with being the bearer of bad news to his former industry cohorts about the need for lower oil and gas prices. He had been roundly branded a turncoat by fellow wildcatters for failing to stick up for their interests, as prices ebbed under Reagan's seeming benign neglect. But Bush's embarrassment was made all the more acute in April 1986, on the eve of a 10-day Persian Gulf trip. With oil trading at barely $11/bbl after the Saudi output jump, Bush told a Washington press conference there was a need for "stability" in the oil market. "I think it is essential," Bush said, "that we not have continued free fall like a parachutist jumping without a parachute." On his trip, the elder Bush raised warnings to the Saudis that Congress might impose import tariffs on oil if prices stayed low, causing confusion and consternation among Yemani and Saudi leaders over what Washington really wanted.

When Bush returned from his trip he was given a rare dressing-down by President Reagan for contradicting and undoing many months of effort by White House NSC staff who had been trying to bring down the price of oil.[12] Bush was further humiliated when the White House publicly disavowed his "stability" remarks, noting

---

11. "Correction," *Platts Oilgram News*, Vol. 76, No. 246, Dec. 23, 1998, p. 5.
12. Schweizer, pp. 259-261.

US policy was to "let the free market work."[13] All the while, Reagan's NSC had been scheming to achieve exactly the opposite, by rigging prices downward through political intervention.

In 1998, George H.W. Bush would be vindicated. In the weeks after the September gathering, NYMEX crude prices initially skidded from more than $16/barrel to under $11 on November 30, in what the Iranians branded as a Saudi scheme to ruin its rivals. The oil price then began to rise as the Saudis and other OPEC countries cut production. By June 1999 the kingdom's output of 7.6 million b/d was down 13%, or more than 1.1 million b/d, from early 1998. By November 1999 prices had risen to near $28/bbl, and a year later would peak at more than $36/bbl in late 2000. The US majors all embarked on a spree of cost-cutting and mergers that dramatically shrank the number of industry players, and their rate of upstream reinvestment. There was also an unusual jump in the net "long" position of non-commercials in NYMEX crude futures during that period. Had someone been tipped to the game plan?

That price run to $36/bbl was capped, however, when outgoing President Clinton decided to release 30 million barrels of crude from the Strategic Petroleum Reserve seven weeks before that year's George W. Bush-Al Gore presidential election. Though widely viewed as another callow political ploy (Clinton had released 900,000 barrels from the SPR in 1996 during his re-election run against Robert Dole, supposedly to compensate for a clogged pipeline), it took the wind out of the oil market's sails just as the US economy was heading into recession and soon the trauma of 9/11. On Sept. 10, 2001, the front-month NYMEX crude contract had closed at $27.65/bbl. In the wake of 9/11 it would briefly fall to barely $17/bbl in November 2001, before OPEC and the Saudis intervened to curb production. From about 8.1 million b/d before 9/11, Saudi output dropped 10%, or almost 1 million b/d, by early 2002. Even so, crude prices would not regain their late 2000 peak of $36/bbl until early 2004, due to weak world demand growth and still-ample non-OPEC crude supplies. More firepower would be required on the NYMEX to get the price up.

Meanwhile, talks droned on over possible upstream deals in Saudi Arabia. In May 2001 the Saudis tentatively awarded three

13. Yergin, p. 756.

major "core venture" gas projects totaling $25 billion of spending commitments to consortia of eight Western majors. ExxonMobil, Shell, BP and Phillips Petroleum were allocated Core Venture 1 for South Ghawar in the Empty Quarter. ExxonMobil was also picked to head a group with pre-collapse Enron and Occidental Petroleum for Red Sea development. A third venture at Shaybah was given to Shell, Total and Conoco.[14] Detailed negotiations on those projects would drag on for more than two more years, however, amid worsening US-Saudi relations.

Ultimately, both ExxonMobil deals would be dropped by mid 2003. Early on, the Red Sea venture was deemed uneconomic. The much larger $15 billion South Ghawar project, involving pipelines, desalination and petrochemical plants, was also considered only marginally attractive, unless ExxonMobil and its partners could get access to existing gas reserves of Saudi Aramco. In the end, the Saudis rejected ExxonMobil's proposal, citing its required mid-teens rate of return. Of the three Saudi core ventures, only part of the Shell-Total deal was signed in 2003, minus a merged ConocoPhillips, to explore for "non-associated" gas in the Empty Quarter. The costly downstream part of that deal was scrapped. Whether due to unrealistic Saudi terms, Western corporate greed, or other geopolitical factors, Saudi Arabia had missed out on a badly needed injection of substantial foreign capital into its upstream gas and downstream petrochemicals, power and water infrastructure. It also meant up to 1 million b/d of Saudi oil production would have to remain in the kingdom to fuel plants that could be running on much cheaper gas.

In what then appeared to be a snub of the US and its majors, the Saudis signed scaled-down 40-year gas exploration deals with Russia's LUKoil, China's Sinopec, Spain's Repsol YPF and Italy's Eni for three blocks in the Rub al-Khali desert. The foreign companies agreed to spend a total of about $800 million to drill 20 gas exploration wells. But the terms were marginal: Any gas would have to be sold for what was then only $0.75/Mcf to Saudi Aramco, which would have a 20% equity stake. The foreign companies could sell condensate and gas liquids at world prices, but would have to give

---

14. "Saudis, majors to sign gas deals June 3," *Platts Oilgram News*, Vol. 79, No. 103, May 30, 2001, p. 2.

up any sizeable oil reserves found.[15] LUKoil got Contract Area A near the super-giant Ghawar field, with plans to spend $215 million. Sinopec got the 38,000 sq km Contract Area B, with plans to spend $300 million, and Eni-Repsol got the 51,400 sq km Contract Area C.

Four years later, however, with well costs in that harsh desert running double the original estimates of $30 million each, there had still been no commercial discoveries declared.[16] Total has exited its venture with Shell after a series of costly dry holes. LUKoil's Luksar and Sinopec's Sino Saudi Gas ventures, with Aramco as a partner, have claimed signs of hydrocarbons in some wells but have no development plans yet. Eni and Repsol have found nothing. This could be trouble for the Saudis. Since collapse of the "core venture" deals, they have separately let dozens of contracts worth many billions of dollars for downstream desalinization, petrochemical and power plants, predicated on vast new gas supplies. But, "If there was a lot of gas there, we would have been exploring it ourselves," retired Aramco E&P head Sadad al-Husseini told the *Wall Street Journal*. "It is just unfortunate that so much money has been spent to confirm what we knew already."[17]

Throughout this period of "core venture" negotiations, the Saudi-US friendship had been under strain. That tension came into stark public view with the 2001 terror attacks of 9/11. Allegedly, 15 of the 19 Al Qaeda aircraft hijackers were Saudi nationals, although a number of the hijackers appear to have had stolen identities.[18] Published reports of prior Saudi financial support for Osama bin Laden and Al Qaeda, as a payoff to avoid terror attacks there, and strong support by Saudi Crown Prince Abdullah for fundamentalist Muslin causes, had raised suspicions about Saudi loyalty and friendship to the US. The *Wall Street Journal* reported soon after the attacks that Abdullah had sent a critical letter to President Bush on August 29, 2001, warning, "A time comes when peoples and nations part.

---

15. "With big gas deals, Saudis welcome in new partners," *Platts Oilgram News*, Vol. 82, No. 45, Mar 9, 2004, p. 1.

16. Guy Chazan, Neil King Jr., "Saudi desert's gas mirage," *Wall Street Journal*, Mar. 25, 2008; p. B1.

17. Ibid.

18. "Hijack 'suspects' alive and well," BBC News, Sept. 23, 2001.

We are at a crossroads. It is time for the United States and Saudi Arabia to look at their separate interests. Those governments that don't feel the pulse of their people and respond to it will suffer the fate of the Shah of Iran."[19]

After 9/11, the Saudis may have had more to fear from the US than from Al Qaeda in terms of "regime change." The rapid invasion of Afghanistan in late 2001 and the March 2003 conquest of Iraq made it clear the US was on a global crusade, and that those who were not its firm allies would be treated as enemies. Relocation in 2003 of the main US command center for the region from Saudi Arabia's Prince Sultan air base to Qatar was an ominous sign of worsening relations, and hinted at possible trouble ahead for Riyadh. All it would take to trigger US armed intervention to garrison the Saudi oil fields would be a terror incident of some kind that might raise international fears about access to Saudi crude, which the US has vowed to protect with military force. In fact, in early 2007 Saudi authorities broke up a major Al Qaeda ring planning just such a terror blitz, including Kuwait and the UAE, to lure in US troops, destabilize Gulf governments and run up oil prices.[20] More than 500 "extremists" were rounded up by the Saudis in June 2008 on charges of plotting a similar round of major terror disruptions.[21] No doubt a nagging question remains for the Saudis: Would the US have secretly preferred that outcome?

It is beyond the scope of this book to psychoanalyze the US-Saudi relationship, or the murky dealings that go on in private between the two. But a sound rule to apply is simple: Watch what they do, not what they say. It is in that spirit one must view the flurry of visits by top Bush Administration figures to Saudi Arabia and other Persian Gulf oil states in early 2008, supposedly for the purpose of talking up the need for "more oil" on the market. In a span of less than three months, the Saudis had house calls from President George W. Bush, Energy Secretary Sam Bodman and Vice President

---

19. Review & Outlook, "The Saudi Contradiction," *Wall Street Journal*, Oct. 30, 2001.

20. "Saudi terrorist network planned 'huge' attacks on oil units: report," *Platts Oilgram News*, Vol. 85, No. 99, May 21, 2007, p. 4.

21. "Saudis foil plot to attack oil installations," *Platts Oilgram News*, Vol. 86, No. 125, June 26, 2008, p. 4.

Dick Cheney. Press reports said all three would urge the Saudis to add more oil to world markets. To which the Saudis consistently replied, "No," and blamed high world prices on "speculators."

If the US really wanted more Saudi oil production and lower prices, it is highly likely that such talks would be carried out away from the glare of news media "photo ops." And the Saudis would be unlikely to issue such a public and humiliating rejection. Logic and common sense suggest something else has been going on. Some speculate this has been preparatory discussion for eventual military action against Iran.[22] Whatever is going on, the Saudis are adhering to the game plan of keeping a snug fit between physical oil demand and supply.

Although it announced a token 200,000 b/d increase in June 2008, to about 9.7 million b/d, that increase mainly appears to have been to prove the Saudis were not to blame for runaway crude prices. Since the added barrels will be mostly heavy and sour Saudi crude, China will see little or no price benefit. But it could mean wider discounts for US and European refiners less dependent on light, sweet crude. Coinciding with the announced Saudi June increase, sweet-crude producer Nigeria was hit with more large-scale production shut-ins of up to 1 million b/d due to ongoing rebel activity there.

Overall, physical crude markets remain well-supplied and the Saudis have stuck to their decision in April 2008 to suspend their $50-billion capacity expansion plan when it reaches a targeted 12.5 million b/d in 2009. That will add about 1.2 million b/d to current capacity of 11.3 million b/d, which was only about 80% utilized as of the end of 2007. "All the latest projections, at least up to 2020, do not require anything higher," Saudi oil minister Ali Naimi told the *Petroleum Argus*. Then in a reference to what the Saudis view as phony oil demand on the NYMEX, Naimi declared, "Unless we see really genuine demand, we have to pause right now and see what happens."[23]

---

22. Editorial, "Cheney's Mideast mission," *Washington Times*, Mar. 17, 2008.
23. Spencer Swartz and Natalie Obiko Pearson, "Saudi Arabia to Pause Adding New Oil Capacity after 2009," Dow Jones Newswires, Apr. 19, 2008.

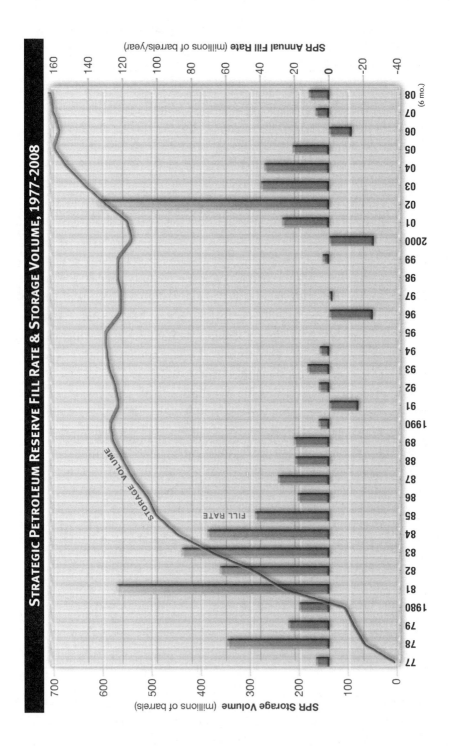

Strategic Petroleum Reserve Fill Rate & Storage Volume, 1977-2008

SPR Annual Fill Rate (millions of barrels/year)

SPR Storage Volume (millions of barrels)

STORAGE VOLUME

FILL RATE

11

The SPR and Other Oil Price Levers

The modest fill rate (of the Strategic Petroleum Reserve) does not put undue pressure on markets. It's a minimal amount of oil.
—Katharine Fredriksen, Principal Deputy Assistant Secretary, DoE Office of Policy and International Affairs

We're going to put $100 oil underground? I think that's nuts, frankly.
— Senator Byron Dorgan, (D.-ND)[1]

Among the arsenal of weapons we have seen to be available to the US national security establishment for affecting the price of oil, there is one small but potent tool uniquely at Washington's discretion. It is the Strategic Petroleum Reserve. Created in 1975 in the wake of the 1973 Arab oil embargo, it is quite literally a giant sinkhole for taking crude oil off the market and sequestering it indefinitely. Officially, it is a "rainy day" oil supply in case of a catastrophic supply interruption and is *not* to be used to manage market pricing. Indeed, the Department of Energy takes pains to insist the buying and selling of crude stocks for the SPR have little or no price impact. But as a practical matter, the SPR has been regularly toyed with to affect oil prices over the years, and its impact has at times been substantial. Price manipulation, in fact, may be about the only thing the SPR is good for, since critics rightly note this costly insurance policy would offer little protection in a real crude supply crunch such as might happen with a shut-down of Saudi Arabian or Persian Gulf exports.[2]

1. US Senate, Committee on Energy and Natural Resources, hearing "To receive testimony on US oil inventory policies, including the Strategic Petroleum Reserve," Feb. 26, 2008.
2. Jerry Taylor, Peter Van Doren, "The Case against the Strategic Petroleum Reserve," Cato Institute, Policy Analysis No. 555, Nov. 21, 2005.

The SPR is a network of 62 underground caverns created in rock-like salt formations at four locations along the US Gulf Coast. Ranging in volume from 6 million to 35 million bbl of capacity, or as big as Chicago's Sears Tower, these cylindrical caverns were created by dissolving the salt with fresh water. Current capacity of 727 million bbl of oil is nearly full. But capacity is being expanded to 1 billion bbl under the Energy Policy Act of 2005. In his 2007 State of the Union address, President Bush called for further expansion to 1.5 billion bbl, "to further protect America against disruptions to our oil supply." That would take the SPR from a current level of about 2.5 months of US crude imports to almost 6 months of import "cover." Since most US imports are from Canada and Mexico, the SPR would swell to a year or more's worth of other US sea-borne crude intake.

Though it has had a lot of emotional support from Congress in the past, the SPR has not been treated as if it were an essential strategic necessity. The few times it has come into play have generally involved price manipulation ploys. For instance:

- Ronald Reagan, at what was presumably the height of the Cold War in 1983, with the imminent threat of nuclear holocaust, cut inputs to the SPR by more than half, to leave more barrels on the market and try to drive down world crude prices. In 1984 the Reagan Administration let it be known it would draw quickly on the SPR in any emergency, further damping market expectations.

- The first Bush Administration released what turned out to be a token 17.3 million barrels in 1991, at the time of the first Iraq war. It was the only formal "emergency" declared under the law that created the SPR, the 1975 Energy Policy and Conservation Act. That was barely half the volume planned to be released, because NYMEX prices quickly tumbled from more than $32/bbl on January 16 to $19.25 on January 18, for a record-breaking 40% drop.[3]

---

3. Interestingly, a huge beneficiary of that SPR release was oil trader Roy William Harris, who is said to have made up to $50 million by presciently making a big bet in the futures market that oil prices would collapse, rather than rise, just as the bombing was about to start in Iraq. Rivals have long marveled at Harris' good fortune and wonder if he had an insider tip. Barely a year later, Harris' Arochem

• The Clinton Administration slowed and then suspended SPR purchases in 1995 as a budget-balancing move. The volume then was just shy of 600 million bbl.

• In 1996, as Bill Clinton was running for re-election, his administration began to auction off 28.1 million bbls of the SPR. When the sales were concluded in early 1997, they had raised $545 million, or less than $20/bbl.[4] NYMEX crude went from the mid-$20s to around $19/bbl. The US economy was humming with low inflation, the stock market was roaring upwards and Clinton could claim to have nearly closed the federal budget deficit.

• In January 1999, soon after the fateful Saudi Washington meeting of September 1998 which signaled the sea-change in US oil price policy, the DoE said it would begin refilling the SPR to its prior 600 million bbl.[5] Prices then began their ascent from the low teens to more than $36 in late 2000.

• To damp home heating oil prices as winter neared in 2000, the Clinton Administration released about 30 million bbl of SPR crude in the form of oil loans to be paid back with interest. Viewed as an election-year ploy, that capped a two-year tripling of oil prices.

As of mid-April 2008, the SPR held just over 700 million bbl of crude, including 280 million bbl of light, sweet crude, and 421 million bbl of sour (more than 0.5% sulfur) crude. Its fill rate was being stepped up from about 1.4 million bbl/month to 3.8 million

Corp. was in Chapter 11 with some $200 million owed to a consortium of banks led by Chase Manhattan. A 1995 *Forbes* cover story by the author detailed how Harris and Arochem had been tightly tied to US-supported Iraq oil-for-arms trading by Carlos Cardoen though the Bayoil empire of David Bay Chalmers Jr. Harris was tried and convicted in 1992 on 20 counts of fraud and a money-laundering count and was sentenced to 15 ½ years in prison. Chalmers, who had paid all Harris' legal bills, later pled guilty in August 2007 to a single federal criminal count of conspiracy to commit wire fraud and was sentenced to 46 months in prison for his role in circumventing the UN Iraq Oil-For-Food program with kickbacks to the Saddam Hussein regime.

4. US Senate, Committee on Government Affairs, US Strategic Petroleum Reserve: Recent Policy, Mar. 5, 2003, p. 13.

5. Department of Energy, press release, "Richardson Announces Plan to Re-Fill the Strategic Petroleum Reserve," Jan. 11, 1999.

bbl in May 2008, and then to more than 2 million bbl/mo, or about 70,000 b/d.[6] Most of that would come from "royalty-in-kind" crude owed to the government by offshore producers in the Gulf of Mexico, or on other federal leases, requiring no spending authorization. But almost $600 million of cash purchases were also planned, using funds collected from "interest" on some 11 million bbl of SPR crude released to refiners after Hurricane Katrina in 2005.

SPR buys buoy oil prices

Compared to overall US petroleum consumption of around 20 million b/d, including imports of just under 10 million b/d, those SPR additions would seem to be a trivial amount of oil "demand." In early 2008 Energy Secretary Bodman, who had just been visibly lobbying the Saudis for more crude on the market, insisted at a Senate hearing that buying crude oil for the SPR "does not affect the price to any meaningful degree." But as oil economist Philip Verleger has noted, even that modest volume can have a substantial price impact in a tight market. In the late-2007 run-up toward $100/bbl oil, Verleger testified to a Senate panel: "DoE's SPR program probably added $10 per barrel," or more than 10%, to crude prices.[7]

Verleger noted there was a close correlation between resumption of SPR crude buys in August 2007, after a year and a half in abeyance, and the sharp rise in NYMEX crude prices, from around $70/bbl at that time. The reason, he calculated, was that one-third of the SPR purchases were light, sweet crude, at the rate of more than 21,000 b/d from August through January 2008, then ramping to almost 40,000 b/d through mid 2008.

Similarly, in May 2008, oil prices abruptly halted their rapid run-up to $135/bbl and briefly eased about 8% when a distraught Congress swiftly passed the Strategic Petroleum Reserve Fill Suspension and Consumer Protection Act of 2008 while President Bush was in Riyadh appearing to unsuccessfully beg publicly for more Saudi crude on the market. He signed the bill into law May 19 despite his

6. DoE, "Strategic Petroleum Reserve Inventory," as of June 5, 2008.

7. Philip K. Verleger Jr., prepared testimony before the Permanent Subcommittee on Investigation of the Senate Committee on Homeland Security and Governmental Affairs, and Subcommittee on Energy of the Senate Committee on Energy and Natural Resources, Dec. 11, 2007, p.14.

prior strong criticism, slowing down a planned topping-off of the SPR from 704 million bbl to 727 million bbl. It defers until 2009 all scheduled royalty-in-kind crude acquisitions through year-end 2008, which were slated to total about 76,000 b/d.

Half of those incoming SPR barrels were to be light, sweet crude, which is the basis for the benchmark NYMEX WTI contract, the benchmark which provides the underlying cost basis for most Chinese oil imports. As previously noted, Chinese refineries are generally not configured with the metallurgy and support units needed to process sour, high-sulfur crudes. So they have to pay up for better grades of sweet crude, whose prices tend to be driven by the NYMEX WTI quote.

Worldwide production of such light, sweet crude with less than 0.5% sulfur is only about 20 million b/d, or less than 25% of total global supply. Of that, Verleger notes, only about 5 million b/d is available to be freely traded. The rest is tied up under long-term contracts or captive barrels within China or other producer countries. So DoE's added daily demand for SPR fill could actually have been taking up to half a percent of the available crude behind the NYMEX contract. With no surplus world capacity to produce light, sweet crude, he noted, "DoE is shrinking the market."

Clean-fuel rules add to price pressure

While the supply of light, sweet crude has been limited in recent years, partly by the low capital investment by Western oil majors noted earlier, demand has been rising even faster than the overall world average crude consumption. In addition to Chinese requirements, the US has also created much more competition for that high-grade crude by imposing much tougher sulfur limits in gasoline and diesel fuels. The US Environmental Protection Agency had been on a long-term quest to clean up air pollution from motor fuel sources. But in July 1998, about the time of the apparent sea-change in US oil policy, the EPA presented to Congress plans for its "Tier 2 Vehicle and Gasoline Sulfur program." It was finalized in late 1999 after hearings and required US refiners to slash sulfur content in gasoline from a prior maximum of 300 parts per million to an average of no more than 30 ppm, starting in 2005, with a cap of 80 ppm in every gallon of gasoline produced. In 2006, 80% of highway diesel fuel had to be cut to no more than 15 ppm of sulfur from the prior 500 ppm allowance. It must be 100% at 15 ppm by 2010.[8]

These huge sulfur reductions drove the US refining industry to spend tens of billions of dollars on hydrogen processing and other units to remove sulfur from their crude, and also tilted demand toward light, sweet grades. Differentials between light, sweet and heavy, sour crudes mushroomed from a few dollars a barrel at times in the late 1990s to around $20/bbl, as refiners bid up the better grades. In economic terms, demand for light, sweet crude became very "inelastic."

The inelastic demand for light, sweet crude

The price impact of even seemingly small volumes of added SPR light, sweet crude demand has been magnified by this inelasticity, Verleger explained. He cited a recent study showing the overall world price elasticity of demand for crude oil at a slim -.04, and estimated the elasticity for light, sweet crude might be only half that. If the elasticity for WTI-grade crude were -0.02, Verleger noted, a 1% drop in supply would theoretically require a 25 to 40% price hike to balance the market. "One can estimate DoE's actions added between 5% and 20% to the price of oil" in late 2007, Verleger testified, implying the impact could have been as much as $18/bbl.[9]

As if that were not bad enough, Verleger also lifted the skirts a bit on the murky business of oil-market derivatives trading, which probably had the effect of further magnifying the late-2007 price run-up. That relates to "delta hedging," a dynamic risk-management practice of the major Wall Street banks that can greatly amplify upward and downward price swings. It stems from the sometimes large volume of put and call options written by the commodity desks of the big investment banks as part of their offering of risk-abatement services to clients. The vast bulk of these options are written when they are "out of the money" and nowhere near worth being exercised. But as prices move up, the value rises quickly for call options, which give the holder the right to acquire oil at a given "strike price."

---

8. For details on Tier 2 sulfur rules, see www.epa.gov/tier2/.

9. Verleger, prepared testimony, p.14.

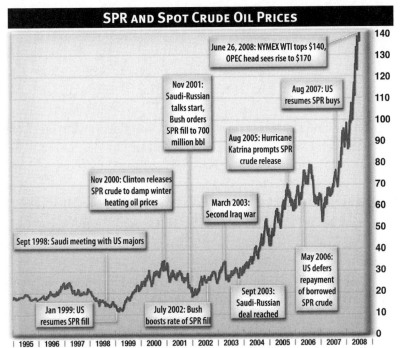

SPR AND SPOT CRUDE OIL PRICES

June 26, 2008: NYMEX WTI tops $140, OPEC head sees rise to $170

Nov 2001: Saudi-Russian talks start, Bush orders SPR fill to 700 million bbl

Aug 2007: US resumes SPR buys

Aug 2005: Hurricane Katrina prompts SPR crude release

Nov 2000: Clinton releases SPR crude to damp winter heating oil prices

March 2003: Second Iraq war

Sept 1998: Saudi meeting with US majors

May 2006: US defers repayment of borrowed SPR crude

Sept 2003: Saudi-Russian deal reached

Jan 1999: US resumes SPR fill

July 2002: Bush boosts rate of SPR fill

1995 | 1996 | 1997 | 1998 | 1999 | 2000 | 2001 | 2002 | 2003 | 2004 | 2005 | 2006 | 2007 | 2008

As the difference, or "delta," between the market and the option's strike price closes, the banks systematically buy futures to cover their exposure. It amounts to "short covering" of options in the futures market. A rising crude price can thus trigger more demand for paper barrels, rather than less. "Data indicate that the price increases tied to DoE's purchases of light, sweet crude were magnified by option hedging," Verleger testified.

"Delta hedging" kicks in

A falling price can likewise generate more sales of futures, to offset the impact of "puts" that have been sold by the banks. Verleger credited such delta hedging with helping to temporarily drive down the price of WTI to as low as $51/bbl in early 2007, from $77, during the 18 months when US SPR buying had been halted after the 2005 hurricane season. But the stepped-up SPR filling in 2008 would be certain to put a renewed upward spin on prices, which, Verleger warned, would be likely to trigger yet more delta hedging. "Prices [of NYMEX WTI could run] as high as an unbelievable $120/bbl if adult supervision is not brought to bear on DoE," he

185

drolly observed in December of 2007.[10] Just six months later they would, in fact, top $135/bbl.

None of this was likely a surprise to veteran professionals inside the DoE, who for some time had been advising against any steady, fixed pattern of SPR crude buying that disregarded the price. In 2002, however, higher-ups in the second Bush Administration overruled DoE's "market-based" approach to buying SPR crude, which had allowed deliveries of royalty-in-kind crude to be deferred with interest when prices seemed high. One senior SPR official warned the administration's new buying policy had been "discredited years ago" and "appears irrational to the market place." "Insisting on [SPR] deliveries in a tight market," he further noted, "would be heavily criticized as mismanagement and would be difficult to defend." He was ignored.[11]

SPR market-based deferrals had saved taxpayers more than $175 million in 2000 and 2001, and added 7 million bbl to the reserve, according to a 2003 Senate probe. Subsequent continued buying, rather than buying on market dips and selling incoming government-royalty crude on the upswings, "cost taxpayers an additional $1 million per day." Moreover, the relentless SPR buying steadily drove up market prices. "In a 1-month period in mid-2002, crude oil price increases caused by SPR deposits spiked the US spot price of home heating oil by 13%, jet fuel by 10%, and diesel fuel by 8%, imposing on US consumers additional crude oil costs of between $500 million and $1 billion," Senate investigators concluded.[12]

Adding a sense of futility, the Senate probe found that *overall* US crude stocks showed no increase whatever after all this SPR buying. By adding 40 million bbl to the SPR in 2002, bringing it up 7% to 600 million bbl, the DoE triggered a 10% drawdown of commercial crude stocks to 280 million, and then to 270 million in 2003.[13] Partly that was due to pushing the forward curve of oil futures prices into backwardation, which, Verleger notes, discourages the holding

---

10. Ibid., p. 17.
11. US Senate, Committee on Government Affairs, US Strategic Petroleum Reserve: Recent Policy, Mar. 5, 2003, p. 6.
12. Ibid., p. 2.
13. Ibid., p. 3.

of commercial inventories and prompts inventory liquidation.[14] If anything, loading up the SPR and drawing down US commercial stocks have helped to illustrate a long term secular trend in the US for less and less working inventory needed to make the refining and distribution system work. As the network of pipelines, terminals, refineries and ports gets more and more efficient, fewer days' worth of crude and refined products need to be kept sitting around at ever-increasing financial cost.

The global drive for strategic reserves

Various attempts by Congress to slow or halt the SPR filling have been rebuffed by the White House, as well as have all recent suggestions that some SPR crude be sold to damp market prices. Energy Secretary Bodman chided Rep. Edward Markey (D.-Mass.) in January 2008 that Markey's proposed sale of SPR crude or the 2.8 million bbl Northeast heating oil reserve would be an "unnecessary market intervention," and leave the region "vulnerable to a true supply shortage."

Instead, the US and its western allies have consistently encouraged the International Energy Agency to push for higher global strategic stockpiles, including pressure for China to build up its own long-planned SPR. From 2000 to early 2007, global strategic oil stockpiles rose 14% to 4.1 billion bbl.[15] As of early 2008, the IEA reported global crude reserves were down slightly, at 4 billion bbl, including 1.5 billion of emergency stocks held by governments and 2.5 billion bbl of commercial inventories. But under its "outreach" strategy, the IEA aims to "promote emergency stock building" in China and India. The IEA claims China has plans for 500 million bbl of crude stockpiles, and that India is embarked on stockpiling 100 million bbl.[16]

Whether China could ever reach such a huge reserve level is doubtful, however. In April 2008 China said it had finished construction of the third of four strategic reserve sites, at Huangdao, in what was termed the 100-million-bbl first phase of its SPR ef-

---

14. Verleger, prepared testimony, p. 8.
15. International Energy Agency, Oil Supply Security: Emergency Response of IEA Countries 2007, executive summary, released Nov. 29, 2007, p.12.
16. Ibid., p. 13.

fort.[17] But even though much of the capacity there had been available since mid-2007, it appears no crude had yet moved into storage at Huangbao. And China has revealed no plans yet for further phases of the SPR effort. As of year-end 2007, Beijing claimed that one of the first two tank farms, in eastern Zhejiang province, had 33 million bbl of crude in storage. Other reports put the volume at only 15 to 20 million bbl, or less than one week's worth of Chinese crude imports.[18] Moreover, the reserves are managed by Chinese state oil companies, who may treat the crude like commercial inventories. "I have repeatedly said that our stock-building will be gradual, based on oil prices," vice minister Zhang Guobao of China's new State Energy Bureau told reporters.

In reality, nobody outside of China really knows how much in the way of "rainy day" crude oil stockpiles the PRC may have salted away over the years. Analysis of statistical data from China's customs arm seems to indicate far more crude has been imported annually than has been run through refineries. This has created a mystery over "missing barrels" in China which has left analysts scratching their heads. It may be explained by bad recordkeeping, non-reporting small teakettle refineries processing crude, or under-reported refinery runs by Chinese majors trying to hide refined product in advance of the next expected state price increase.

Given the serious strategic ramifications of such information, it is no surprise the Chinese would be secretive. But one thing is certain: If they did not hide away sizeable crude reserves in years past, they will be paying through the nose to build a strategic reserve now. And without a crude supply cushion of many months, it would be economic suicide for the PRC to launch a hostile takeover of Taiwan that would most certainly invoke a protracted oil embargo.

---

17. Reuters, "China 3rd oil reserve ready; no oil fill yet-source," Guardian.co.uk, Apr. 18, 2008.
18. Xinhua News Agency, "China sets up oil reserve center," Dec. 24, 2007.

MONTHLY NET FUNDS FLOWS INTO COMMODITY INDEX INVESTMENTS

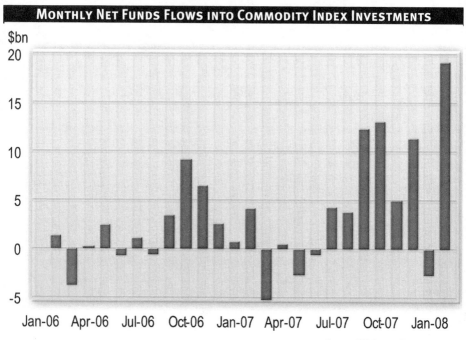

Source: JPMorgan Energy Strategy

HOW INDEX SPECULATORS HAVE BLOATED THE COMMODITY FUTURES MARKET

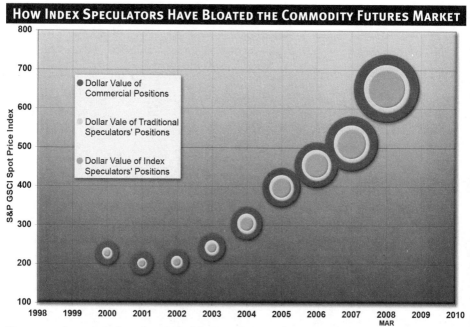

Since 2005, investment flows by pension funds and other managed money into unlimited speculative positions on the NYMEX and other commodity exchanges has coincided with the steep rise in prices, and now overshadows the "commercial" players and traditional "speculators."

Source: Masters Capital Management, Bloomberg, CFTC reports

12

The Role of
the Futures Market

Markets work if we let them.[1]

— ExxonMobil CEO Lee Raymond

T he conventional wisdom is that a large, global market in a highly fungible commodity like crude oil cannot possibly be manipulated up or down for very far or for very long. In fact, that "wisdom" is wrong. We saw how oil prices were successfully manipulated significantly downward for a decade or longer to deprive the Soviet Union of its main source of hard currency. Those same mechanisms, with some refinements, can be employed in reverse to sustain upward pricing well above normal market-clearing levels. To be sure, it is not any easy endeavor, and can only be accomplished by a determined superpower like the US pulling on all its available levers, and motivated to achieve a key national security objective.

This is what we have been witnessing in the oil markets since the late 1990s, and it could go on for another decade or longer until the objective is reached, or the policy abandoned. Moreover, with the price of oil now unhitched from the fundamentals of supply and demand, there is no theoretical limit to how high it can be driven with sheer financial pressure. When Goldman Sachs warns crude prices could go to $150, or even $200/bbl, be forewarned.[2] They very well could.

1. US Congress, Senate, Committee on Commerce, Science and Transportation and the Committee on Energy and Natural Resources, joint hearing on Energy Prices and Profits, 109th Congress, 1st sess., Nov. 9, 2005, p. 8.
2. In March of 2005, with NYMEX crude selling in the mid-$50 range, Goldman Sachs astoundingly predicted the price could hit a "super spike" of up to $105/bbl. Just three years on Mar. 7, 2008, with crude trading slightly above $105/bbl, Goldman analyst Arjun Murti issued an update predicting prices could spike to $150 to $200/bbl on a supply disruption. Two months later on May 6, with crude

The essential ingredients of a sustained oil price rise are as follows:

• Reduction of surplus world crude output and tightening of the physical supply/demand balance. This we have seen in the behavior of the Western oil majors, Russian and Saudi production restraint, and the crippling of Iraq as an oil exporter.

• Aggressive accumulation of strategic stockpiles to sop up excess crude supply, led by the US but also driven by the International Energy Agency and other OECD nations.

• Persistent anxiety over geopolitical disruption of crude movements, most recently seen in the turmoil surrounding rebel action in the Niger Delta, and in Persian Gulf tension relating to Iran.

Send in the traders

With these underlying elements of the game plan in place, the stage is set for employing the real driving force to lift and sustain oil prices: money. It is here that US economic warriors have brought to bear the heavy guns of deep-pockets funding on the oil futures market, which, with its minimal margin requirements and thus high inherent leverage capability, can act as a kind of hydraulic lift to magnify the financial inputs.

As with the short-driven downward NYMEX price movement in the 1980s, there are no overt signs of government intervention in the oil markets. However the plan may be implemented, it is designed to appear like normal market dynamics. But we will see that the upward sea-change in pricing has coincided with a series of timely and odd US regulatory changes. It has been accompanied by aggressive commodity market activity by major investment banks such as Goldman Sachs, which could be regarded as extensions of the national security establishment. There has also been unprecedented commodity market activity by quasi-governmental pension plans like CalPERS. And there are telltale indications of involvement by the government's secretive market intervention group: the "Plunge Protection Team," formally known as the President's Working Group on Financial Markets (WGFM).

---

above $120/bbl, Murti warned: "The possibility of $150-$200 per barrel seems increasingly likely over the next 6-12 months." He cited supply/demand "fundamentals" while downplayed speculation.

Avoiding overt "market manipulation," the game plan appears to have been to create a structural market change. Rather than carrying water, as it were, the econo-warriors have dug a diversionary canal to channel part of the mighty river of US financial flows into what had long been a market backwater: oil futures. The effort has been a resounding success. Pulled up by the NYMEX, world oil prices have risen more than 12-fold since late 1998, to above $140/bbl, as trading volume has mushroomed.

At the end of the first quarter in 2008 there was "open interest" of about 2.5 million matching buy/sell contracts in the three main contracts for light, sweet crude oil futures traded on the New York Mercantile Exchange and the new Atlanta-based electronic IntercontinentalExchange (ICE).[3] Each contract is for 1,000 bbl, delivered at either New York Harbor or Cushing, Oklahoma. Almost none of that crude actually is taken as an "exchange for physicals" when a futures contract expires. The deals are nearly all unwound before maturity in purely financial settlements. The same is true for a wide-ranging "complex" of contracts for refined products like gasoline and heating oil, and crude derivatives for a myriad of price differentials by grade, location and timing.

At the recent market price of around $130/bbl, those 2.5 million open contracts equate to about $325 billion of nominal transaction value pending at any given time, spread over several years of maturities. This is triple the 750,000 or so contracts open, at far lower crude prices, in the late 1990s, and five times the volume in the mid-1990s. All told, there has been a more than 20-fold increase in transaction value for the NYMEX and ICE crude contracts over the past decade. Most of this has occurred in just the past two years.

That describes just the volume in actual futures. If options—the future right but not the obligation to buy (call) or sell (put) the commodity—were included, open interest in NYMEX WTI (light, sweet crude) would have been 3 million contracts in early 2008. The total, with the ICE contracts for WTI and North Sea Brent, would have been more than 4.1 million. That would be a notional value of

3. The CFTC Commitments of Traders report for Apr. 1, 2008, showed open interest of 1.35 million WTI contracts on the NYMEX. The ICE website reported open interest on Apr. 1, 2008, of 591,000 contracts for Brent crude and 533,000 for WTI.

more than half a trillion dollars, and equate to one and a half months of total worldwide oil consumption.

Of course, not all that value means hard-dollar investment. Margin requirements on NYMEX and ICE are usually only about 5% of a futures contract's face amount. That is because they are regarded mainly as performance bonds. This is fundamentally different from the down payment on a broker loan on a stock purchase, also termed "margin," which is usually at least 50% of the stock's value. Still, posted margins equate to about $13 billion in deposits down on exchange-traded crude futures. And that does not count the large volume of exchange-traded futures and options on a myriad of refined product categories, nascent crude oil futures exchanges in Dubai and Shanghai, or the vast volume of customized over-the-counter crude-based futures and derivative contracts bought and sold by the big investment banks. Those OTC deals, which sometimes end up being hedged with offsetting exchange-based futures and options, are estimated to be *three to five times* the reported volume on NYMEX and ICE.[4]

In terms of daily oil futures volume, the 2.8 million of NYMEX and ICE crude contracts bought and sold *per day* in early 2008 equated to more than a month's worth of the entire world's crude oil demand, and probably more than 100 times the volume of physical crude actually changing hands each day in market-based arms-length deals. The "paper" traffic now dwarfs the physical crude traffic by perhaps two orders of magnitude.

The absurdity is actually far worse if compared just to the world volumes of light, sweet crude changing hands daily in arms-length deals, which may be only a tenth of total world oil consumption. More and more crude production is in heavier, higher-sulfur grades selling at substantial discounts to WTI of $20 or more per barrel. US refineries are well equipped to handle these cheaper crudes. The Chinese are not, and must pay prices close to the WTI level for most of their crude imports, mainly from the Middle East and West Africa. Thus, artificially inflated NYMEX WTI prices disproportionately hurt PRC refiners versus those in the US.

It is worth noting here a crucial difference between commodity futures and the stock or bond markets. Stocks and bonds are for the long haul. Futures mature and have to be unwound with an opposite

---

4. Based on discussions with exchange staff.

purchase or sale before they expire, or else you have to physically deliver or take the commodity itself, which we've noted almost nobody does. Options expire, too, and most expire "out of the money" and worthless. Stocks and bonds, on the other hand, are "securities," traded in "capital" markets. They are designed to raise long-term equity and debt, and are regulated to protect "investors." Futures are designed mainly for risk management and are seen as a zero-sum game in which for every winner there is a loser. "Insider information" is considered essential for the commodities market to work; it is illegal in stock trading. Those fundamental tenets are now being muddied beyond recognition as the US government moves to unify the rules and regulations for futures and securities.

Who are the real speculators?

Where on earth has all this trading activity originated? The official explanation is that it is from "speculators." But that is an unfortunate historical term derived from the weekly reports by the Commodity Futures Trading Commission, which break out US futures volume according to "commercial" and "non-commercial" buyers and sellers. The crude oil "commercials" are generally the physical producers and consumers: upstream oil companies (the natural "longs"), refiners (the natural "shorts") and physical traders with inventory price risk. These were historically thought to be the smart-money players with the best market information, engaged mainly in hedging the inherent risk of their ongoing businesses by buying or selling futures or options. When prices get out of whack, high or low, it has been generally presumed the "commercials" would step in to right the market. No more.

The "non-commercials," in CFTC lingo, were the outsiders gambling on price movements with no physical interest in the commodity itself. In years past, the weekly CFTC "Commitments of Traders" reports referred to them as "speculators."

In another unfortunate twist of terminology, some of the key players now on the non-commercial side are "hedge" funds, so called because they may tend to take both long and short positions in whatever investment category they are pursuing this week for their well-heeled clientele. Ironically, these "hedge" funds do not qualify for the preferential treatment given by the CFTC to the "commercial" hedgers, because they presumably do not hedge physical volumes. That means they are held back by "position limits" on the number of open contracts they can hold. We will see this limitation may be severely restricting the number of sellers in long-dated NYMEX oil futures, just as that market has been hit with a tidal wave of unrestricted buying. The CFTC has stacked the deck in favor of rising commodity prices.

A series of profound changes in the commodity markets in recent years has turned these old definitions of "commercials" and "speculators" on their heads. The traditional "commercials" or "hedgers" have been eclipsed by the inflow of speculative money coming, again ironically, from long-term investors and professional money managers, including hedge funds. The vast bulk of this new money has tended to come into the market on the "long" or "buy" side, straining the capacity of the usual "sell" side market players (the commercials) to keep up with the demand for futures dated longer than their usual comfort range of a few months out. The result has been a strong and relentless upward bias in oil futures prices, regardless of industry supply and demand fundamentals.

Far from the classic image of a swashbuckling "speculator," jumping in and out of a market to make a quick buck, the new breed of oil futures player may be the epitome of the staid, conservative trust fund manager. Public employee and private pension funds, institutional money managers and banks have started allocating to commodities a small, but growing, share of the trillions of dollars they administer as fiduciaries. If even only a few percentage points of this managed wealth were to flow into the oil market, the impact would be huge. And it has been.

Among the pacesetters in this regard has been the giant California Public Employees Retirement System or CalPERS. It is a role model for most other state and private pension managers, and has thus legitimized a massive and growing rush of otherwise cautious investment money into commodities. As of early 2008, CalPERS had poured about $1 billion, or about 2%, of its $240 billion of assets into oil and other commodity funds in the span of just a few years. That could grow to $5 billion in just three more years, a CalPERS official told Reuters in early 2008, with other reports hinting at an allocation of more than $7 billion by 2010. CalPERS later damped speculation on the timing, but not necessarily the amounts, after oil prices surged above $100/bbl. "We plan to ramp up the program," a spokesman told Reuters. "There's no rush," he added: "As a long-term investor, we can afford to be patient."[5]

As goes CalPERS, so goes the rest of the pension fund industry. Soon after betting $450 million on commodities in March 2006, CalPERS was followed by Hermes Pensions Management Ltd., the biggest UK pension plan, which invested more than $2 billion of its assets in commodities. Since then, there has been a rush of other pension funds into the commodity pits.[6]

Getting CalPERS to capitulate and take on commodities was a major sea-change. Until then, commodity futures were a clear no-no for pension fund managers. They were regarded as far too risky. Professional portfolio managers knew they might get lucky and make an occasional killing. But the inevitable losing position would be a career-wrecker. The main function of commodity futures had always been to lay off price risk from or between producers or consumers, with the help of the non-commercial speculators. They were never meant to be a long-term investment vehicle.

An added feature of the commodity futures market, which became a preoccupation of government, was the open window it provided for "price discovery." The whole tenor of commodities regulation in the past had been to damp speculative forces that would skew prices away from the fundamentals dictated by physical supply and demand. In fact, under Title 7 of the U.S. Code, Section 6(a), the Commodity Futures Trading Commission is given the job of "diminishing, eliminating, or preventing" what is termed "excessive speculation" that causes "sudden or unreasonable fluctuations or unwarranted changes in the price" of a regulated commodity. That includes oil. Section 5(b) of the code tells the CFTC to "deter and prevent price manipulation or any other disruptions to market integrity." Instead, since the late 1990s the CFTC has stood by and effectively enabled runaway oil prices by

5. "CalPERS plays down talk of commodities buying spree," Reuters, Mar. 7, 2008.
6. Saijel Kishan, "CalPERS Beats Pickens as Commodity Indexes Clobber Hedge Funds," Bloomberg.com, Nov. 12, 2007.

allowing the crude futures market to be turned into a sinkhole of speculative excess.[7]

Until the NYMEX oil contract gained credence in the mid-1980s, government and industry were almost completely dependent on private price-reporting services like *Platts* to assess prevailing markets in oil and refined products. Those services are still relied on to assess prices by specific locations and grade and their differentials to the NYMEX price, but they are now subservient to the exchange-traded futures quotes.

The zero-sum risk-management nature of commodity futures is in stark contrast to the investment nature of the capital markets for stocks and bonds, where there is presumed to be inherent underlying value in securities that should grow over time as a rising tide of value eventually lifts all boats. Indeed, it took more than a decade of clever and persistent salesmanship by Goldman Sachs and other Wall Street houses to persuade CalPERS and other pension managers to put money into commodity futures. The fee-hungry brokers had been trying since the early 1990s to end the long stigma against commodities, and to cajole the pension funds into buying a raft of new futures-related financial services.[8] Their efforts got a fortuitous boost from some academic studies, using statistics from the recent years of steady price gains, which defended commodities as an "investment" category that can rival the returns on stocks and bonds. In theory, a properly structured commodities investment could actually lower the overall risk in a portfolio because commodities are considered to be negatively correlated to the performance of stocks and bonds.[9]

To diversify risk, much of the institutional investing in commodities has been tied to the performance of two broad-based commodity price indexes. They are the heavily oil-weighted Goldman Sachs Com-

7. Chairman of the CFTC from December 2001 to August 2004 was James E. Newsome. He then became president of the New York Mercantile Exchange. Newsome had been named to the CFTC as a commissioner in 1998, the critical sea-change year in US oil pricing strategy. As CFTC head, Newsome was also a member of the President's Working Group on Financial Markets.

8. Philip K. Verleger Jr., "Impacts of Passive Commodity Investors on Energy Markets and Energy Prices," *Comments on Energy Markets*, May 16, 2007, p.1.

9. Gary B. Gorton and K. Geert Rouwenhorst, "Facts and Fantasies about Commodity Futures," *Financial Analysts Journal*, CFA Institute, Vol. 62, No. 2, March/April 2006.

modity Index, now managed by Standard & Poor's, and the broader Dow Jones-AIG Commodity Index. Other indexes are also emerging from JPMorgan and BNP Paribas, geared especially to track the performance of very long-dated futures, up to three years out.[10] CalPERS, for instance, made its $450 million bet in March 2006 in the form of a "swap" designed to match performance of the GSCI. At the time that index was around 475. Two years later it was more than 700, and oil prices had doubled.

For its GSCI deal, CalPERS apparently traded directly with a swap dealer, or broker: a big investment bank or specialized commodity trading firm that would structure a pattern of futures contracts to mimic the GSCI, then "swap" an equivalent payment stream to CalPERS. As we will see further on, this has the virtue of evading CFTC position limits on what would otherwise be considered a speculative investment.

But smaller, individual investors, as well as pension and institutional fund managers, now have their pick of an array of specialized commodity pools and managed funds to invest in with much smaller amounts, which are then aggregated into similar swap deals. These intermediaries are similar to mutual funds, but invest in commodity futures and options, usually trying to match the commodity index performance. More than 50 of these commodity fund groups have emerged in recent years. They have rapidly accounted for an estimated inflow of $200 billion into the overall commodity markets, with about half that apparently focused on oil and energy contracts. The biggest such commodities index fund is Pimco Real Return (ticker: PRTNX), which since its inception in early 1997 had grown from $8 billion of assets to more than $14 billion in early 2008.[11]

This trend has spread into the retail investor realm as well with the recent emergence of stock-like Exchange Traded Funds (ETFs) in oil, such as United States Oil (Amex:USO). These are geared to the little guy, with low entry minimums and easy exit. Launched in 2006, USO mushroomed to almost $1.3 billion in assets before it was a year old.

To give themselves an aura of conservatism, most of these managed funds tend to take futures positions on a "fully funded" basis.

10. Brad Zigler, "JP Morgan and BNP Paribas' Commodity Indexes Battle Contango," Seekingalpha.com, Nov. 21, 2007.
11. Gene Epstein, "Who's behind the boom?" *Barron's*, Mar. 31, 2008, p. 32.

That is, a small portion of incoming investor money goes to cover the 5% margin requirement on a futures position, while the bulk of the cash is invested in interest-bearing securities. That has helped woo long-term investment and retirement money from thousands of institutional accounts for millions of beneficiaries, many of whom probably have little idea where their money is going and don't care, so long as the returns are positive.

Because of the "fully funded" futures investing by the pension giants, higher margin requirements on futures trades would likely do very little to curb their appetite for commodity index plays. It would mean slightly less of their money allocated to that sector would be earning a nominal interest yield. In fact, raising margin levels on commodity futures might serve instead to drive prices even higher by further discouraging sellers, who are less likely to be operating on a "fully funded" strategy.

As of late March 2008, the S&P GSCI had drawn some $143 billion worth of investment in commodity futures and the DJ-AIGCI had $88 billion, for a total $231 billion. That was more than double their combined value a year earlier, according to CFTC data. Crude oil (WTI and Brent) accounted for $68 billion of that total with another $20 billion in heating oil, distillate and gasoline contracts, or almost 40% of the total index values. Together these two indexes accounted for a stunning 27% of all open interest in WTI contracts on the NYMEX and ICE, and 29% of the ICE Brent contract. In NYMEX heating oil, their value equated to almost 36% of the open interest.[12]

In early 2008, economist Philip Verleger calculated that just since early 2006 at least $130 billion of new pension and other passive institutional investment funds had been directed into the oil markets, mainly through these indexes. CFTC reports show such index-based and other managed-money investment now accounting for about 40% of the open interest in the NYMEX WTI contract. The vast bulk of that has gone into the "buy" side of futures and options. As one NYMEX veteran explains it: "That money tends to go long, because it's scared." And it tends to be invested many months or even years out on the forward "curve," which Verleger notes is inherently speculative

12. Verleger, "Tracking Commodity Investments by Passive Investors," *Notes at the Margin*, April 2008.

and uncomfortable ground for any traditional "commercial" futures player. In the past, nearly all the action in oil futures was concentrated in the nearest three months of the curve, with almost no activity farther out. No more. In a 2006 Senate hearing, Verleger noted that long-dated oil futures (30 months or longer) had made up only 4.5 % of open interest in NYMEX crude in July 2001, but had climbed to 15% of a much larger volume by July 2005.[13] As of May 2008 they were still running about 12% of NYMEX WTI contracts, even as overall volume had exploded.[14]

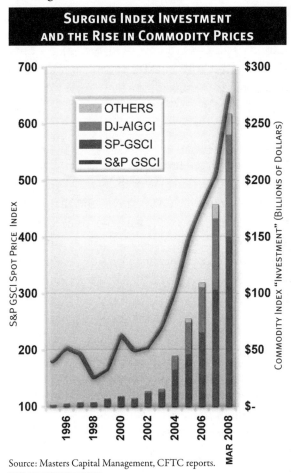

SURGING INDEX INVESTMENT AND THE RISE IN COMMODITY PRICES

OTHERS
DJ-AIGCI
SP-GSCI
S&P GSCI

S&P GSCI Spot Price Index

Commodity Index "Investment" (Billions of Dollars)

Source: Masters Capital Management, CFTC reports.

As those index-fund "long" contracts approach maturity, they have to be sold. The funds are rolled over again into the outer months or even years into the future. So the money just keeps being recycled in the futures market with a kind of flywheel effect, putting steady "long" (buying) pressure on the far end of the curve. The ironic result, as noted by a CFTC

13. Verleger, *The Petroleum Economics Monthly*, July 2005, p. 1, as cited by the staff report of the US Senate Permanent Subcommittee on Investigations, Committee on Homeland Security and Governmental Affairs, "The role of market speculation in rising oil and gas prices: A need to put the cop back on the beat," June 27, 2006, p. 25.
14. Calculated from NYMEX website data

study in 2006, is that the emergence of these supposedly speculative passive futures index investors has actually tended to damp the volatility of short-term price swings. In other words: Take heart, we're drowning in calm seas.

This serves to draw in yet more pension and managed money seeking to lower the "beta," or volatility, risk in those portfolios (versus stocks and bonds). But it is a recipe for disaster.

One predictable bit of volatility from all this "long" futures buying is noticeable, however. It is dubbed the monthly "Goldman Roll," which tends to push down the near-month contract by about 5% over several days, as institutions trade out of a wave of maturing GSCI positions. Conveniently for federal policymakers, the low point of this monthly dip in oil prices tends to coincide with the survey date for government inflation statistics, after which prices bounce back and carry on their rise.

But the implication of that 2006 CFTC study, that such fund investment has not affected the overall level of prices, was refuted by a Senate investigation in June of that year. Staff of the Senate Permanent Subcommittee on Investigations concluded flatly: "Speculation has contributed to rising US Energy prices."[15] That report said the only question, due to "gaps in available market data," is "the extent of the market impacts." Various oil market analysts have put the "speculative" impact on prices at anywhere from $20/bbl to $50 or more (at NYMEX quotes of $80 to $100/bbl).[16]

There are two basic ways to make or lose money on oil or other futures. One is if the overall price level along the whole curve goes up or down. The other depends on the shape of the curve. If the pattern of monthly futures prices is higher in the near months than farther out, the curve is said to be "backwardated." So if you buy a long-dated contract in that case, you might sell it for a gain even if overall prices fall. The other situation, however, is a "contango" market in which the near-months sell for less than father out on the curve. In that case, the futures holder can lose money even if overall prices on the curve go up. Likewise, a "short" who sells a long-dated contract and buys it back near maturity can lose money even in a contango market if the overall price curve rises too fast.

---

15. Permanent Subcommittee on Investigations, p. 6.

16. Gheit testimony.

For every buyer or "long" in commodity futures, there has to be a seller or "short." In classic commodities theory, as mentioned, the "commercial" producers of oil would always step in as sellers if prices went haywire on the high side, or buyers if they sank too low. But in the current run-up, buy-side demand for long-dated contracts has swamped the usual sellers, who have pulled back in the face of this torrent of new funds pushing up the curve. Into that void have stepped the hedge funds, proprietary trading desks at the big banks and other risk-takers willing to sell long-dated futures and options. By and large, however, anyone who has been on the short side of long-dated oil futures in the past two years has been clobbered. This includes many independent upstream oil and gas companies who thought they were locking in profits on forward production by selling futures, only to incur big losses when they had to buy their way out of those positions at prices vastly higher than they ever imagined.

Adding to the surging volume in long/short oil futures has been a groundswell in "spread" trading, which tries to profit from month-to-month or seasonal price variations along the forward price curve. Of the 2.72 million contracts of open interest in NYMEX WTI futures and options as of late May 2008, fully 30% was in "spreading" positions.

This pummeling of the "shorts" has led to further imbalance in oil futures. The steady buying pressure has outweighed the appetite of the sellers, even at nosebleed price levels for crude oil. Badly bruised, the shorts have opted to get out of the way of this freight-train of buying rather than try and "fight the tape." The result has been that fairly modest amounts of new money entering the market have been able to keep aloft a veritable lead balloon of inflated oil prices. With any concerted increase in pension fund commodities "investment," prices could see a further sustained run-up. In theory, there is no reason they could not be pushed to $200/bbl or beyond. It's just a matter of money now, and the commodity professionals are skittish about going short.

China gets stung

A classic example of this battering of the shorts was PRC-controlled, Singapore-listed China Aviation Oil (CAO), which had a virtual monopoly on the sale of jet fuel to China's three major airlines.

As a buyer of jet fuel, CAO was a natural short. But in late 2003 it began moving even farther to the short side in what became a futile and disastrous bet that rising oil prices would subside. CEO Chen Jiulin, later sentenced to 51 months in prison, persisted in rolling over and expanding a losing short options position, until it had mushroomed from about $6 million to some $550 million in the red.

Just before CAO's collapse in late November 2004, state parent China Aviation Oil Holdings sold down its 75% stake to 60%, to raise about $100 million to fund the losses, without telling the institutional buyers or underwriter Deutsche Bank. Even with that infusion, CAO failed when it was hit with margin calls on its 52 million barrels of exposure. It ran out of cash and bank creditors began liquidating its positions.[17] The company was eventually recapitalized in a debt restructuring with $130 million of new equity from BP and Singapore state investment arm Temasek. It resumed operations in March 2006. PRC ownership was cut to about 51%, through what is now China National Aviation Fuel Holding Co.[18] For Beijing, it was an expensive lesson in the relentless power of money and markets.

But it is not just the "shorts" at risk in a rising oil market. The dirty little secret of the managed commodity funds crowd is that much of the institutional investor money being churned along on the forward oil curve actually earns a rather poor return, and would be generating losses were it not for the rapid inflation of oil prices. The reason is that the influx of demand for long-dated futures has shifted the oil curve away from profitable backwardation for the "longs" to contango, or to a flat "curve." So as those long futures mature, they have to be closed out at little or no gain, or a loss, while incurring hefty fees and expenses. The net result is that while many oil commodity funds linked to the indexes have shown year-over-year gains of 50% or more, that falls far short of the doubling in crude prices over that time. As perhaps a sign of what is to come, the US Oil ETF has seen its asset value skid to barely $500 million in early 2008, or barely a third of its year-earlier peak.

---

17. "China Aviation Oil hedge details surface, assets frozen," *Platts Oilgram News*, Vol. 82, No.233, Dec. 6, 2004, p. 1.

18. "China Aviation Oil returns to futures trade," *Platts Oilgram News*, Vol. 86, No. 43, Feb. 29, 2008, p. 2.

That exposes the real risk inherent in the recent oil price run-up. If crude prices ever lose the support from a steady influx of new funding and enter a sustained downward correction, there could be a bloodbath of losses. Spooked pension funds and other institutions could be rushing for the exits when they realize the oil market has been more of a Ponzi scheme than a true capital securities market built on underlying fundamentals. With oil futures prices more a function of cash inflows than industry realities, the bubble is set for eventual deflation. And it could come with a bang. After all, ExxonMobil has said its all-in cost of finding and developing a new barrel of oil in 2007 averaged less than $10.

We're forever blowing bubbles

The key problem now for the US economic warriors is to generate and sustain an adequate flow of investment dollars into oil futures to raise and maintain prices. This is a matter not to be left to chance, and we will see that there has been a continuing series of subtle but profound regulatory and policy moves undertaken by various parts of the government in recent years to insure just that. "Reality based" shorts betting on a fundamentals-driven correction in the oil markets any time soon could be further bloodied. Stand back. The price run is far from over and could go on for another decade, as did the low-price oil war against the Soviets.

There can be no doubt about one salient fact: The torrent of direct and indirect speculative investment into oil and other commodity futures by pension funds and institutions would not have been possible without the acquiescence and outright encouragement of the US government. Indeed, it has required the wholesale stand-down of market regulators to let speculation run wild, in direct contravention of historic legal mandates. Critics will argue the government is not smart enough to orchestrate such a price rise in oil. But the more relevant question is the opposite: How could Congress and the regulators appear to have been so stupid and derelict as to enact and leave in place policies which have had such a disastrous price effect, unless this was intentional?

A watershed event in channeling this torrent of speculative money into oil futures occurred with passage of the Commodity Futures

Modernization Act of 2000, signed into law December 21 of that year in the waning days of the Clinton Administration. Curiously, the impetus for the new law came not from the CFTC. Rather it was drafted at the recommendation of a murky and now controversial inter-department government body called the President's Working Group on Financial Markets.[19] The WGFM is better known by its dubious popular nickname as the "Plunge Protection Team," and has been reported to be behind a series of price-rigging market interventions in the stock, bond and currency markets.[20] Dabbling in commodity pricing would be a natural extension of that intervention.

The CFMA of 2000 was mainly designed to remove from CFTC jurisdiction a wide range of financial and commodity futures transactions being done in the over-the-counter market or on electronic principal-to-principal trading platforms. This had been a burgeoning gray area of regulation over which the CFTC theoretically could have imposed disclosure rules and position limits. It also gave the SEC jurisdiction over securities futures, other than broad-based stock index futures. Along with the proposed legislation, the CFTC and SEC agreed in 2000 to work out rules to allow trading in single-stock futures. That had been effectively banned in 1982 after a turf fight over how it would be regulated.[21] The line between commodities and securities was going to get more blurry, and funding from the huge securities markets would soon be sloshing over into commodity futures in tsunami fashion.

---

19. The WGFM was first formed in March 1988 under Executive Order 12631 by President Ronald Reagan in response to the stock and bond market gyrations of 1987. Headed by the Secretary of the Treasury, it includes the heads of the Federal Reserve Board, the Securities and Exchange Commission and the Commodity Futures Trading Commission. Published reports and comments by government officials since then have confirmed it has been informally expanded to include the heads of some of the major Wall Street investment banks, stock exchanges and the commodity bourses to constitute what a headline writer dubbed the "Plunge Protection Team" in a story by Brett D. Fromson in the *Washington Post*, Feb. 23, 1997.

20. John Embry and Andrew Hepburn, "Move over, Adam Smith: The Visible Hand of Uncle Sam," Sprott Asset Management, August 2005.

21. The 1982 Shad-Johnson Accord was signed by SEC head John Shad and Philip McBride Johnson of the CFTC. It gave the CFTC sole jurisdiction on the trading of broad-based, cash-settled stock market index futures, such as the S&P index, but banned single-stock and narrow index futures. GSCI futures began trading on the Chicago Mercantile Exchange in 1992.

The Enron Loophole

A particular feature of the 2000 CFMA was a bit of wording slipped in at the last moment which allowed "electronic trading of excluded and exempt commodities."[22] By "excluded," that meant OTC or electronic futures trading one-to-one by "eligible contract participants." The "exempt commodities" included "energy derivatives." That wording came to be known as the "Enron Loophole," because it was pushed through at the last moment by Enron and other OTC and electronic trading interests. It soon became an eight-lane highway for the onslaught of unregulated energy futures speculation. As we saw earlier, Houston-based energy merchant Enron and other natural gas traders promptly ran up gas prices in the last week of 2000 to nearly $10/Mcf, four times their year-earlier level. That put the equivalent energy value of a barrel of oil at $60, when crude had actually slumped briefly from $30 to barely $20. It soon rebounded in response and, after a dip in early 2002, crude began a steady six-year climb past $100/bbl.

A key feature of the newly emerging electronic trading systems like EnronOnline and ICE is that they impose no overall limits on the volume of positions that can be held by speculators. On futures exchanges regulated by the CFTC, particularly in agricultural commodities, non-commercial participants are closely monitored to make sure they are not taking unduly large positions that could let them "corner" a market or create a "short squeeze," distorting prices. It is the abdication of control over position limits which has allowed the piling-on of what amounts to huge speculative long positions in oil, and now other commodities in the major indexes. These have grown out of all proportion to actual physical volumes traded.

EnronOnline disappeared in the collapse of Enron in late 2001, which was due mainly to bad debts Enron had been lugging along out of sight on its balance sheet and the imaginary, cashless profits it had been booking under aggressive "mark-to-model" accounting for its energy derivative positions. When news broke of Enron's shady dealings, and of a formal SEC probe, its trading counterparties head-

---

22. Library of Congress, summary of H.R.4541, Title: "To reauthorize and amend the Commodity Exchange Act to promote legal certainty, enhance competition, and reduce systemic risk in markets for futures and over-the-counter derivatives, and for other purposes," Oct. 19, 2000.

ed for the exits and raced to unwind their positions on EnronOnline. That led to a hemorrhaging of cash held as deposits, desperate borrowing, a falling stock price and finally ratings downgrades that sealed Enron's doom.[23]

Still surviving and flourishing, however, was ICE, which had been trading OTC natural gas contracts since 1997. It also moved into OTC oil futures trading with ICE's 2001 purchase of London's International Petroleum Exchange, which had been allowed since 1999 to

---

23. The mortal blow to Enron, in terms of investor and counterparty confidence, was news revealed by the company in October 2001 that the SEC had opened an informal investigation. Court documents later revealed that probe was launched Aug. 28, 2001, one week after the SEC received a heavily annotated copy of a *Platts Oilgram News* story by this author, detailing how Enron was using the manipulation of its forward curve assumptions on gas and other energy pricing to manufacture bogus profits. The story, headlined "Doubts linger on Enron after CEO's exit," ran Aug. 21, 2001, and included the following:

According to some analysts and institutional investors interviewed by *Platts*, the problem with Enron is not that its numbers don't look good. Rather, they may look *too* good. And the company's complexity, shifting business mix and limited disclosures make it impossible to analyze from the outside. "It's a black box," says one big institutional money manager who has given up on Enron: "It all boils down to 'trust me.'" By all accounts Enron has done a remarkable job in delivering on its promises of ever-higher reported profits. Just before [CEO Jeffrey] Skilling's departure Enron revised upward its "guidance" to Wall Street for earnings next year of $2.15/share, up from last year's $ 1.47.

There seems little doubt Enron will meet or beat that target, since the vast bulk of its reported profits are theoretical, non-cash "mark-to-market" earnings on over-the-counter energy derivatives it creates and trades as part of its investment banking business. Though subject to fluctuation in changing markets, those valuations are based largely on Enron's own, propriety in-house forward curves. Those are price assumptions out as much as 10 years or more on a myriad of commodities in which Enron seeks to make markets, from gas and power to coal, weather and bandwidth.

Since verifiable exchange-traded transactions occur in relatively few of its commodities, and seldom more than a year out, Enron and its trading peers build their own forward curves, subject only to a "reasonableness" test by auditors. In Enron's case, that is Arthur Andersen, which got $25-mil in audit fees and $27-mil for consulting at Enron last year. Skeptics say those huge fees, and the domination of AA's audit team by Enron's bonus-driven pros, has given Enron great leeway in setting its curve, and thus booking profits.

trade North Sea Brent futures electronically in the US without formal CFTC oversight. From under 2 million Brent contracts a month trading on ICE in early 2005, the volume had swelled by early 2008 to 5.7 million contracts a month.

In January 2006, the CFTC agreed to let ICE trade US WTI contracts, with those volumes now rivaling Brent at more than 5.2 million contracts a month. That was soon followed by CFTC permission for ICE to trade US gasoline and heating oil contracts. All that volume is run through London-based ICE Futures, overseen by the UK Financial Services Authority, but with no CFTC oversight, and no position limits on speculators. The CFTC seems to have thus gone out of its way to encouraging rampant oil market speculation in venues not subject to its control, or to its legal mandate to control speculation.

In mid-June of 2008, under intense pressure from Congress, the CFTC belatedly required ICE to adopt NYMEX-style position limits for speculators, and make added disclosures on energy trades.[24] But even on the NYMEX, where the CFTC has clear authority to rein in speculators with position limits, that key regulatory tool has been abdicated. Using a convoluted and circular rationale, the CFTC in 2006 decided to treat as "commercials" the swap dealers being used by the commodity pools and by the rising tide of institutional commodity index players. As such, the swap dealers are no longer subject to position limits, which have been required since 1936 to shield the thin commodity markets from manipulation and distortion. The reasoning is that those dealers are "bona fide hedgers." In reality, that was an excuse to let the onrush of new speculative money in the oil market escape position limits. To be a "bona fide hedger" traditionally has required having offsetting positions involving the physical commodity, not just a paper exposure.[25]

Under the glare of Congress, the CFTC said in June 2008 it was "revisiting" its decision to classify swaps dealers as commercial hedgers, but has set no timetable for resolving this "area of concern."[26] Meanwhile, however, the agency has proposed that speculators in

---

24. US CFTC news release 5511-08, "CFTC Conditions Foreign Access on Adoption of Position Limits on London Crude Oil Contract," June 17, 2008.
25. Epstein, p. 32.
26. Telephone response by a CFTC spokesman to questions June 17, 2008.

commodity index plays be exempt from *all* position limits.[27] That would "throw the door open for unlimited index speculator 'investment,'" warned fund manager Michael W. Masters of Masters Capital Management in congressional testimony in May 2008. "Is this what Congress expected when it created the CFTC?" Masters chided.[28]

It gets worse. The CFTC has essentially exempted the speculative "longs" from position limits. But those tight limits remain in place for other bona fide speculators who might want to go short on long-dated NYMEX crude contracts without using the big-bank swap desks. That tends to restrict the supply of sellers and force up prices in a one-way spiral.

Yet another feature of the 2000 CFMA was a provision that lets the CFTC authorize exchange clearinghouses for OTC energy and other futures and options. That has served to draw in yet more outside money managers, by offering a means for playing in OTC futures without the risk of counterparty default. The clearinghouse stands in the middle between all buyers and sellers as a guarantor to absorb that credit risk. This has expanded the universe of acceptable OTC oil futures players far beyond the clubby circle of industry commercials and big-name banks to include much smaller fry, hedge funds, and purely financial players. Both NYMEX and ICE now have booming OTC clearing operations, which cleared a combined 224 million contracts in 2007.[29]

The CFTC touts these rising volumes of "cleared" OTC deals as providing a window into market activity. But while there might be some visibility of traders with very large volumes, due to clearinghouse reporting requirements, there are no position limits for those deigned to be commercial hedgers.

A pattern of market manipulation

As mentioned earlier, the impetus for the 2000 CFMA was the President's Working Group on Financial Markets, headed since

---

27. US CFTC, Notice of Proposed Rulemaking, Risk Management Exemption From Federal Speculative Position Limits, Federal Register, Vol. 72, No. 227, Nov. 27, 2007, p. 66097.

28. Masters testimony, p. 8.

29. CFTC Chief Economist Jeffrey Harris, written testimony before the Senate Committee on Energy and Natural Resources, Apr. 3, 2008.

June 2006 by Treasury Secretary and former Goldman Sachs CEO Henry ("Hank") Paulson. Though originally formed under Ronald Reagan to deal with market turbulence in 1988, the secretive WGFM appears to have quickly morphed into a joint government-Wall Street fire brigade, charged with dousing any financial conflagration that might seriously unsettle the stock and bond markets. Taking an apparent cue from a 1989 *Wall Street Journal* op-ed piece by former Federal Reserve governor Robert Heller, the "Plunge Protection Team" has reportedly made repeated surreptitious interventions in the stock, bond and currency markets in times of severe stress.

This has been all but openly admitted by former government officials, including a Sept. 17, 2001, statement on ABC's *Good Morning America* by correspondent and former top Clinton policy advisor George Stephanopoulos, detailing steps the government was taking to shore up the stock market after 9/11. According to Stephanopoulos, "Perhaps most important, there's been – the Fed in 1989 created what is called a plunge protection team, which is the Federal Reserve, big major banks, representatives of the New York Stock Exchange and the other exchanges, and there – they have been meeting informally so far, and they have kind of an informal agreement among major banks to come in and start to buy stock if there appears to be a problem."[30]

In 1992, *New York Post* reporter John Crudele quoted former Reagan-era NSC economist Norman A. Bailey as confirming Plunge Protection Team stock market interventions in 1987, 1989 and 1992. Those moves had already been widely suspected after stories by the *Wall Street Journal, BusinessWeek* and other publications pointed to suspicious concerted futures buying activity in the obscure but powerful Dow Jones Major Market Index at the bottom of those drops. Those mysterious waves of futures buying rallied the broader market and prevented steep selloffs that would have wrecked the balance sheets of major financial institutions. "People who know about it think it is a very intelligent way to keep the market from a meltdown," Bailey told Crudele, adding that the brokerage firms may not even know for whom they are buying the futures

---

30. Transcript of ABC News *Good Morning America* broadcast Sept. 17, 2001, as cited by Embry and Hepburn, p. 25.

contracts. They are told it is for "foreign clients, perhaps the central banks of other countries."[31]

That last revelation about "foreign" bank clients has led researchers John Embry and Andrew Hepburn of Toronto-based Sprott Asset Management to speculate the funding for these periodic market-mending expeditions by the Plunge Protection Team may be coming from foreign bank reserve accounts managed by the Federal Reserve Bank of New York as custodian. The New York Fed also has jurisdiction over a kitty called the Exchange Stabilization Fund, created in 1934 to damp volatility in the currency market. The ESF is technically under Treasury control. Indeed, because of its dual role with both the Treasury and the Federal Reserve, the New York Fed appears to be the locus of market surveillance and response efforts by the Plunge Protection Team.

"We believe we can establish that the government has intervened in the stock market," Embry and Hepburn conclude in their 2005 Sprott report. This may not be altogether bad, they note, since healthy financial markets have become synonymous with national security. The nagging questions remain, however: How much of this is really going on? Has it become routine, as the Sprott report suggests? Have these market manipulations extended to other arenas, such as commodities?

From stocks, bonds and currencies, it seems a small leap to the oil market. And with small change. Compared to what's needed to move those much larger markets, a well-run intervention effort could rather easily stanch price falls and provide an occasional upward boost to oil futures when needed. By thus "painting the tape" to give the appearance of more market strength than might otherwise exist, the manipulators could lure in private investment funds to do the heavy lifting, wooed by the impression that the crude market was on a one-way trip to the stars.

The Sprott report notes a troubling and intriguing hint of just this sort of wide-ranging tinkering dropped by Alan Greenspan, and captured in two 1995 transcripts from meetings of the Fed's Open Market Committee. When questioned on January 31 of that year by one Federal Reserve Bank president about the political wisdom and legality of

---

31. John Crudele, "Evidence Suggests Government Manipulating Stock Market," *Buffalo News,* Sept. 1, 1992, as cited by Embry and Hepburn, p. 9.

using the ESF to bail out Mexico, Greenspan responded cryptically: "The dangers politically at this stage and for the foreseeable future are not to the Federal Reserve but to the Treasury. The Treasury, for political reasons, is caught up in a lot of different things."[32]

Greenspan shrewdly avoided saying more on that occasion. But on March 28, he was recorded as saying, "We have to be careful as to precisely how we get ourselves intertwined with the Treasury; that is a very crucial issue. In recent years I think we have widened the gap or increased the wedge between us and the Treasury.... In other words, we have gone to a market relationship and basically to an arms-length approach where feasible in an effort to make certain that we don't inadvertently get caught up in some of the Treasury initiatives that they want us to get involved in. Most of the time we say 'no.'"[33]

What are these Treasury "initiatives"? How often does the Fed say "yes"? Is oil pricing just one of many key economic variables being manipulated? Is the WGFM the economic warfare equivalent to the Joint Chiefs of Staff at the Pentagon? Perhaps John Crudele summed up the issue in his 2008 April Fools Day column for the *New York Post*. "Does the Working Group live up to its nickname of the Plunge Protection Team by rescuing the stock market in times of distress? There is strong circumstantial evidence that this is exactly what the group does today and has done for years. If these stock market rescues do occur, then capitalism and free markets were changed long ago. And we were all fools."

---

32. US Federal Reserve, Transcript of Federal Open Market Committee meeting for Jan. 31-Feb. 1, 1995, p. 136.

33. Federal Reserve, FOMC Transcript, Mar. 28, 1995, p. 6.

—13—

Conclusion

As world oil prices climb ever upward from $100/bbl to $120, $150 or even $200, it should be useful to keep in mind the basic points we have surveyed in this book. There is a reason prices are high and climbing, and it is not that China and India are exhausting supplies, that the earth's crust is running out of oil, or that a few crafty Wall Street speculators are profiteering on the woes of beleaguered motorists from Los Angeles to Hong Kong.

The reason is economic warfare, waged by the US national security establishment against what it sees as a relentlessly rising and ultimately threatening China. We have seen that oil pricing, or availability, has long been used as an economic weapon, and was the single most important factor in breaking the Soviet Union in the 1980s. We are witnessing that again, in reverse, aimed at curbing the growth and power of the PRC. And the trend likely extends from oil to a myriad of other raw materials and industrial commodities required by the PRC to sustain its export-driven employment growth: from iron ore and bauxite to soybeans, wheat, corn and rice.

The same mechanisms employed and documented in the 1980s to push oil prices dramatically downward for a decade or more are equally available to the US now to push prices upward, and to sustain them there for a protracted period. These include:

- Oil production rates of the international majors (from loose to tight).
- Saudi Arabian oil production, surplus capacity and reserve perceptions (from loose to tight).
- NYMEX futures trading (now augmented with massive inflows of passive investor funds into commodity index plays).
- US and other global strategic petroleum reserves (sopping up excess supply and driving up prices).

• Well-managed public perception of looming shortage (vs. perpetual glut in the 1980s) and environmental constraints: the "Peak Oil" scare and "global warming" mantra.

• US and Western government policy and regulatory moves to boost demand for benchmark light, sweet crude by imposing tough new sulfur limits in gasoline and diesel; inaction on further improving car and truck fuel efficiency rules; regulatory hindrance of new and upgraded refining capacity.

• Add to these the additional strong weapons of cartel-like Russian crude output restraint, outright military occupation of the Number Two world oil reserve holder Iraq, and persistent threats and violence in other key producing states like Iran, Nigeria and Sudan.

Taken together and applied over time, as was done in reverse against the Soviets, the US and its allies are quite able to drive up the world price of oil and other basic commodities. Prices can be sustained well above market-clearing levels for many years. Indeed, it is probably easier to move prices up than to move them down, since most of the key players make lots of money. We need merely to encourage the cartel-mongers do a better job, help enforce their market discipline, and fund the resulting commodities bubble with diverted pension monies (if not outright government-controlled funds). The developed countries get a cold; China could get pneumonia. If American consumers feel pain at the gas pump, they need only to consider the alternative to economic war: *real war* with body bags.

The purpose of this book has not been to make value judgments, or to declare the policies of either the US or China to be "good" or "bad," moral or immoral. It is not meant to impugn the leaders of Big Oil, or regulators, who may be merely doing what they are told. Rather, it has been to simply describe the oil market mechanisms and realities, and to explain why prices seem so irrationally and artificially high. Nation states behave with logics, moralities and imperatives all their own. Who can know them? When these elephants rage, we pygmies are trampled. It pays to know when to get out of the way.

Who will win this economic war? The prevailing perception is that the People's Republic of China is an unstoppable juggernaut on its way to claiming inevitable ownership of the 21st century. But cooler heads behind the scenes on both sides can see the PRC as a seriously unbalanced economy, fraught with structural problems, panting hard on the treadmill of job-creation and, with no democratic safety valve for blowing off steam, ever at risk of exploding in civil unrest. It is precariously financed with non-performing bank loans and fickle foreign capital, dangerously exposed on most of its key input costs, and hooked on government subsidies, price controls and protective trade barriers. It is playing a much weaker hand than it lets on. And it is up against the US and its ally Russia, who have the high ground of geography, alliances, unfathomably deep pockets and a wealth of experience in waging economic war.

My own hunch is that Beijing is going to fold its hand at some point, but not before there are serious economic and social dislocations for all involved. China could devolve into regional fiefdoms, or even democracies, and could even prosper by abandoning aspirations of geopolitical dominance. More likely, it will be a very messy ending, strewn over many years. As with the failed Soviets, a collapsing totalitarian empire leaves a chaotic vacuum that can take decades to fill.

The insight for the investor in all this is to realize that arbitrarily high commodity prices can just as easily become arbitrarily *low* commodity prices. If there were a catastrophic collapse of the PRC government, or a fundamental Sino-Russian realignment against the West, the motivation for punishingly high oil prices would vanish, and we could see a return to the doldrums. Based on cost fundamentals in a non-bubble commodity environment, crude oil could again gravitate to its long-term level of around $20/bbl, adjusted for inflation. The oil majors know this, which is one reason they have held back on capital spending.

The main counter-argument to the thesis expressed here is that the US government could not possibly be smart enough or strong enough to cause such a profound change in commodity prices and sustain it over such a long period. But I have posed the issue in reverse. Could the US government and its allies be so obtuse and downright *stupid* as to put in place a series of flawed and disastrous policies that set up this situation, and then to leave them in place for years and years as oil prices climbed skyward? Would they have unwittingly added yet more actions to worsen the oil price spike, even in the face of persistent warnings?

Those policies include a series of seemingly small overt steps, such as the CFTC's waiver of position limits on what speculative NYMEX trading, draconian reductions in allowed fuel sulfur and relentless SPR sweet crude purchases. There are also the many points of *in*action by the government, including: allowing unimpeded the great merger wave among the US oil majors, then standing by while they slashed reinvestment, and dawdling on tougher fleet fuel economy rules, which had so dramatically reduced US fuel consumption in the 1980s. In short, Washington has been the proverbial "dog that didn't bark" when it comes to rising oil prices. And as Sherlock Holmes would have noted, that is strong evidence of an "inside job."

Those are the visible actions. What we cannot see is the behind-the-scenes cajoling, arm-twisting, coercion and manipulation required to sustain such an economic war. Indeed, if the battle goes on so fiercely on the oil front, how many other skirmishes, ambushes and frontal assaults are going on elsewhere? Seen through the dark glasses of an underlying economic war between the US and China, an array of other murky global phenomena take on a different tint, from the Iraq war and the Global War on Terror to currency gyrations and monetary policies. The realities are no less devastating, but at least they become more understandable. Unfortunately, the thesis here explains *a lot*.

Another critique of this thesis is that you could not possibly maintain a conspiracy on the scale required to move oil prices this way. But I hope it is clear from this book how few conspirators are required to accomplish these things. At bottom, it may only take phone calls to a handful of oil majors, the Saudis, the Russians, a few Wall Street banks, and one or two giant pension funds. With those players on board, the rest of the details almost take care of themselves, with some guidance from the national security establishment. Everybody else falls into line, or they get their knuckles rapped.

Welcome to the brave new world of economic warfare.

Appendices & Index

—Appendix 1—

Unocal: A Deal Too Far

The sad reality is the CNOOC-Unocal situation confirms China's perception and strengthens those in the Chinese government who argue energy is a national security issue.
— University of Alberta China expert Wenran Jiang.[1]

No single event better crystallizes the high-stakes global geopolitical oil rivalry between the US and China than the thwarted attempt in early 2005 by CNOOC Ltd. to take over US upstream independent Unocal. In June of that year, CNOOC fielded an offer of $18.5 billion to buy the former Union Oil Company of California, which already had an agreed deal pending to be bought by US major Chevron for $16.4 billion of cash and stock. It set off a firestorm of political reaction in Washington, laying bare the suspicions and animosities on both sides of the Pacific.

For several years prior, century-old Unocal had been rumored as a likely takeover candidate. Having sold off all its downstream refining and marketing assets in 1997 to Tosco, later acquired by ConocoPhillips, Unocal had been pared back to being a modest-sized oil exploration and production company. At year-end 2004 it had about 1.8 billion boe of proved oil and gas reserves, one-third in the US and Canada and two-thirds abroad. It had key operations in near-China venues like Indonesia, Thailand, Myanmar, Bangladesh and Azerbaijan. It was a logical fit for any of the world majors, and rumors had periodically surfaced that Unocal CEO Charles Williamson had been holding exploratory informal merger talks since taking over at Unocal in 2001.[2]

Speculation about a looming deal in the works with China's CNOOC Ltd. began to push up Unocal's stock price in early 2005.

1. "Petrodollars," *Platts Oilgram News*, Vol. 83, No. 156, Aug. 15, 2005, p. 4.
2. "Unocal at center of merger speculation on who's next," *Platts Oilgram News*, Vol. 80, No. 21, Jan. 31, 2002, p. 1.

It was later revealed those talks had been under way since December 2004. After press reports of Unocal-CNOOC talks in early January, Chevron CEO David O'Reilly called Williamson to explore a possible merger or buyout. At least one other international major, believed to have been Italy's Eni, also expressed interest.

Though Unocal would be a big meal to swallow, the Chinese clearly had a head-start in the takeover play, and had the trump card of virtually unlimited cut-rate financial backing from Beijing. Unocal was roughly half the size of CNOOC and would more than double its daily production to more than 800,000 boe/d. Their combined reserves would be just under 4-billion boe. But before the dawdling Chinese offshore major could formulate a firm offer, Chevron had stepped in to negotiate its own agreed deal for Unocal, signed April 4, 2005. Per share, Chevron offered 1.03 of its own shares or $65 in cash, or a combination of cash and stock: notably less than what the market had been expecting CNOOC to offer. Based on Chevron's stock price at the time, Wall Street valued the deal at about $61/share for Unocal.

Rather than quickly counter with its own higher bid, however, CNOOC continued to dither. Its CEO, US-educated Fu Chengyu, finally called Williamson June 1 to say an offer would be forthcoming. But when it finally arrived June 22, CNOOC's taxable all-cash offer of $67 a share for Unocal was only marginally better than Chevron's cash deal and much worse than Chevron's stock-swap, after tax. Analysts, who had been expecting at least a $70/share deal to top Chevron, were puzzled and disappointed. Moreover, CNOOC indicated Unocal itself would have to pay the $500 million breakup fee on the Chevron deal: a particularly glaring and noxious bit of Chinese penny-pinching.

Unocal directors, understandably, decided to stick with their sure-thing deal from Chevron, but got permission to hold detailed talks with CNOOC about raising the Chinese offer. On July 19 Chevron raised the cash part of its offer a modest 5% to $69 to match an expected small increase by CNOOC. That gave the Chevron deal a blended value of $64/share, still less than CNOOC's offer. But given the growing doubts about US approval of the deal, even after many months of expected review, analysts had downgraded the discounted present value of CNOOC's cash offer to about $65/ share, which in the view of advisory group Institutional Shareholder service "did not justify ... the risks."[3] In the end, CNOOC offered no sweetener and eventually withdrew its bid amid a rising chorus of US political criticism.[4] Chevron had won, and the Unocal merger was consummated in August 2005.

"They had no game plan," Oppenheimer & Co analyst Fadel Gheit chided CNOOC. "I don't know if they had bad advice or did not listen or if the bureaucracy just couldn't move fast enough. I think they could have had Unocal," Gheit told *Platts* at the time: "They just blew it."[5]

Bad Chinese opera?

Indeed, CNOOC's bumbling approach to what could have been a stunning strategic victory, despite having Wall Street powerhouse Goldman Sachs as its advisor, raises a troubling question: Was it designed to fail? A somewhat diabolical view reported by *Platts* at the time is that CNOOC knew it had no chance of winning Unocal. But it fielded its half-hearted, belated and technically flawed offer merely to smoke out the vitriolic US anti-China political wrath Beijing knew would be sure to ensue from such a perceived raid on key international and US energy assets. In fact, CNOOC dubbed the project "Treasure Hunting Ship," after a legendary Chinese buccaneering expedition.[6]

Though 70% controlled by the PRC, CNOOC had four outside directors who apparently were dubious of the foray, including former Swiss ambassador to Iraq, Erwin Schurtenberger. He quit CNOOC's board in the heat of the Unocal takeover maneuvers Apr 1 "due to ill health."

As noted by *Platts*, "From the get-go, CNOOC was a day late and a dollar short. After goading Unocal into a self-auction, CNOOC then failed to meet Unocal's lenient bid deadline. Then it came back

---

3. Unocal press release and Form 425, Aug. 1, 2005.

4. For a detailed chronology of the Unocal-CNOOC-Chevron negotiations, see Unocal's SEC proxy statements of July 25 and June 29, 2005.

5. "CNOOC abandons effort to buy Unocal," *Platts Oilgram News,* Vol. 83, No. 148, Aug. 3, 2005, p. 1.

6. "Petrodollars," *Platts Oilgram News,* Vol. 83, No. 156, Aug. 15, 2005.

with an iffy cash deal only marginally better than Chevron's sure-thing tax-advantaged offer. When CNOOC could have then stolen the show by jumping its bid to $70 in July, Fu balked, reneging on even the obvious need to pay Chevron's $500-mil breakup fee. Makes you wonder if the CNOOC-Unocal courtship drama was just bad Chinese opera."

Vigorous US opposition to a CNOOC-Unocal deal should have been assumed from the start. For years, top Chinese energy officials had been chaffing under what they saw as US-led efforts to tighten world oil markets, manipulate crude prices upward and choke off Chinese access to foreign equity crude. Among those critics was Xu Ding Ming, director of the energy bureau at the powerful National Development and Reform Commission, China's former top central planning arm. Xu had recently blasted the "international petroleum crocodiles" he blamed for jacking up New York Mercantile Exchange WTI futures to what was then $67/bbl with speculative buying and conspiring to restrict world oil supplies.

"The sad reality is the CNOOC-Unocal situation confirms China's perception and strengthens those in the Chinese government who argue energy is a national security issue," University of Alberta China expert Wenran Jiang told *Platts* at the time. "The deal shows the US is not budging and that China can't just naively seek cooperation. The result will be not to weaken, but rather strengthen China's resolve to get more energy. So the competition is on."

The hollowness of US objections to the CNOOC-Unocal deal was apparent to anyone in the oil industry. While Congress was bewailing the possible ownership loss of Unocal's oil and gas reserves, the stark reality was that CNOOC was aggressively prospecting and drilling to put more barrels on the world market, while Chevron had recently shown a remarkably poor ability to sustain even existing production and replace its reserves year to year. Chevron ranked last among the international majors in a 2005 Bear Stearns analysis of reserve replacement at only 49%. Soon after making its bid for Unocal, Chevron reported first-quarter 2005 results that showed continuing output declines in the US, where liquids production was down 15% from a year earlier at 452,000 b/d. Its US natural gas output was off 22% at 1.6 Bcf/d. Deutsche Bank analysts termed the decline "horrible ... even allowing for disposals." Chevron's international volumes also fell 38,000 boe/d to 1.7-mil boe/d, for an overall drop of 195,000 boe/d, or 7.5%, to 2.4-mil boe/d.[7] If aggressive oil and gas exploration were really the goal of US policy, Chevron would have been the last buyer allowed for Unocal.

Coda: China and the demise of Bear Stearns

In mid-March 2008, venerable New York investment bank Bear, Stearns & Co. suddenly imploded under the weight of unmarketable assets and a capital crisis that threatened a "run on the bank." Within a matter of hours, over one weekend, what had been a Wall Street major with $25 billion of equity value less than an year earlier had been subsumed into the maw of rival JP Morgan Chase for what eventually would be a mere $1.4 billion of JPMC stock. It was a stunningly swift collapse and "rescue," effected behind closed doors under the auspices of US Treasury Secretary Henry Paulson. Rather than give Bear Stearns adequate time to line up more capital, or let it borrow from the Federal Reserve "window" as other Wall Street banks would soon be permitted, the company was summarily forced to be sold or face complete collapse.

One cannot help but wonder if the unusual circumstances of Bear's demise were related to the fact it had been negotiating to sell 6% of its equity to Chinese state-run investment giant CITIC, which could have been in position to snatch a much larger stake or even outright control as Bear spiraled downward. Did then-Bear CEO Jimmy Cayne cross that same invisible line in the sand that did in Saddam Hussein and Mikhail Khodorkovsky?

CITIC's original deal in late 2007 was to pay $1 billion for 6% of Bear. Even that small interest had raised concerns in Washington. But when CITIC demanded to renegotiate that deal in early 2008, angling for up to 10% as Bear began to stagger under sub-prime securities problems, alarm bells sounded. New York Senator Charles Schumer, chairman of the joint economic committee of Congress, hinted at the need for more regulation of such investments. Still CITIC was a receptive buyer and increasingly Bear's last line of defense as its balance sheet was disintegrating. The choice of JPMC as

7. "Weak downstream hurts ChevronTexaco 1Q," *Platts Oilgram News*, Vol. 83, No. 83, May 2, 2005, p. 6

buyer may have had less to do with its offer price than its pedigree, or nationality. "Although many potential investors had been invited to invest, Bear Stearns had determined that JPMC was the most suitable bidder," according to the odd wording of minutes from the Federal Reserve meeting which sealed Bear's fate.[8]

As weapons of economic warfare, large money-center investment banks could be compared to aircraft carrier battle groups in conventional naval conflict. Their ability to "project power" through the channeling of financial flows, and their long-range surveillance capabilities by virtue of being able to watch money and deal movements, make them "capital" ships of the line. Before Lord Nelson would let such a prize be boarded and captured, he would no doubt prefer to ground, scuttle and burn the hunk after removing is guns and stores. Bye Bye Bear.

---

8. Minutes of the Board of Governors of the Federal Reserve System, Mar. 16, 2008, p. 3.

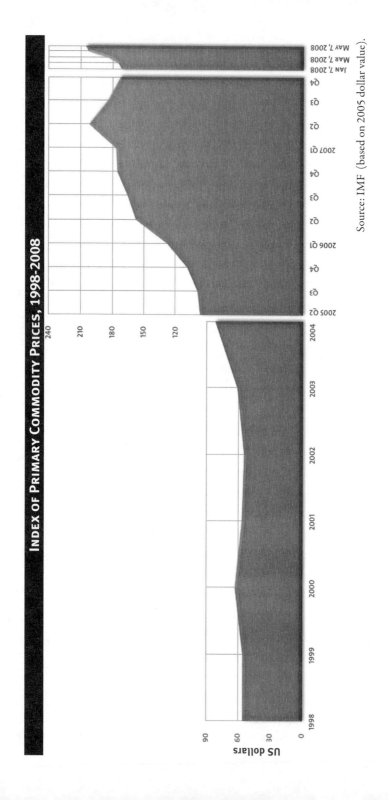

INDEX OF PRIMARY COMMODITY PRICES, 1998-2008

Source: IMF (based on 2005 dollar value).

—Appendix 2—

Other Economic War Fronts?

O il may be only part of a much broader commodity price squeeze being exerted to restrain Chinese growth rates. The run-up in crude prices since China became a major importer has been matched or even exceeded by the surge in other industrial input costs. Indeed, a weighted index of eight key industrial metals tracked by the International Monetary Fund has more than tripled from 2003 to 2008, nearly matching the rise in IMF-tracked petroleum costs over that period.[1]

Included in the IMF index are copper, aluminum, iron ore, tin, nickel, zinc, lead and uranium. Futures and options in all but iron ore and uranium are traded on the London Metal Exchange. Since 2002, annual trading volume on the LME in those contracts has roughly doubled to more than 100 million "lots" worth a notional gross value of some $10 trillion.[2] China is a net importer of all those metals except aluminum, for which the price actually ebbed in 2007. But it is a major importer of the bauxite from which aluminum is made, and that price is soaring.

China's Steel Boom
F rom being a major net importer of steel in 2003, taking in some 43 million tons or 13% of world steel exports, China became a net exporter itself in 2005. By 2007 China single-handedly accounted for 40% of the world steel market with estimated production of more than 500 million tons, up 20% from the prior year and double

1. International Monetary Fund, "Indices of Primary Commodity Prices, 1998-2008," Table 1a, June 4, 2008.
2. Martin Abbott, London Metals Exchange, "2007 and Beyond," presentation Oct. 8, 2007, p. 4.

its output just four years earlier in 2003. It was also by far the world's biggest steel exporter at 72 million tons (65.2 million mt), up 33% from 2006.[3]

China has declared steel to be a major strategic industry focus and has been allegedly aiding its producers with almost $16 billion a year in energy and raw material subsidies. This has spawned an explosion in the number of iron and steel companies there to some 7,000 mostly small and likely inefficient producers as each province and town has sought to have its own steel mill. With government curbs imposed on its domestic construction industry in 2004, damping internal demand, China's steel exports surged and their price fell. Chinese producers in 2006 were selling hot rolled coiled steel at $424 a ton, or almost 20% under US steel prices even after allowing for freight costs from China.

By mid-2008, that delivered-price advantage had narrowed to about 10% under US steel in Indiana, as *Platts* assessed the Shanghai price of hot rolled coil at $950/mt.

Even with that doubling in Chinese steel prices, it is questionable whether any Chinese steel company would be making a profit without hefty subsidies for everything from electricity and natural gas to coking and steam coal. In January 2008 the US Commerce Department imposed anti-dumping duties of up to 85% on Chinese steel plumbing pipe due to below-cost sales in the US, as well as countervailing duties of more than 600%. Those rulings were upheld in June when the US International Trade Commission confirmed US pipe-makers had been harmed by Chinese imports. US trade officials have also protested Chinese steel subsidies to the WTO.

A key vulnerability for China steel is the cost of iron ore. China has to import more than half its iron ore needs, and has to process very low-grade domestic ore for the rest with as little as 20% iron compared to 80% ore from Australia. In 2007 it had to import an estimated 400 million tons of iron ore, projected to rise to 550 million by 2010.[4] But in the 12 months from January to December 2007, the world spot price for iron ore more than doubled from $75

3. Iron and Steel Statistics Bureau, "The World's Top Trading Counties," June 11, 2008.
4. Rio Tinto, "Delivering Exceptional Growth," investor seminar, Nov. 26, 2007, slide 12.

per metric tonne to $185. Longer-term contract prices more than doubled from three years earlier to more than $80/mt.

Fearing another 50% increase in imported iron ore costs in 2008, Chinese steel companies have clamored to block a proposed merger of major Australian iron ore producers BHP Billiton and Rio Tinto launched by BHP in late 2007. The Chinese see that as a prelude to further tightening of iron ore and other raw material supplies akin to what happened after the Big Oil merger wave of 1998. Even though the BHP-Rio deal appears stalled, in late June 2008 Rio Tinto extracted a price hike of up to 96% for 2008 on contract iron ore deliveries to Baosteel Group, which had been negotiating on be-

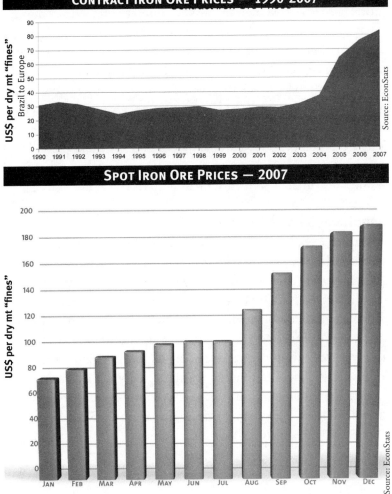

CONTRACT IRON ORE PRICES — 1990-2007

Source: EconStats

SPOT IRON ORE PRICES — 2007

Source: EconStats

half of China's overall steel industry. Earlier in the year, Baosteel had agreed to pay 65% more than in 2007 for iron ore under a long-term supply deal from Brazil's CVRD.

Price-setting on iron ore sales is a murky business, transacted between a small number of major export mining companies like BHP, Rio and CVRD, and a large number of steelmakers, big and small. With no futures market yet in operation to provide transparency, iron ore pricing is tightly controlled by the producers and is said to vary widely by customer.

As with oil, the earth's crust has large amounts of iron. And as with oil, the limiting factor in supply tends to be the willingness of the major mining companies to commit to the large-scale development efforts needed to have a profitable new mine at normal (low) prices.

It could well be the sharp escalation in world iron ore prices is simply a normal function of scarcity economics in the face of a sudden rise in Chinese demand. But overall world steel consumption has been growing only modestly, and there would seem to be ample resource supply available to be brought on line. On the other hand, if there were an effort by the US and its allies to crimp Chinese growth in crucial strategic areas, iron ore pricing would indeed be a key choke point. From a Chinese perspective, this is no theoretical prospect, but rather a real example of economic strangulation using natural resource pricing.

Bauxite as a battleground

Another choke point for China is bauxite, the basic raw material for aluminum. Along with steel, China has set a strategic course to be the world's leading maker of that lightweight and versatile metal. In 2007 China is estimated to have produced more than 11 million mt of aluminum, up more than 50% from 2006 for around 30% of total world output. Of that, more than 2 million mt was exported, mostly as processed metal, making China the world leader. By 2008 its aluminum smelting capacity was expected to approach 15 million mt a year.[5] Even at almost 40% domestic demand growth, that would boost export capacity to about 3 million mt.[6]

---

5. Lou Schwartz, China Strategies LLC, "China's Extrusion Industry," AEC 2007 management conference, Sept. 19, 2007.
6. Tom Stundza, "Aluminum: No trouble sourcing light metal in 2008," *Purchasing*, Nov. 15, 2007.

But China is woefully short on bauxite and as of early 2007 was importing more than half its requirements. Through August of 2007, it had imported 15.5 million mt of bauxite, up 180% from a year earlier and 15 times its bauxite imports in 2005.[7] More than 90% of China's 2006 bauxite imports came from Indonesia. But a move by the Indonesian government to close down illegal mines there has forced China to shop elsewhere, at higher prices for both the mineral and shipping. UK shipping consultants Clarksons calculated Chinese bauxite imports in the first eight months of 2007 at 44.6 billion tonne miles, up almost 250% from a year earlier and 19 times the 2005 import load. The China bauxite trade soaked up what amounted to fully half of all the new dry bulk shipping capacity added in that time. Moreover, freight rates doubled to more than $32,000 a day for a "handysize" 30,000 dwt bulk carrier.

The cost of the bauxite itself has also skyrocketed in price. Delivered to China, the cost in 2006 jumped 28% to around $45/mt. It climbed another 12% or more in 2007 and some sellers see the price rising another 30% in 2008 to around $65/mt delivered to China.[8] It takes two to three tonnes of bauxite to make one tonne of alumina. Two tonnes of alumina are needed to make one tonne of aluminum, plus large amounts of electricity. To feed its fast-growing aluminum industry, China encouraged the building of alumina capacity to reduce its dependence on high-cost imports of that intermediate material. In 2007 China's alumina output leaped more than 40% to almost 20 million mt. But after overbuilding its alumina industry, China has found itself struggling for want of affordable bauxite just as the market price of aluminum has faltered. From more than $1.30/lb in early 2007, the spot price for primary aluminum was below $1.10/lb in early 2008.

What's next?

As Chinese subsidies lurch from overbuilding one industry to the next, huge distortions occur with sharp swings from being a net importer to net exporter. Professor Usha C.V. Haley, di-

---

7. David Jordan, "The Logic Behind China's Booming Bauxite Imports," *Clarkson Research Studies*, Oct. 29, 2007.
8. "2008 Bauxite Prices to Soar, Says India," *Russian Metallurgy and World*, Oct. 5, 2007.

rector of Connecticut's University of New Haven Global Business Center, pointed out to a House Ways and Means subcommittee in early 2007 that the world price of ethylene for plastics fell by half as Chinese capacity rose 35% in 2007 and is slated to double again in the next few years. "Soon, smelted copper will join the ranks," she noted: "China has 2.5 million tons of annual production capacity and another 2.5 million tons under construction. Similarly, in stainless steel, China's annual production capacity approximated 2.5 million tons at the end of 2004. Industrial projects and subsidies will expand this to 10 million tons in five years."[9]

After hovering under $1/lb for many years until mid-2003, finished copper prices then quadrupled to almost $4/lb by mid-2006 as China became the world's largest copper importer. Copper prices on the LME have remained in the $3-$4 range even though overall world demand growth has been minimal.[10] As its new smelters come on line, Chinese imports of finished copper are slowing, but imports of concentrate continue to rise and were up 23% in the first four months of 2008 from a year earlier.[11] Chinese copper mines can supply only about 20% of Chinese copper demand, exposing smelters to the same raw material cost risk faced by China's steel and alumina industries.[12] In 2007 Chinese imports of copper ore and concentrate rose 25% to 4.52 million tons, according to state statistics.

Food costs

China is also affected by a range of agricultural commodity prices which have been soaring along with crude oil as the torrent of pension fund and other managed money rushes into US commodity index plays. The price of soybeans on the Chicago Board of Trade has skyrocketed from barely $6/bu in late 2006 to more than $15 in mid-2008. Wheat spiked from less than $5/bu to more than $12 in early 2008 before easing to about $9. Corn has rocketed from barely

9. US House of Representatives, Committee on Ways and Means, Subcommittee on Trade, prepared testimony of Usha C.V. Haley, Mar. 15, 2007.

10. International Copper Study Group, "Trends in World Refined Copper Stocks and Price."

11. Glenys Sim, "China May Copper Imports Forecast Above 100,000 Tons," Bloomberg.com, June 3, 2008.

12. "Resource shortage challenges China's copper industry," Chinamining.org, Mar. 14, 2008.

$2.50/bu in early 2006 to almost $7.50 in mid-2008. Rice doubled in barely six months from $12/cwt to $24 in April 2008 before easing to around $20.

China is self-sufficient in corn, wheat and rice, but only barely so. It is the world's largest importer of soybeans and soy oil, both for food consumption and for processing into export goods. Even if it can supply its own food needs, it will feel the inflationary effects of rising global prices. Chinese food costs in April 2008 were up more than 22% from a year earlier, mainly on sharply higher pork prices due to diseased hogs. This drove China's overall consumer inflation rate that month to a worrisome 8.5%.[13]

As with crude oil and petroleum products, the huge run-up in agricultural commodity prices can be directly traced to the massive buying of index futures by pension and other managed-money accounts in the US. As of mid-2008, such unrestrained speculative buying has risen to account for 64% of the "long" interest in US wheat futures, 35% in corn, 42% in soybeans and 63% in both live hogs and live cattle. Except in corn, that vastly exceeds the long interest of either physical hedgers or traditional speculators.[14]

Put another way, this surge of index-related commodity futures buying has built up a huge "stockpile" of paper bushels in a kind of hoarding process, notes trader Michael Masters in his Congressional testimony. The 1.3 billion bushels of index-related long wheat positions, he notes, equates to two years' worth of US wheat consumption. (Likewise in crude oil, index-fund paper stockpiling over the past five years of nearly 900 million bbl almost matched the increase in Chinese physical oil demand over that span.) "Index speculators' trading strategies amount to virtual hoarding via the commodities futures markets," Masters warned.[15]

Surging prices of agricultural commodities have a tendency to engender the physical hoarding of foodstuffs as well, as nominal exporter countries fret about their own future supply, and importers scramble to protect their populace. Thus frantic buying by the Philippines in early 2008 helped jack up rice prices, while export limits by India and Vietnam curtailed supply and leading exporter Thailand

---

13. "Food prices drive China inflation," BBC News, May 12, 2008.
14. Masters testimony, p. 13.
15. Ibid., p. 5.

talked of forming a producer cartel for the grain akin to OPEC.[16] That cartel idea was quickly shelved. But the threat remains of panic buying, hoarding and restricted sale of key foodstuffs on a global scale due, one way or another, to the decisions of financial regulators in Washington.

* * *

This is the face of modern economic warfare, waged globally and targeting the very lifeblood of rival nations. "Collateral damage" is rife. Defenses are few. The stakes are very, very high.

---

16. "As Prices Surge, Thailand Pitches OPEC-Style Rice Cartel," *Wall Street Journal Online*, May 5, 2008.

Index

Index

Index

Index